WAR IN OUR TIME

A comprehensive and analytical history in pictures and text of the first eleven years of World War II, beginning with the invasion of Manchuria by the Japanese, showing the rise of Fascism and its conquest of Europe and attack on United States, and ending in 1942 with the tide beginning to run in favor of the democracies and free peoples of the world.

By HARRY B. HENDERSON AND HERMAN C. MORRIS

SAM SHAW, Art and Picture Editor

DOUBLEDAY, DORAN & COMPANY, INC. GARDEN CITY, NEW YORK

Contents

Acknowledgements

PRODUCTION OF THIS BOOK has required a great deal of effort and time on the part of many people and would not have been possible without their help. Undoubtedly our greatest debt is to the news photographers of the world, most of whom are anonymous, who secured the pictures which tell the story of war in our time, often at the risk of their lives. We are indebted to Stewart Hopkins and C. M. Weil of International News Photos, Inc., who made available to us their organization's great collection of pictures as well as space in which to work. Most of the pictures in the book came from INP. Likewise, we are indebted to the staff of the INP file room, especially Joseph Miller, John Cirigliano, Thomas Carolan, John Priestly, Dennis Burke, who aided our picture research. We are also indebted to Miss Helen Black and Charles Rikon of Sovfoto for picture research on the Russian war; all Russian pictures in this book come from Sovfoto. We are indebted to Ernest Cabat who drew especially for this book the excellent maps of the Nazi military campaigns in Poland, France, and Russia. We are grateful for the assistance given us by the British Library of Information, the Free French Delegation, the Inter-Allied Press Committee, Miss Ruth Maier of the Royal Yugoslav government-in-exile, the Office of Production Management, the Office of Emergency Management, and the New York Public Library.

We are indebted also to Beatrice C. Henderson and Anne Ruben who typed the manuscript, to Sherman Lurie for special research. In addition to pictures from INP files, others came from News of the Day, Press Association, U. S. Signal Corps, U. S. Navy, U. S. Marines, Office of Emergency Management, Farm Security Administration, Acme, British Combine, Three Lions, and European picture agencies.

We regret that lack of space has made it impossible to identify the source of the material in the captions and text. This material was drawn from the widest variety of sources and a complete bibliography would run to several pages. However, the main sources were the New York *Times, Herald-Tribune,* and *World-Telegram, Time, Life, Newsweek, Look, Fortune, Business Week, Foreign Affairs Quarterly* and *Bulletins,* Facts on File, and Who's Who. Other sources were *A Diary of World Affairs* by Marcel Hoden, the Encyclopedia Britannica, Prof. Edward MacInnes' two-volume chronology of events entitled *The War,* the U. S. *Infantry Journal,* the U. S. *Field Artillery Journal,* Winston Churchill's books, *Step by Step, While England Slept,* and *Blood, Sweat and Tears, Red Star over China* by Edgar Snow, *J'Accuse!* by André Simone, *Betrayal in Central Europe* by G. E. R. Geyde, *Italy Under Mussolini* by William Bolitho, *Inside Europe* and *Inside Asia* by John Gunther, *Military Strength of the Powers* by Max Werner, *Berlin Diary* by William L. Shirer, *Peace In Our Time* by Hamilton Fish Armstrong, *Ethiopia* by John H. Shaw, *Ethiopia and the Italo-Ethiopian Conflict* by D. C. Haskell, *Italian Facism* by Salvenini Vaetano, *Failure of a Mission* by Nevile Henderson, *Sawdust Caesar* by George Seldes, *Nazi Germany Means War* by Leland Stowe, *Hitler and I* by Otto Strasser, *Hitler Speaks* by Hermann Rauschning.

For some of the pictures and much of the information about the underground movements in conquered Europe we are indebted to several persons whose identity must remain, at least until Nazism has been crushed, anonymous.

Introduction

WAR HISTORIES are generally dull, tedious recitals of places, dates, almost meaningless figures, and pale thin characters. Today the news camera has freed us of our dependence on the written word and made possible a new historical technique. It takes us directly to the scene, gives an eye-witness, on-the-spot report of what happened. Most of all this technique makes it clear that history is not cold names, places, and dates, but people, good and bad, what they did and had done to them. We see the pompous Mussolini's straggling march on Rome. We are on the beaches at Dunkerque, in burning Shanghai, on the sinking *Panay's* deck, watching the scrawny Chamberlain shake a clammy hand in that of dee-lighted Adolf Hitler. The invasion of Russia becomes, not a phrase wholly undescriptive of the action that took place, but hardened, fighting, smoke-grimed men and monsters of steel smashing one another. These are images that are retained long after names and dates have been forgotten. What the editors have done is arrange these images in their relation to one another and historical importance to tell the story of war in our time.

The war which today engulfs the world and in which we are fighting for our very lives as free men did not begin on that crisp September morning when Adolf Hitler sent his Nazi legions rolling across Poland's plains. It began on September 18, 1931, when the Japanese invaded Manchuria. All that has happened since has been part of the same war.

The peace which the armistice of November 11, 1918; brought was to be permanent. A million men had died for it and everyone said they had not died in vain. Yet little more than a decade of peace followed. During that decade Fascist parties developed in most European countries and in Japan. War is an integral part and an avowed aim of Fascism. Once the Fascists had conquered and enslaved their own people World War II began. It took many forms. The actual invasion of Manchuria was a military action, but the real struggle was fought in the League of Nations halls in Geneva. No battles were fought when Czechoslovakia fell to Nazi Germany. Yet who can maintain that it was not war, the same war we are fighting today? As World War II developed it was described by various names: a war of nerves, a psychological war, a diplomatic war. Indeed it has been all these things. But its main characteristic has been that it is a war waged by the fascists in every country against the democracies of the world in an attempt to enslave all peoples. Thinly disguised for a time as a war against Communism, World War II has always been directed against the democracies. The sides have never changed: Japan, Germany, Italy vs. Britain, France, Russia, China and the United States.

The terrible tragedy of World War II is that it need not have been, that it was preventable. Each new demand, each new aggression by the Fascist powers was merely building the foundation for the ultimate struggle for world conquest. At any point the Fascist advance might have been checked—in Manchuria, Ethiopia, the Rhineland, in Spain, Austria, China, Czechoslovakia, even after Hitler demanded Danzig. It was prevented because selfishness, fear of Communism, and isolationism dominated the statesmen of the democratic countries and barred the erection of a strong system of collective security pacts. What we have had in these years since 1931 has not been "Peace in our time," as Neville Chamberlain put it, but war in our time.

World War II Began in Manchuria, 1931

RICHEST PLUM IN THE ORIENT, Manchuria has been the cause of almost continual war-fare since 1900. The full extent of its great mineral deposits, including coal, iron and lead, is unknown, even to the Japanese. Strategically its importance lies in the fact that it offers access to China, Russia and Japan. Its central region is a vast rolling plain, much like Kansas; its biggest crop: soya beans.

WORLD WAR II began on September 18, 1931, when Japan, charging that Chinese soldiers had bombed the Japanese-owned South Manchuria Railway five miles north of Mukden, launched a full-scale invasion of Manchuria "in self-defense." Thus began the attempt of the fascist nations to conquer the world, an attempt that was eventually to involve every major power, cost millions of lives, and untold billions in destruction. The press paid scant attention to it; in the New York *Times* and *Herald-Tribune* it won less than a column of space and editorially it was dismissed as a "problem of the League of Nations." Yet within a few short years it was to seriously affect the lives of every American. Since 1890 Manchuria had been the scene of almost continual battle between Russia and Japan. The Russo-Japanese war of 1904 gave Japan control of Manchuria, although it was nominally Chinese. Through the South Manchuria Railway, owned by the Tokio government, Japan began the economic development of Manchuria's vast mineral deposits, adding much rail mileage, building huge steel mills. Until 1929 China did nothing, largely because Manchuria was ruled by Chang Tso-lin, a war lord often in the pay of Japan. But after his murder by the Japanese, the Chinese, objecting to Japan's economic control because it interfered with Chinese sovereignty and deprived her of her own resources, built railroads to compete with the South Manchuria line. Millions of Chinese migrated to Manchuria, where they settled as farmers. By 1930 Japanese investments in Manchuria totaled $850,000,000 and their coal and iron holdings had been developed to the point where Japan's industrial and economic life was largely dependent on them. Thus it became necessary for the power-mad Japanese to invent an incident which would permit them to seize and hold Manchuria.

MASSACRE OF CHINESE IN KOREA by Japanese-inspired Koreans in July, 1931 was the first incident provoked by Japan to furnish an excuse to seize Manchuria. This picture shows Japanese and Koreans mopping up after massacre. On August 27 Chinese troops discovered a Japanese Captain Nakamura mapping inner Manchuria, promptly executed him as a spy. Then on Sept. 18, between 10 and 10:30 a.m., according to Japanese, Chinese soldiers dynamited a section of South Manchuria track just north of Mukden. No one was allowed to visit the scene and strangely enough the Changchun-Mukden express arrived on time although it could not have passed over damaged track. Some time later the Japanese produced a slightly bent 100-pound rail. This was the Sarajevo of World War II.

INSTANTLY, ATTACKING "IN SELF-DEFENSE," Japanese armies struck at all the cities along the South Manchuria Railway. Japanese troops poured in from Korea and Japan so rapidly that it was obvious that they had been organized for the attack for some months. In answer to diplomatic inquiries the Japanese replied they were merely protecting their nationals from Chinese bandits. Chinese troops fell back deliberately before the onslaught while China appealed to the League of Nations and the United States to cite Japan as the aggressor, aid her by applying sanctions against Japan. Then the Japanese branched out, seized the competing Chinese railroads and the surrounding territory, murdering thousands of helpless Chinese. Meanwhile they ignored a request from the League to withdraw.

7

WITHIN A MONTH FAST-MOVING JAPANESE TROOPS, unhampered by any real opposition, had occupied the three provincial capitals of Manchuria—Mukden, Tsitsihar, and Harbin. At Geneva ex-Premier of France, Aristide Briand, head of the League Council, listened to Chinese and Japanese and, after months of delay, appointed a committee to "investigate" whether there was a war.

DR. ALFRED SZE, CHINESE REPRESENTATIVE at Geneva (right), argued against the "investigation," pointing out that it was a "mere device to condone and perpetuate the unjustifiable occupation of China's territory by an aggressor who already virtually had attained his unlawful objective while the League discussions were going on." But the investigators went on to China.

MEANWHILE, JAPAN BOMBED AND SHELLED the defenseless town of Chinchow, inflicting terrible loss of life. Soon this ruthlessness was to become a standard part of the Fascist attack. As the Japanese neared the Soviet frontier the Soviets rushed their Far Eastern armies to the border to show the Japanese they were ready to fight. But the Japanese stopped short of the border.

REPRESENTING JAPAN, MATSUOKA argued at Geneva that China was not a nation since her people were disorganized, that the Manchus had to be protected from the Chinese, that Japan had no territorial ambitions. It was a slippery path to walk.

NEITHER RAMSAY MacDONALD, Prime Minister of Britain, nor Briand did anything to check Japan, and with England out of the picture Japan's success was assured. But the Chinese people instituted an anti-Japanese boycott which hurt Japan seriously, for China bought more than 30% of all Japanese exports. On January 21, 1932, the Japanese fleet steamed into Shanghai under Admiral Shirosawa, who demanded the boycott's end. The Chinese refused. On January 28 the Japanese invaded Shanghai.

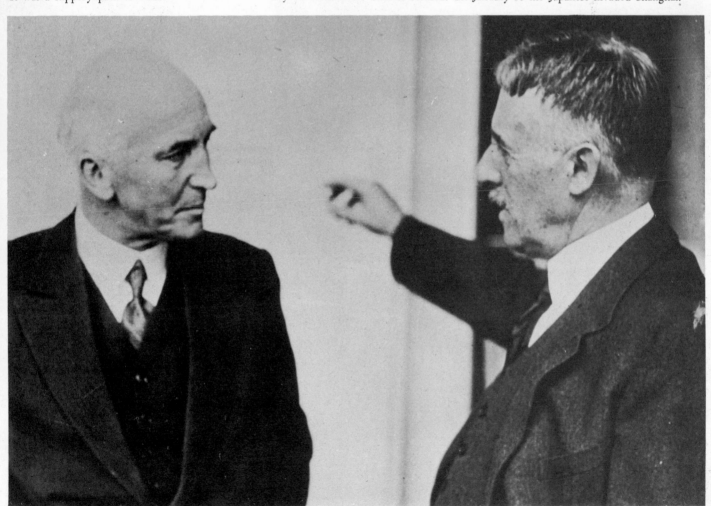

THE ONLY VOICE TO PROTEST was that of U.S. Secretary of State Henry L. Stimson, who tried to convince Sir Samuel Hoare and other British leaders Japan should be checked. But he convinced no one. Stimson, declaring Japan was violating her treaties, announced U. S. would not recognize her conquest. The League of Nations, attempting to save face, announced it would adopt the U. S. program.

The conservative London *Evening Standard*, approving Japan's act, said: "Now is not the time for interference from sentimentalists." Few Americans paid much attention; millions were in breadlines in an America which was turning bitterly introspective. Thus Hitler, Mussolini, and Hirohito got their first concrete proof that the democracies would not resist aggression.

As a warning to others a Japanese-paid Manchurian soldier hangs up the severed head of Chinese who dared to resist the invaders.

THE ATTACK ON SHANGHAI BY THE JAPANESE smashed what few illusions there were about Japan's real intent in China. It was at Shanghai that the Chinese began their heroic resistance to the invaders. Despite their lack of air power and artillery, the ragged Chinese army drove the Japanese back time and again. In retaliation the Japanese shelled and bombed the defenseless Chapei district of Shanghai, inflicting a great loss of life upon the civilian populace. Finally, their munitions gone, the Chinese agreed to a truce.

THE BLACK DRAGONS OF JAPAN

BEHIND every important move Japan has made since 1880 has been the secret, terroristic Society of the Black Dragon, the most powerful organization in Japan. Its purpose has been to wipe out "Western" parliamentary government, replacing it with a military dictatorship of the samurai (warriors), and the building of a world empire through pan-Asiaism. The Sino-Japanese War of 1895 was started through the activity of Black Dragon agents in Korea. The Russo-Japanese War of 1904–5 was declared only after the Black Dragon gave anti-war Premier Ito the choice of war or death. Assassination has been the main Black Dragon weapon. Most of the military and political leaders belong. It controls more than a hundred less-important secret societies.

FOUNDER OF THE BLACK DRAGON MITSURU TOYAMA has headed the organization since 1878. He has been the most feared man in Japan for sixty years. As a Zen priest he once ate only leaves and grass; on another occasion he sat silent, sleepless, waterless, foodless, motionless for five days and five nights. In 1905 he told Premier Prince Ito to either declare war on Russia or be murdered. In 1932 the Black Dragon and affiliated societies staged an uprising, murdering Premier Inukai because he refused to expand the Manchurian invasion to China. Later investigation showed the uprising was financed by the Japanese controlled South Manchuria Railway which was headed at that time by Black Dragon leader Yosuke Matsuoka, who was later to become Japan's Foreign Minister.

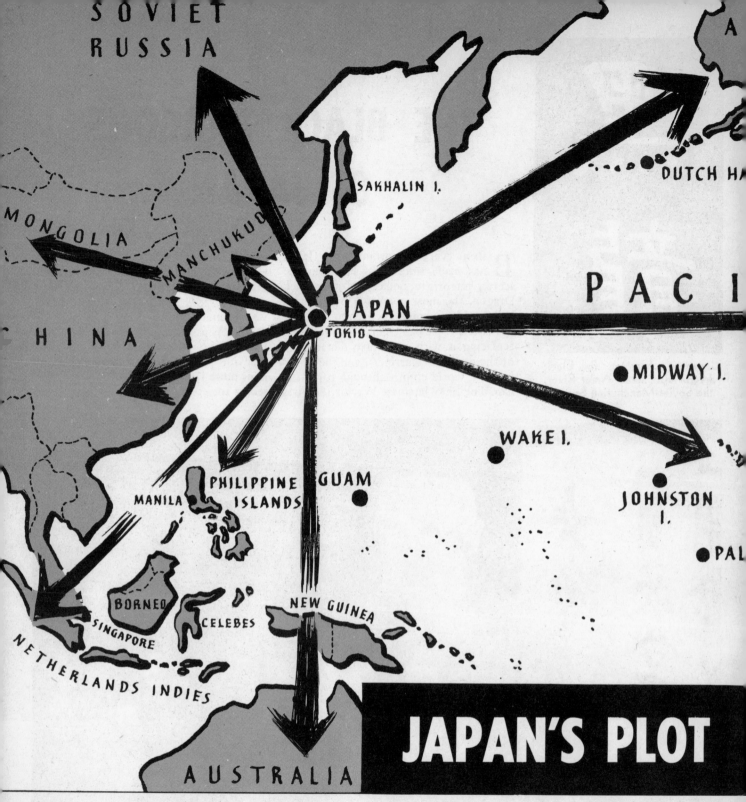

SOVIET RUSSIA

MONGOLIA

MANCHUKUO

CHINA

SAKHALIN I.

JAPAN
TOKIO

PHILIPPINE ISLANDS
MANILA

GUAM

BORNEO

CELEBES

SINGAPORE

NEW GUINEA

NETHERLANDS INDIES

AUSTRALIA

PACI

DUTCH HA

MIDWAY I.

WAKE I.

JOHNSTON I.

PAL

JAPAN'S PLOT

The Secret Report of General Tanaka in 1927 to the Emperor

IN 1927 the ex-bandit head of Manchuria, Chang Tso-lin, bought from a Japanese a rough translation of a confidential report to the Emperor of Japan written by Baron Giichi Tanaka, then Premier. The report was allegedly a Japanese plan for the conquest of the world. Japanese promptly denied its authenticity. For years it was laid aside as a fraud. Only after Japan's treacherous attack on Pearl Harbor was the Tanaka Document remembered. In it is laid down the empire program which Japan has been stead-fastly following for more than a decade. It is the Japanese *Mein Kampf*.

Tanaka himself was a son of a samurai of the Choshu class and a member of the Black Dragon, which has made his program that of all Black Dragons. He was Premier from 1927 to 1929, when he committed suicide in the apartment of his favorite geisha.

Here are some key quotations from the grandiose scheme for conquest outlined by Tanaka:

" . . . Japan cannot remove the difficulties in Eastern Asia unless she adopts a policy of 'blood and iron.' But in carrying out this policy we have to face the United States. . . In the future, if we want to control China, we must first crush the United States. . . But in order to conquer China we must first conquer Manchuria and Mongolia. . . . Having China's resources at our disposal, we shall proceed to conquer India, the Archipelago (Dutch East Indies), Asia Minor, Central Asia, and even Europe. . ."

FOR CONQUEST

Baron Giichi Tanaka, author of the Tanaka Document, pulls on his boots before going to see the Emperor.

TANAKA PROVIDED FOR FIFTH COLUMNISTS: ". . . we should appropriate 1,000,000 yen from the 'secret funds' of the Army . . . so that 400 retired officers disguised as teachers and Chinese citizens may be sent into Outer and Inner Mongolia to mix with the people, to gain the confidence of the Mongolian princes . . . to lay the foundations of our national interest for the next 100 years."

WAR ON RUSSIA WAS ALSO PLANNED: "In our struggle against . . . Soviet Russia, we should drive China before us and direct events from behind. . . That we should draw swords with Russia again in order to gain the wealth of North Manchuria seems a necessary step. . . We shall pour our forces into North Manchuria as far as we can. When Soviet Russia intervenes, as she must, that is our opportunity for open conflict. . . . Looking into the future, a war with Russia is inevitable. . . After completion of this line (Changchun-Taonan railroad) we shall be able to . . . advance on Siberia through three directions. . . ."

IN SUMMARIZING, TANAKA AGAIN COMES BACK TO RUSSIA AND THE UNITED STATES:

" . . . The Yamato race is . . . embarked on the journey of world conquest. . . . Our first step was to conquer Formosa and the second step to annex Korea. Having completed these, the third step is yet to be taken, and that is the conquest of Manchuria, Mongolia, and China. When this is done the rest of Asia, including the South Sea Islands, will be at our feet. . . .

For the sake of self-preservation and of giving warning to the rest of the world we must fight America some time. The American Asiatic squadron stationed in the Philippines is but a stone's throw from Tsushima. . .

Manchuria and Mongolia are the Belgium of the Far East. In the Great War Belgium was the battlefield. In our wars with Russia and the United States we must make Manchuria and Mongolia suffer the ravages. . . ."

These Black Dragons Follow

Crafty, tough Hideki Tojo, Premier and head of army, follows Tanaka's plan ruthlessly. Very active in the Black Dragon, he plotted treacherous attack on the United States.

General Hajime Sugiyama, Black Dragon leader and army chief of staff in 1937, carried out the attack on China called for by the Tanaka plan after Manchuria had been seized.

COLONEL SHUITU MATSUMURA, Chief of Information of the army section of Japanese Imperial Headquarters, who announced the Vichy government of French Indo China had permitted Japanese troops to march through en route to Singapore, is a leading Black Dragon. The Black Dragons have never hesitated to murder anyone, even the Premier, if he seemed to be in their way.

Tanaka's Plan for Conquest

Ambitious Koki Hirota, Premier following Black Dragon assassinations of 1936 and once Ambassador to U. S., will probably succeed aged Mitsuru Toyama as Chief Terrorist.

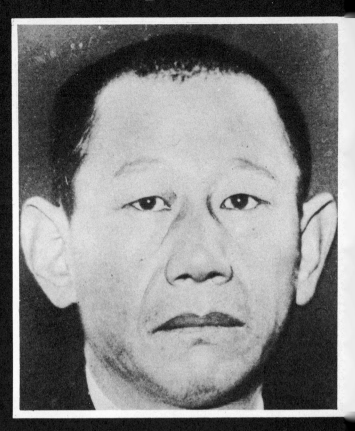

Ruthless Kingoro Hashimoto, liaison man between Black Dragon and Konoye. Ordered the attack which resulted in Sinking of U. S. Gunboat Panay in 1937.

BIG FOUR OF JAPAN who plotted attack against United States included Prince Konoye, Matsuoka, Admiral Yoshida, and General Tojo, who ... rightened by a resist... enough "Panay" Defen... of the United States and then Russia are the last steps in the Tanaka program for building Japan's empire. Under the "Big Four" the last vestiges of democ... disappeared from Japan.

The Rise of Hitler

ADOLF HITLER will go down in history as the most underrated man of our time. A hypochondriac, possessed by complex and contradictory emotions, a non-German filled with a desire for a world-dominating Germany led by himself, he rose in twenty years from a nondescript water-colorist to a tyrant capable of challenging a world which had steadfastly refused to take him seriously. No thinker, no soldier, no organizer, he had an intuitive political sense, a sinister, completely cynical approach to propaganda, and a fanatical single-mindedness—though his tactics might change—about his true object, a Germany that would dictate to the world.

He began his political life as a spy for the German army among labor groups, being assigned to spy on the German Workers' party in 1919. Seeing in this organization a chance to gain control of Germany, he changed its name to National Socialist so that it would appeal to both nationalist and labor groups. The fraud of his "socialist" aims was maintained for years; indeed, after the war began he announced it was against the "plutocratic" democracies. His creed is stated in *Mein Kampf*. "People will believe a big lie more easily than a half-lie." Though he was an astute propagandist, Hitler might have remained a street-corner anti-Semite had the army and the industrialists not seen in him a means to their own greedy ends for more power and the crushing of German labor. Once in power, the terror he unleashed reached bestial depths. Thousands were murdered and tortured by his storm troopers. Schools, libraries, colleges became the instruments of his vicious race propaganda. Scientists like Einstein and writers like Mann were forced to leave their country. Yet the rise of Hitler was not entirely of German doing. He had the passive, occasionally active, support of many of the financiers, industrialists, politicians of Europe who believed, if left alone, he would attack their No. 1 bogey: Soviet Russia.

A corporal in World War I, Hitler began his career in 1919 spying on labor groups for the German army.

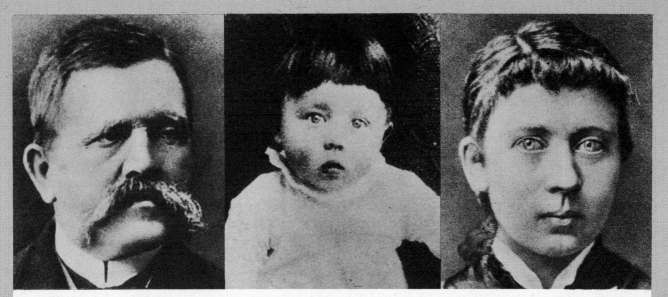

HITLER'S FATHER was Alois Schicklgruber, a cobbler who later changed his name to Heidler and through misspelling to Hitler. Thrice married, his first wife bought him a job as an Austrian customs inspector. His third wife, Klara Poelzl, gave birth to Adolf in Braunau, April 20, 1889. The above baby picture was taken when he was just over a year old. Hitler grew up hating his overbearing father, and his father regarded him as a worthless dreamer. Hitler loved his mother deeply, which had much to do with his development.

POSTWAR GERMANY was an economic wreck and a national psychopathic case. The Versailles Treaty had heaped enormous debts on it, slashed off the Ruhr and Rhineland, broken up the old empire, barred it from the League of Nations. Inflation made the mark worthless, ruining the lower middle class and starving the working class. The German people felt ashamed and that their "punishment" was undeserved. Hitler fed upon their misery and desire to hold their heads up. Promising all things to all men, demanding the German people follow him, Hitler screamed, "You are humiliated. You are degraded. Germany is a sick nation. . . . You have been trying to persuade yourselves that you are content with this miserable republic." He blamed everything on "Jewish Communists."

THE FIRST PHOTOGRAPH OF HITLER to reach America showed him reviewing members of various nationalist societies, including his own brown-shirted SA storm troopers, at Nuremberg, Sept. 2, 1923. One of the labor groups Hitler had spied on for the army was the German Workers' party. He had joined it, taken over control, changing its name to National Socialist party (Nazi). From the start he had the backing of the army. Note the helmeted ex-army officers in the picture above. As the party grew, Hitler put most emphasis on his violent anti-Semitism and attacks on Communists and shed the anti-capitalist program of the original party.

FIRST BIG HITLER BACKER was General Erich von Ludendorff and in Nov. 1923 they attempted a *putsch* at Munich which failed when authorities fired upon the Hitlerites, killing 16 of them, wounding Hermann Goering.

THIS HITHERTO UNPUBLISHED PICTURE shows Hitler on trial for treason after the *putsch*. Convicted, he was imprisoned in Landsberg fortress where he wrote *Mein Kampf*, outlining Nazi program.

The Men Behind
HITLER

Adolf Hitler in Jail: 1924.

THE *putsch*, though it failed, brought Hitler to the attention of Krupp, German munitions king who was then serving a jail sentence for having incited anti-French riots, and Fritz Thyssen, head of the powerful German steel trust. After publication of *Mein Kampf* in 1925 they began contributing heavily to Nazi party funds through Goering, who was Hitler's chief contact with industrialists. Thyssen later named the chief financial supporters of Hitler as himself, Von Papen, Von Schroeder, Kirdorf, Krupp von Bohlen und Halbach. They backed Hitler because they were certain Germany would become Communist. Hitler promised them he would smash the trade unions and deprive the working class of all its political rights, give Germany "Christian" Fascism.

THIS UNPUBLISHED PICTURE shows Krupp von Bohlen. German munitions maker, playing cards in prison while awaiting sentence for having incited a riot which resulted in many deaths.

This early picture shows Fritz Thyssen, German industrialist and Nazi backer, with Hitler at a review of the Nazi Storm Troopers.

ANOTHER EARLY HITLER BACKER was wealthy Dr. Alfred Hugenberg, shown here with Von Papen. Hugenberg, who owned the film trust UFA, the publishing trust Scherl, and the official German news agency, gave him good publicity, won him industrialists.

NAZI STORM TROOPERS, shown here parading behind the flag of piracy, were encouraged by Hitler to beat up and murder Jews and trade-union leaders. Composed of riffraff, they were periodically whipped up to anti-Semitic outrages by Jew-baiter Streicher.

HITLER PICKED CAPABLE BUT RUTHLESS MEN as sub-Fuehrers: 1. Goering, a World War I pilot, a dope fiend, brutal but a good organizer; 2. Wilhelm Frick, loyal, unambitious, the "perfect bureaucrat"; 3. Gregor Strasser, brilliant theorist, good organizer, a murderous gangster. Strasser had headed a northern Nazi-like party and the rivalry between him and Hitler, who developed the southern party, was intense after consolidation of the two. In 1934 Hitler had him, Ernst Roehm, Karl Ernst, and other mistakes in judgment executed in a "blood purge." Hitler came to power easily. At midnight, Jan. 29, 1933, Hitler, Von Papen, and Hugenberg awoke President Hindenburg to tell him Chancellor von Schleicher, later murdered in the purge, planned to use the army against the Nazis. They had the bewildered old man appoint Hitler Chancellor, Von Papen vice-Chancellor to avoid "civil war."

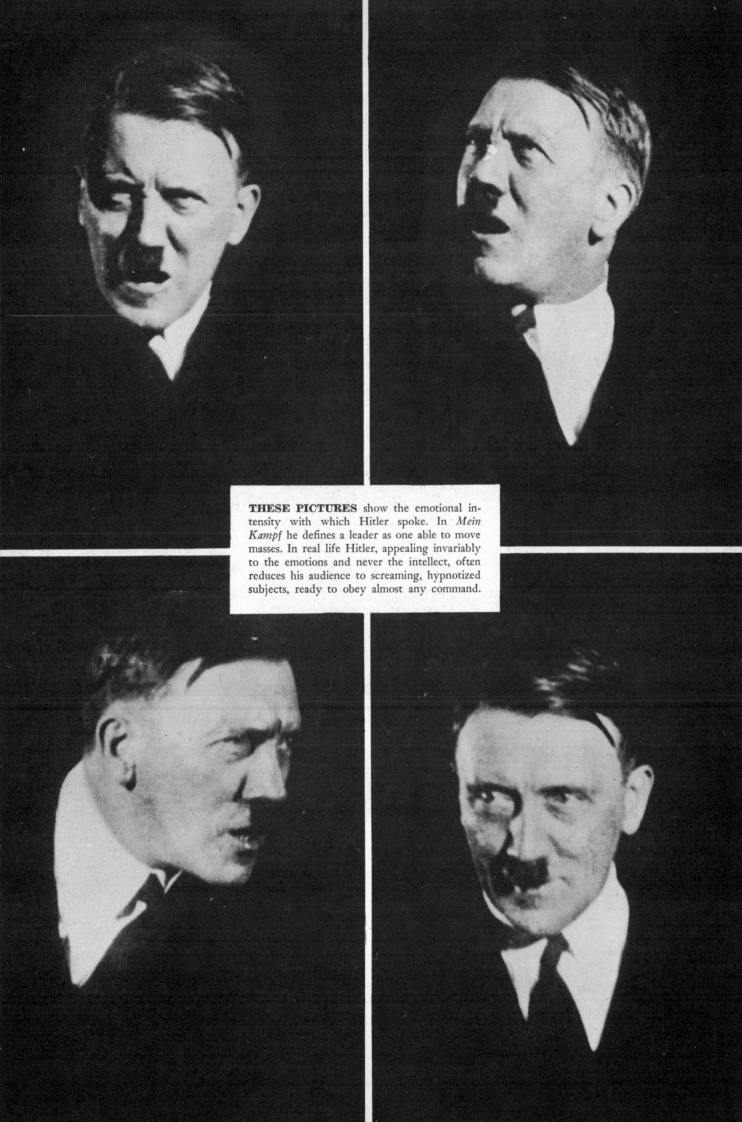

THESE PICTURES show the emotional intensity with which Hitler spoke. In *Mein Kampf* he defines a leader as one able to move masses. In real life Hitler, appealing invariably to the emotions and never the intellect, often reduces his audience to screaming, hypnotized subjects, ready to obey almost any command.

Hitler assumed power legally, backed by the might of Hindenburg, who was at first contemptuous of him, later liked him.

These died outside the Reichstag from Nazi blows in riots that followed. German people themselves were Hitler's first victims.

JUST BEFORE THE ELECTIONS to confirm Hitler's chancellorship, the Reichstag was fired. Nazis blamed Communists. A Dutch half-wit, Van der Lubbe, above, and Communists Dimitrov and Torgler were arrested as the Red arsonists. Nothing could be proved against the Communists. Evidence indicated Nazis had set the blaze to drive hesitant Germans into the Nazi fold. This it did.

BOOK-BURNING BEGAN the intensive Nazification of Germany. Books on democracy, liberalism, freedom, and scientific works that refuted Hitler's lie about Nordic superiority were burned by the ton by wild storm troopers everywhere. Pogroms against the Jews were encouraged and they were deprived of their civil rights. The schools were among the first instruments taken over for propaganda.

IMPRISONED FOR OPPOSING NAZISM, these men were photographed at Dachau, largest and worst of the Nazi concentration camps. They included Catholics, teachers, Communists, scientists, trade unionists, Jews, democrats, writers. Thousands of them have been beheaded by the medieval ax—reintroduced to Germany by Goering. More thousands have been tortured, beaten, and starved to death. These horrors aroused the protest of the world.

IN AMERICA, TOO, Hitler started his campaign to gain converts for the Nazi cause. This picture, snapped in the Yorkville section of New York City the day Hitler assumed power, shows the office of the National Socialist party, later the German-American Bund—proof that Hitler had already established his fifth column here. But most Americans, if they noticed Hitler at all, put him down as "the new dictator who looks like Charlie Chaplin."

23

Nazi Sub-Fuehrers

Pictured on this and the opposite page are the men who with Hitler led the Nazi party to power. With him they developed their terrible criminal plans and executed them ruthlessly. They are among the most brutal and depraved men ever to win power in any country. Hand-picked by Hitler himself, they must bear with him the responsibility of Nazi crimes.

HERMANN GOERING . . . No. 2 Nazi . . . Big Business contact man . . . A World War I ace . . . an ex-dope addict . . . ruthless . . . an organizer and executive.

RUDOLF HESS . . . No. 3 . . . Hitler' closest friend . . . well educated . . . mys tic and fanatic . . . quiet . . . a believer ir faith healing. . . . Nazism's "gentleman."

KARL ERNST . . . an ex-waiter . . . Roehm's chief protégé . . . top-ranking Storm Trooper . . . murdered by Goering's orders in purge.

GREGOR STRASSER . . . once No. 2 Nazi . . . its first theoretician . . . powerful . . . terrorist . . . also murdered in the purge of 1934.

WILHELM FRICK . . . a colorless law-yer . . . obedient . . . drafted anti-Semitic laws . . . made hatred of England part of Germany's educational program.

HJALMAR SCHACHT . . . a Prussian aristocrat . . . shrewd monetary wizard . . . won financial support for Hitler's arms

WALTHER FUNK . . . an obese yes-man . . . friend of many financiers . . . Nazis gave him a party job to make contact with

ALFRED ROSENBERG . . . born ir Lithuania . . . taught draftsmanship . . . mystic philosopher of Nazism . . . edito

JOSEPH GOEBBELS . . . a frustrated author . . . a violent orator . . . reckless . . . vindictive . . . inventor of many anti-Semitic lies.

JOACHIM VON RIBBENTROP . . . a champagne salesman . . . once worked in Canada . . . very ambitious . . . cynical . . . slick . . . wealthy.

ERNST ROEHM . . . ruthless . . . homosexual . . . Chief of the Storm Troops . . . violent . . . murdered in the blood purge of 1934 with von Schleichter.

JULIUS STREICHER . . . a Bavarian gauleiter . . . exponent of brutality . . . publisher of pornography . . . violent, crude anti-Semite.

HEINRICH HIMMLER . . . an ex-policeman from Munich . . . head of the secret Gestapo and SS (Hitler bodyguard) . . . ambitious and utterly ruthless . . .

REINHARD HEYDRICH . . . cold-blooded . . . No. 2 Chief of Gestapo . . . personally shot Roehm . . . assassinated in Prague in May 1942.

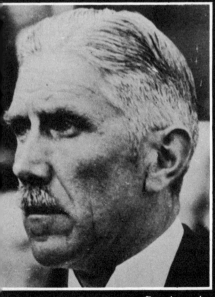

FRANZ VON PAPEN . . . Prussian aristocrat . . . ex-Chancellor . . . head of spy ring in U.S. in World War I . . . too am-

FRITZ WEIDEMANN . . . Hitler's commander in World War I . . . entrusted with fifth-column missions . . . served as a consul

ROBERT LEY . . . World War I pilot . . . ex-chemist . . . head of the fake Nazi trade unions . . . a notorious drunkard . .

Mussolini Defies the League and Grabs Ethiopia

AFTER YEARS OF WARLIKE BELLOWING Mussolini openly began picking a quarrel with Ethiopia in the fall of 1934 and mobilized his armies.

BUT HAILE SELASSIE, ETHIOPIA'S EMPEROR, felt certain that the League of Nations would protect his country as it had a few years earlier.

DURING the summer of 1934 Mussolini, pompous dictator of Fascist Italy, openly began to assemble large quantities of war materials at Mediterranean bases. For twelve years he had been preaching the right of might, promising to restore the Roman Empire itself as well as the grandeur of Rome. When the Italian governors of Eritrea and Somaliland began bickering with Haile Selassie, Emperor of Ethiopia, the mystery of where Mussolini intended to strike was solved. Only the question of when remained unanswered.

Known as the "garden of Africa," Ethiopia is a land of fertile plains and valleys, separated from the Red Sea and Indian Ocean by the scorching Danakil Desert. In 1896 the Italians had been defeated in an attempt to conquer the country. In 1926 Britain, France, and Italy attempted to divide the country into three zones for their exclusive exploitation. But calm Haile Selassie had beaten off that scheme by bringing their secret plan before the League of Nations where the British, French, and Italians were forced by world opinion to give up their contemplated spoils.

On Dec. 5, 1934, Mussolini charged that an outlying Italian post at Wal Wal had been attacked by Ethiopian troops. This was an incredible blunder for Wal Wal, even on Italian maps, was some sixty miles within Ethiopia. Selassie protested to the Italians and asked for arbitration under a 1928 Italo-Ethiopian pact of eternal peace. But Mussolini, accusing Ethiopia of aggression, invaded. A week later Selassie appealed to the League, and on Jan. 3, 1935, he asked the League to name Italy the aggressor and impose sanctions. But meanwhile the French Prime Minister and Foreign Minister Laval had secretly agreed to give Il Duce a free hand, and signed an accord with him granting twenty-five per cent of the Franco-Ethiopian railway shares, cultural autonomy for the 250,000 Italians in Tunis, and—most important of all—control over one of the Seven Brothers islands; this gave Il Duce strategic control over the narrow passage leading from the Red Sea into the Indian Ocean.

Even as the League began its debating, Italian armies plunged into Ethiopia from three directions, under the command of aging Marshal de Bono, one of Mussolini's early followers.

JAMMED TROOPSHIPS LEFT NAPLES almost daily during the summer of 1935 for Eritrea, from which the aging Italian General Emilio de Bono planned to attack. Despite more than a decade of continuous propaganda for war, riots and strikes against the war broke out in many parts of Italy. By closing down the Suez Canal through which the Italian troopships had to go, the British might have stopped the war. But the Italians were paying $2.50 a head for the passage of their troops and the British were not inclined to close it. Meanwhile, in Addis Ababa Haile Selassie began assembling his untrained, primitively equipped soldiers to meet the highly motorized invaders. He found none of the munitions factories of Europe would sell him arms. But he still kept his faith in England and the League.

These terror-stricken Ethiopian soldiers had never seen planes before. Mussolini's warriors bombed helpless villages mercilessly.

Ethiopian artillery amounted to only a few pieces from the War of 1896. They had no tanks, few planes, old rifles.

The Italians had modern artillery plus tanks and poison gas. Thus Ethiopia learned to appreciate "civilization."

AFTER SANCTIONS HAD BEEN HALF-HEARTEDLY applied, Sir Samuel Hoare met with Laval in December. Together they worked out a secret "peace" plan which gave Italy two thirds of Ethiopia. The battle for sanctions had been a tremendous one, waged mainly by Anthony Eden, Maxim Litvinov, and the British people. But the British government, anxious not to annoy Mussolini, approved the Hoare-Laval plan. However, when the terms became known to the British public, overwhelmingly anti-Mussolini, such a roar of disapproval went up that the plan had to be dropped, Hoare had to resign. Meanwhile, in Ethiopia the Italians were doing so poorly that Mussolini, faced with disaster on all sides, replaced De Bono with Badoglio, and threw all his mechanized forces into the war. The Ethiopians, not taking advantage of guerrilla warfare, were massacred by the thousands. The Italians advanced 120 miles in nine days and seized Addis Ababa May 5. Selassie fled to London. Thus the League failed in its second test.

Litvinov urged collective security as the only way to stop aggression.

Eden, defying Hoare, led the fight for sanctions against Mussolini.

Selassie himself pleaded for aid in the halls of Geneva, but to no avail.

Bombastic, pompous Mussolini got his Fascist salute, later adopted by Hitler, from the Poet D'Annunzio. "Der Fuehrer" is the German equivalent for "Il Duce."

MUSSOLINI: *Governor by Gag*

CRUDE, violent, temperamental, vain, and flamboyant, Benito Mussolini began life the son of a village blacksmith and Socialist. He was born July 29, 1883. When he was nineteen, he fled Italy to escape military service. In 1904 he returned a journalist, a Socialist, and a violent anti-cleric, lecturing on *The Crimes of the Popes*—a career that landed him in jail frequently. Expelled from the Socialist party for advocating Italian intervention in World War I, he was sent to the front where he was wounded, shipped home to found a pro-war paper, *Popolo d'Italia*.

The end of the war filled northern industrial Italy with disgruntled, jobless soldiers whom Mussolini began organizing into a Socialist party which had as its base a fierce nationalism. Then, under the pretext of "liberating" the unions from Communists, he began gangsterlike attacks on them, breaking strikes, murdering union leaders, wrecking clubhouses. His smashing of offices of *Avanti*, labor paper, by the Fascisti attracted the attention of the General Confederation

of Industry, which began financing him.

Now that he had funds, Mussolini's party began to grow, and he announced his program: "Law and Order," saving Italy from the chaos of Communism. The army backed him. So did the southern landowners. The industrialists continued their support. With these behind him he marched on Rome—after the government and the King had assured him his Black Shirts would not be met with force.

Mussolini brutally crushed all opposition which he felt could not be won over. He reserved his most ferocious treatment for his ex-comrades—the Socialists. Behind all his bombast lay a shrewd, coldly calculating mind seeking only aggrandizement in power and fame for Mussolini alone. He has betrayed every pledge he ever made. He crushed fellow-Fascists without hesitation if their popularity seemed to jeopardize his own. Through all the early years of his rule by gag, not one of his dramatic, seemingly daring moves was made without coldly arranging for its success beforehand.

30

AS A SOCIALIST AGITATOR AND ANTI-CLERIC Mussolini was arrested eleven times. The tiny confines of his cell gave him a severe case of claustrophobia. In Rome his office was sixty by forty.

MUSSOLINI'S FAMOUS MARCH ON ROME was not begun until the King gave him assurances his Black Shirts would not be attacked. The King did so by phone; Il Duce insisted on a telegram.

KING VICTOR EMMANUEL received Il Duce as a savior, turned down Badoglio's offer to blow the Black Shirts "out of history" with a whiff of grapeshot. Il Duce's LAW and ORDER program was begun by beating, murdering, torturing anti-Fascists.

THIS RARE PICTURE SHOWS THE SECRET FUNERAL OF MATTEOTTI, labor leader, who was bestially murdered in 1924. His murder gave Mussolini his first real crisis. Admitting the murder boldly, Il Duce weathered the storm with more violence. Under the pretense of saving Italy from Communism, his gangs' victims totaled 3,000 in two years. Their favorite torture: castor oil. The press was suppressed and editors who defied Il Duce were horsewhipped and their presses wrecked.

TO IMPRESS ITALIANS AND THE OUTSIDE WORLD Mussolini posed for this picture with two lions. Hundreds of American papers fell for this "strong-man" publicity stunt; years later Pierre van Paassen, foreign correspondent, revealed the lions' teeth had been extracted, that they were fed on macaroni. Other pictures showed Il Duce in an imitation of Napoleon's uniform with his left hand inside the coat, skiing while stripped to the waist, jumping horses over barriers, fencing ferociously. The American press gave no other dictator so much favorable space.

THE VISIT OF SIR AUSTEN CHAMBERLAIN, British Foreign Minister and half-brother of Neville, to Mussolini in 1926 indicated British Conservatives were inclined to give Il Duce the go-ahead. Earlier Britain absolved the Fascist government from the Italian debt for a negligible sum. This, plus a $50,-000,000 loan from J. P. Morgan, helped Il Duce.

MOST OF THESE CHILDREN ARE PROBABLY DEAD today, killed in Il Duce's wars. Italy's youth was a special target for Mussolini's propaganda. He appealed to its love of action and romanticism. A child entering school was taught Fascism was the "proud passion of the best Italian youth," to obey without question, to sneer at freedom, and to be proud of violence.

MUSSOLINI'S WIFE, VIRTUALLY AN EXILE for many years, has occasionally been permitted to appear publicly since war against England began, usually in the uniform of the women's auxiliary service. Though she bore him five children, Il Duce did not marry her until his desire for Vatican support made a religious rite expedient.

"PEACE" WITH THE VATICAN CAME with the signing of the Lateran Treaty in 1929 by Cardinal Gasparri and Il Duce. Shortly after coming to power the ex-atheist had ordered the crucifix put back in the schools. But at the same time his Fascisti gangs burned Catholic clubhouses because Mussolini dared leave no spot where men could talk freely. The Vatican paper criticized the Fascist regime strongly. The Lateran Treaty was to bring peace between Il Duce and the Church, but, shortly after, Mussolini and the Pope clashed again over Fascist education.

VITTORIO, MUSSOLINI'S ELDEST SON, VISITED HOLLYWOOD in 1937 as the guest of Hal Roach. He is shown here with Mrs. Roach and Dolores del Rio. But Americans, slowly awakening to the menace of Fascism, protested his visit so vigorously that he had to leave the country. Vittorio had flown with his brother Bruno against the Ethiopians. Americans were incensed when Bruno, callously describing how he had bombed a group of helpless Ethiopians, wrote: ". . . the group opened up like the flowering of a rose. It was most entertaining."

IL DUCE'S FAVORITE is his daughter Edda, who married Count Ciano, pulled him into inner Fascist circles. Smart, shrewd, an intriguer like her father, she has often served to win diplomatic victories. Before the outbreak of the war she toured European and South American capitals, winning many friends for her father.

Ja! Hitler Takes the Saar

CEASELESSLY, throughout his rise to power, Hitler raged over the "crimes of Versailles," promising revenge. Nothing won him more sympathy from the German people. A major sore spot in the treaty had been the giving of the vast Saar coal fields to the French. The Saar, whose 770,000 people were 90 per cent German, produced some 13,000,000 metric tons of coal yearly, loss of which greatly cramped German heavy industry. Under the Versailles Treaty political control of the district was to be vested in an international commission for fifteen years, at the end of which time a plebiscite was to determine whether the region went to Germany or to France permanently. The fifteenth year was 1935. Nothing could have suited Hitler better. Its German population insured victory for Germany at the plebiscite—and Hitler could claim he had begun fulfilling his pledge to right the wrongs of Versailles. To heighten the atmosphere of conflict he began a campaign of propaganda, sent his storm troopers in to terrorize dissident Germans, threatened a *putsch*, and glorified himself and Nazism as the saviors of World War I-dismembered Germany.

SECRETLY HITLER HAD BEGUN rearming the Reich although his soldiers carried spades instead of guns. They could be seen drilling in every part of Germany, building a tremendous system of military roads and commercial airports which could be readily transformed into military flying fields.

AS THE JANUARY PLEBISCITE NEARED international military forces took over policing of the Saar to curb outbreaks of violence. Geoffrey Knox, head of the League's Commission which had governed the region for fifteen years, is shown here inspecting the Italian contingent of the international forces with Major J. E. S. Brind, commander. A small, articulate anti-Nazi group carried on an intense campaign against Hitler's propaganda and fought Saar Nazis in the streets. Hitler's campaign was spectacular; he even brought Nazi Saarlanders back from America to vote. Everywhere it was conceded that the German populace would vote "*Ja*" for the return to the Reich. In the end some ninety per cent voted for the Reich. Hitler, righter of the wrongs of Versailles, drove into Saarbrucken, where his Nazi storm troopers staged a tremendous welcoming demonstration. Few Germans did not rejoice. And now Hitler had coal.

THE SECRET TRAINING OF THE GERMAN ARMY WAS revealed to Germany's people at a Nazi party rally, Sept. 6, 1934, when German labor squads, marching smartly across the stadium, suddenly broke into the goose step. It was as a signal to the hundreds of thousands of spectators, who went wild with joy. The fall before Hitler had withdrawn the German delegation from the League of Nations because it refused his demand for military equality with all nations. Hitler boasted: "We are strong and getting stronger."

Hitler Secretly Rearms the Reich, Defies the League

THE Versailles Treaty imposed drastic restrictions on German armaments. It limited the army to 100,000 men, barred conscription, and a general staff. The navy was limited to six small battleships. But the most drastic provisions forbade any submarines and any air force. Only a strong league could have prevented rearming of the Reich and the League was weak. Shortly after seizing power the Nazis began secret rearmament; of their intention to rearm, they made no secret. By 1934 they had a well-trained, well-equipped army of 400,000. On March 16, 1935, Hitler defied the League, announced universal conscription, and his intention of having an army of 1,000,000 men by the spring of 1936.

THE GERMAN GENERAL STAFF, SECRETLY IN EXISTENCE SINCE 1920, had set up classes for the development of young officers for the rapidly expanding army. Here an officer instructs student officers drawn from the regular army in strategic tactics. Rearmament plans endeared Hitler to Junkers.

USING GLIDERS INSTEAD OF MILITARY PLANES, which were barred by the Versailles Treaty, Goering began the secret training of an air force in 1933. Germany became one of the most air-minded countries in the world. Simultaneously Goering began developing commercial airlines. His purposes: the big commercial planes could be easily converted into bombers; it gave the glider-trained pilots opportunities to gain experience with heavy-motored planes; factories and laboratories could be used for war purposes.

GERMAN TANK CORPS WERE SECRETLY TRAINED with canvas and wooden dummy tanks, such as these, while the artillery corps were developed with wooden guns. Most of the Nazi tank tactics came from Russia.

NOR WAS THE NAVY NEGLECTED. Secret construction of submarines, barred by the Versailles Treaty, began in 1934, and by November 1935 twenty-one 250-ton subs were in service. To the murmured protest of England, Hitler replied they were "defensive."

Ja! HITLER GRABS THE RHINELAND

Reichstag für Freiheit und Frieden

Wahlkreis

Nationalsozialistische Deutsche Arbeiterpartei

Adolf Hitler

Heß   Frick   Göring   Goebbels

○

THE GERMAN PEOPLE VOTED APPROVAL of Hitler by putting an X in the circle. There was no way of voting disapproval of him.

WITH each new step Hitler promised peace, no new territorial demands, and implied, by his violent harangues against Communism that, if left alone, he would throttle the Soviet Union. On May 21, 1935, he pledged respect of the Locarno Pact which guaranteed the Franco-German-Belgian borders. But on March 7, 1936, with dramatic suddenness, the Fuehrer sent his new armies into the demilitarized Rhineland, scrapping the Locarno Treaty, the main pillar of European peace. His excuse was the ratification of the Franco-Soviet Pact of mutual assistance. The French began mobilizing, then called it off and appealed to the League. Hitler had been shrewd enough to attach a long, though utterly impossible, proposal for a new Locarno to his denunciation of the original pact. This, the French had paused to consider. The time to act passed, although Anthony Eden had immediately pledged Britain's support to France. Another "Ja" election was dutifully run off on January 29.

When the Nazis seized the Rhineland, they carried sealed orders to retreat if the French armies advanced against them.

Hitler's troops were met by cheering crowds who had not seen German soldiers on their streets for seventeen years.

FLANDIN, LAVAL'S SUCCESSOR AS FOREIGN MINISTER, was the Frenchman who couldn't make up his mind whether or not to oppose the Nazi troops. When it was too late to do anything else, he submitted the problem to the League. Colorless, plump, six foot four, Flandin had been elected as a reaction against Laval's appeasement policies. But, as Flandin admitted, he "agreed with the foreign policy of Laval" and had, in fact, supported Laval's fight for the sanctions against Italy which Eden had sought to apply. To Hitler this indicated Anglo-French disunity and he sent his troops marching. In America Hitler's move still attracted only momentary attention. People were busy with the CIO, Roosevelt, and the Supreme Court, Edward Windsor and Wally, Benny Goodman's hot clarinet.

Jubilant over splitting the Loyalist forces, Fascist General Franco walks through Burgos with Generals Mola and Calvanti.

Democracy Fights Back In Spain

On Saturday, July 18, 1936, Fascist-led military garrisons throughout Spain attempted to overthrow the new republican government. In the smaller cities they succeeded, but in Madrid, Barcelona, and Valencia they were crushed by the enraged people who, determined to defend their democratic rights, fought them off. Thus did Spain's long-festering civil war break out.

The revolution of 1931 had destroyed monarchy—but not the forces behind it. These, the real "bosses" of Spain, were the army, the grandee landowners, and the political clergy. As a group they were, as *Life* has said, "probably the world's worst bosses—irresponsible, arrogant, vain, ignorant, shiftless, and incompetent." The army, top-heavy with 21,000 officers and 700 generals, took one fourth the national budget to support these idle gentlemen. The political clergy, because the Church was rich and part of the State, were powerful in influence . . . and anti-democratic. But the land was Spain's greatest problem. One per cent of the people —the grandees—owned 51 per cent of the land. Few grandees, nearly all absentee owners, put back in improvements any of the money they took out of their estates. The peasants lived in degrading poverty. The rightist government which succeeded the republican forces of 1931 wiped out all reforms. It skidded from crisis to crisis until 1936, when the republican parties, forming a Popular Front *which excluded Communists and Socialists*, were elected. This was "Red" Spain against which Franco led his Fascist revolt. In reality, this was the oft-repeated lie of Hitler and Il Duce.

40

THE SPANISH PEOPLE FOUGHT OFF THE FASCISTS with every weapon they could find; many had never used a rifle before. The Fascist plan, backed by Spain's incompetent ex-"bosses," had been to seize power in strategic cities. But they had not reckoned on the determination of the people to fight for their democratic rights. Meanwhile, General Franco, who only a short time before had been imprisoned for disloyalty to the government and then retired at full pay, had flown to Morocco and returned with Spanish Foreign Legion and Moorish troops. On his return he assumed leadership of the Fascists in Spain.

WORKERS POURED OUT OF BARCELONA FACTORIES, armed themselves, and marched off to meet the advancing forces of Franco, who by the end of July had begun to receive assistance from Mussolini in the form of planes. Meanwhile, Moors were flown into the country in great quantities. By mid-August Hitler was sending planes, and soon Italian troops arrived to aid Franco, now an avowed Fascist. The reason for this, as John Gunther has said, was simply that Franco could not find enough Spaniards to fight for him. After a 70-day siege the Fascists took Toledo to rescue the rebels trapped in the Alcazar and advanced on Madrid.

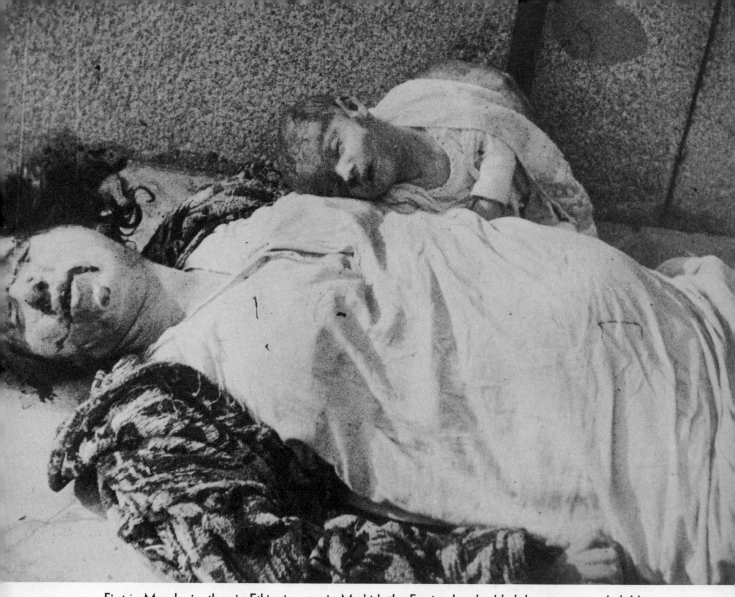

First in Manchuria, then in Ethiopia, now in Madrid, the Fascists bombed helpless women and children.

CARRYING AN ITALIAN FLAG, IL DUCE'S TROOPS are shown marching into the outskirts of Barcelona. They had been rushed into Spain when it became apparent that Franco could not defeat the heroic Spanish people's army alone. By the spring of 1937 there were 10,000 Nazi technicians and 65,000 Italian troops with Franco. With them came tanks, bombers, pursuit ships, and artillery.

NAZI MILITARY EXPERTS EXPLAINED the use of Krupp-made howitzers to members of the Nazi Black Condor Legion. Spain became a testing ground for the Fascists for their planes, tanks, guns, tactics, and men. Russia, the only nation to aid the Loyalists, sent tanks and planes, thus pitting their weapons against the Axis for the first time.

Bombing Barcelona continuously for 41 hours, Nazi pilots killed over 1,000 civilians. Here they acquired their brutal precision.

TO FIGHT NAZI AND FASCIST FORCES, anti-Nazis from all over the world, including 2,700 Americans, trickled into Spain to form the International Brigade, shown here charging a Fascist machine-gun nest near Irún. It included writers, laborers, trade unionists, Communists, seamen, Socialists. They were of every race and creed, men who were convinced Spain was the place to stop Fascism. They fought valiantly, more than once stopping Fascist advances with suicidal counterattacks. Early in the war England and France suggested all the countries of Europe sign a "non-intervention pact," agreeing not to aid either side, to "keep the war from spreading." This monstrous agreement prevented the legally elected government from purchasing munitions to put down the Fascist uprising.

PRESIDENT ROOSEVELT ROCKED THE WORLD with his Chicago speech of October 17 which called for "quarantining the aggressors." Though he mentioned neither the Nazis nor Fascists, howls of surprised pain went up from Berlin and Rome. Roosevelt had invoked the U. S. Neutrality Act at the outbreak of the war but now regretted it. Axis aid to Franco was redoubled in order to win a quick victory before the Neutrality Act, which prevented American guns and material from going to Loyalist Spain, could be revoked.

THE FIRST NAZIS TO DIE FIGHTING DEMOCRACY are brought home for burial. They were killed when a Loyalist pilot bombed the Nazi battleship *Deutschland*. In reprisal the Nazis brutally shelled the town of Almeria, making "non-intervention" a farce.

GERMAN AND ITALIAN OFFICERS EXAMINE a Russian-made tank which had been captured from the Loyalists. In comparison to the aid given Franco by Germany and Italy, Russian aid to the Loyalists was meager. At no time did they send troops.

FASCIST VICTORY CAME ON MARCH 28, 1939, when the armies of Franco entered surrendered Madrid. The Spanish people, despite unbelievable odds, had held off Franco and his Nazi and Italian allies for almost three years. But after they lost Teruel in February 1938, and the Fascists pushed on to the sea, splitting Loyalist Spain, theirs was a steadily losing battle. By the end of the war Franco owed Germany $800,000,000, Italy $500,000,000, and forty per cent of his troops were either German or Italian.

THE REMNANTS OF THE SHATTERED LOYALIST armies fled the Franco terror by crossing the Pyrenees into southern France where they were promptly disarmed and incarcerated in concentration camps by French police. But thousands could not escape and were either murdered or imprisoned by Franco. Meanwhile, faced with the monster they had helped to create, the democracies set about trying to win Franco from his Fascist partners by granting him loans and supplies.

JAPANESE BOMBS CAME FROM U.S. SCRAP IRON which was shipped to the steel mills in ever-increasing quantities. In 1932 U.S. sent 13,000 tons of scrap to Japan's munitions factories; in 1933, 142,133 tons; and by 1939 scrap shipments reached 607,208 tons. High-octane gasoline for Japanese war planes was also shipped in vast quantities as part of the State Department's "appeasement" policy.

THIS TERRIFIED, SCREAMING BABY was almost the only human being left alive in Shanghai's South Station after brutal Japanese pilots bombed it to pieces in September 1937, when Japan, following the Tanaka Plan, began her attempt to conquer all China.

Japan Attempts to Swallow All China

STEP No. 4 in the Tanaka Plan for Japanese conquest was the conquering of all China; its vast resources were to enable Japan to conquer most of the world. The 1932 invasion of Manchuria and seizure of Shanghai aroused China's millions. In December 1936 young Marshal Chang Hsueh-Liang, tired of begging Chiang Kai-shek to fight the Japanese, kidnaped him and forced him to agree to stop his civil war on the Communists, form a democratic government, and resist Japan. The Japanese decided to strike before China became too strong. An incident was needed. It came on July 7, 1937, when Japanese troops, on night maneuvers near the Marco Polo Bridge ten miles from Peking, discovered one of their men missing. Deciding the rebellious Chinese had seized him, they attacked the near-by village of Lukouchiao. Meanwhile, the missing man reappeared—he had been lost in the dark. Disregarding his return, within a few hours 35,000 Japanese troops, ready in advance, were marching through Tientsin toward Peking. Chiang Kai-shek demanded the Japanese evacuation of the Peking area. Their reply was the seizure of Peking itself. The Chinese people rallied behind Chiang and, in August, when the Japanese began pouring into Shanghai's suburbs, they were met by hard-fighting, united Chinese troops. The battle lasted until November.

CHIANG KAI-SHEK SENT HIS BEST TROOPS into the Shanghai area to meet the Japanese, who had filled the harbor with transports and warships. 450,000 Chinese, probably twice as many Japanese, lost their lives in the titanic struggle that followed. The superiority of Japanese arms and planes—the Chinese had practically none—forced the Chinese back. On Nov. 9 the Chinese retreated toward Nanking.

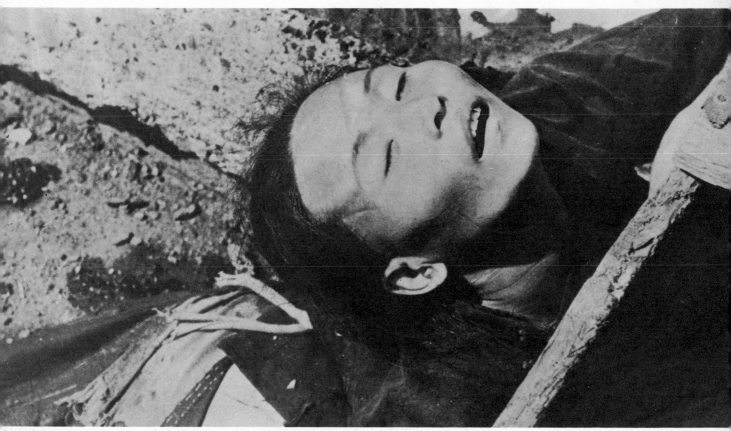

THIS CHINESE WOMAN WAS ONLY ONE OF THOUSANDS of civilians killed by the ruthless Japanese bombers, who carried out their attacks on the civilian populace with the same ferocity they used on the Chinese armies. They bombed, strafed, machine-gunned, beheaded, raped, and looted. They waited until the Shanghai South Station was filled with people waiting for trains before blowing it to pieces. This was the Fascist total war and it was expected to terrorize and subdue the nation, paralyze its morale. But instead of subduing the Chinese, it strengthened them, united them as nothing else ever could. Meanwhile, the Chinese armies, falling back to Nanking, drew the rapacious Japanese deeper into China. Despite all this bloodshed the Japanese maintained there was no war.

47

Enraged at Chinese resistance, the Japanese bound 1,500 Chinese soldiers captured at Nanking and then bayoneted them in pairs.

AS THE CHINESE ARMIES RETREATED, the Japanese, thinking victory lay only a few months ahead, advanced. At Nanking, capital of China, Chiang Kai-shek made another stand. After a fierce battle in which both sides lost heavily the capital fell on December 13, 1937, but Chiang escaped with his armies intact to retreat still further into China. The Japanese, who had been proclaiming their "friendliness toward the Chinese," were enraged when the Chinese did not surrender. They slaughtered captured Chinese soldiers and civilians with a bestial brutality that shocked the world. International protests against Japan's warfare brought cynical assurances from Tokyo that the Japanese were not engaged in a war, that it was only an "incident" which would be settled very shortly.

Captured Chinese being buried alive by Japanese troops. Thousands were beheaded. These atrocities shocked the world.

DAILY THE CHINESE ARMIES DREW the Japanese deeper into China, continually retreating, making occasional stands to exact a huge toll from the Japanese for every foot of ground. They initiated the "scorched-earth" policy of burning and destroying everything on the land they yielded, and behind the ever-lengthening communication lines of the Mikado's men Chinese guerrillas arose to harass every troop movement and every captured village. In the northern provinces the guerrillas actually were able to hold most of Shansi. Meanwhile, the Japanese drove Chiang Kai-shek's armies from Hankow to Szechwan, and in October 1938 Canton, through which most of the Chinese munitions and supplies from Hong Kong had come, fell. It was a disastrous blow to China.

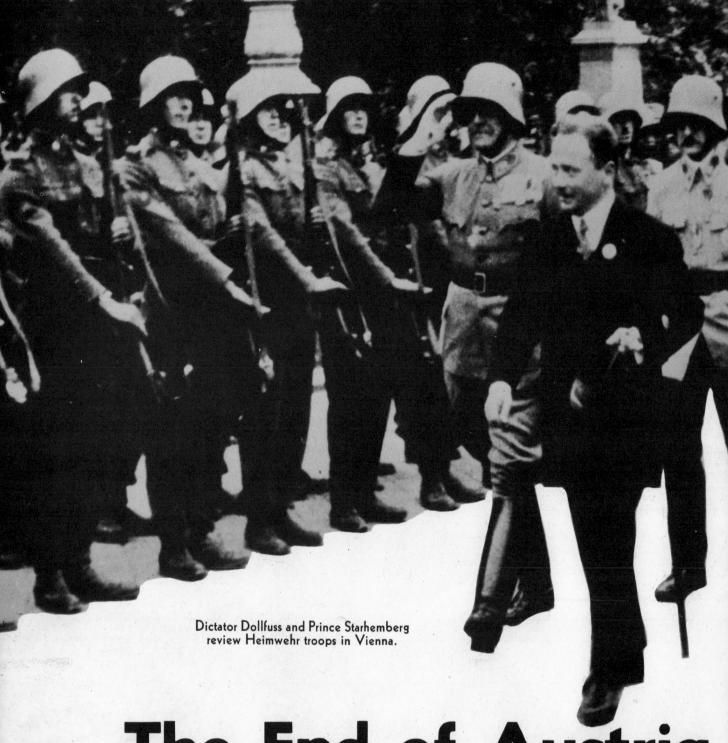

Dictator Dollfuss and Prince Starhemberg
review Heimwehr troops in Vienna.

The End of Austria

Fascism came to power in Austria when a deputy left the parliamentary hall to visit the washroom. He left his ballot for a colleague to vote, but his friend made a mistake and in the ensuing uproar over irregularities in the voting all the speakers resigned. On Sept. 20, 1932, Chancellor Engelbert Dollfuss, four foot eleven, clever, ambitious, took advantage of the situation to declare himself dictator.

In 1932 the Nazis, on the verge of power in Germany, had just begun their Pan-German propaganda in Austria; within a year it was to amount to outright interference with Austrian affairs. World War I had left Austria a small buffer state, internally split between the militant Viennese Socialists and the impoverished, uneducated peasantry controlled by the clerical Fascists. The Socialists had their own defense corps, made up of intellectuals and workers armed with rifles left over from their revolutionary days. The clerical Fascists also had their own army, the Heimwehr, composed mainly of peasant lads and armed by Mussolini, who dreaded both the Viennese Socialists and the prospects of a strong Germany on the other side of the Brenner Pass.

Dollfuss steadily weakened the Socialists by persecution while simultaneously increasing the strength of the Heimwehr. Caught between the Nazis, whose strength among the Heimwehr soared after Hitler assumed power, and the Socialists, Dollfuss put his trust in Il Duce. The Socialists, insisting the Nazis were the real enemies of free and independent Austria, called for a united front against them. But Dollfuss, on Mussolini's orders, attacked the Socialists, murdering and imprisoning them. Against the Nazis he did little. On Feb. 12, 1934, the Fascist Heimwehr shelled the Socialists' model apartments. From the moment the first shells began landing the end of Austria was in sight, for they destroyed

DOLLFUSS THREW HIMSELF INTO MUSSOLINI'S ARMS to save himself from the Nazis, who began threatening annexation in 1932. Il Duce began supplying him with arms to put down the Vienna Socialists. But in 1933 this secret arms traffic was exposed. At Riccione, when Dollfuss and Mussolini signed a new pact, Il Duce insisted that Dollfuss speed up the Heimwehr-Fascist plans, especially liquidation of the Republican Defense Corps. Meanwhile, Mussolini held off Nazis by moving his troops into the Brenner Pass.

THE FASCIST HEIMWEHR ATTACKED THE KARL MARX HOUSE and other Socialist housing projects on Feb. 12, 1934, shelling them with massed artillery before storming them. The workers defended themselves—and what was left of republican Austria —bravely until they ran out of ammunition. Thus Dollfuss eliminated the only force which might have saved Austria from Nazism; against the Nazis he did nothing, relying on Mussolini. A year later Berlin-directed Nazis putschists assassinated Dollfuss. (below.)

the only forces willing and capable of fighting Nazism. A year later Dollfuss was murdered—by the Nazis whom he had not molested.

Schuschnigg succeeded to the dictatorship and the Dollfuss policy of depending on Mussolini. Until it was too late he refused to seek the support of the workers against the Nazis. Meanwhile, Mussolini had become embroiled in the Ethiopian war and needed the support of Hitler, whose first condition was a free hand to develop Nazism in Austria.

Thus the Rome–Berlin Axis was born. Its first victim was Austria.

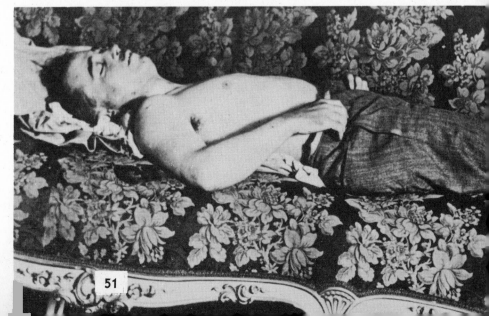

KURT VON SCHUSCHNIGG SUCCEEDED DOLLFUSS when the Nazi *putsch* failed. Shown here speaking to his deputies. Schuschnigg was a very devout Catholic, pro-German, and attempted to make Austrian Fascism more "Christian" than Dollfuss had. Colorless but calculating, he became Minister of Justice in 1932.

LIKE DOLLFUSS, SCHUSCHNIGG DEPENDED ON IL DUCE for necessary help and support against Hitler's National Socialist Germany. But he was coolly aloof from the people and their demands. Meanwhile he managed to get rid of the treacherous Major Emil Fey, Austrian Heimwehr chief.

VON NEURATH, NAZI FOREIGN MINISTER, and Von Papen, Hitler's adroit diplomatic agent, plotted Schuschnigg's downfall with Guido Schmidt (center), violent pro-Nazi Austrian. Schuschnigg, too, was plotting to get rid of Starhemberg. Von Papen went to work on Schuschnigg, playing on his pro-German and Catholic sympathies.

Major Fey was secretly plotting a *putsch* against Chancellor Schuschnigg with the help of German Ambassador Franz Von Papen, by suddenly demanding that the Heimwehr and all other armed groups throughout the country be incorporated into a single "Fatherland Front Militia" under Prince Ernest Rudiger von Starhemberg.

THE ROME–BERLIN AXIS WAS A DISTINCT SHOCK to Schuschnigg who found, in April 1936, that Il Duce, far from guaranteeing his borders, now insisted that he come to terms with Hitler. This Schuschnigg did, signing a pact which permitted the development of the Nazi party and the inclusion of pro-Nazis in his cabinet.

SEYSS-INQUART HAD POSED AS A LOYAL but Nazi Austrian to Schuschnigg, and when Hitler confronted Schuschnigg at Berchtesgaden on Feb. 12, 1938, with a flood of demands, the only thing the harrassed Austrian dictator would agree to was the appointment of Seyss-Inquart as Minister of Security. When Schuschnigg returned word came of the mobilizing of the Nazi armies.

ON MARCH 11 SCHUSCHNIGG CAPITULATED to Hitler's demand for his resignation. At the last moment he had appealed to the labor forces he had driven underground and had attempted a plebiscite which would have wrecked Hitler's plans. But Hitler threatened invasion, forced him to resign. Seyss-Inquart, now a ranting Nazi, took his place, and on Mar. 13 Austria was annexed.

THEN CAME CZECHOSLOVAKIA

HENLEIN, FIRST NAZI FIFTH COLUMNIST TO BECOME WELL known, got his orders from Hitler. He claimed his party was loyal to Czechs and wanted only autonomy for Sudetens. Not until April 24, after Austria was in the Nazi bag, did he demand Nazification of Sudetenland.

W ITH Chamberlain, who had refused to take cognizance of Austria's seizure, still hypnotized, with Eden out of the British Cabinet, Hitler unloosed his war of nerves on highly industrialized, well-armed Czechoslovakia. The Fuehrer himself had made it clear in his Feb. 20th speech that the Czechs were next on his death list, ridiculously charging them with subjecting 3,500,000 Sudeten Germans within their borders to continuous suffering because of "their sympathy and unity" with Nazism. Actually the Sudeten minority, aggressive and well organized, suffered no political persecution. Hitler's front man, Konrad Henlein, ex-gymnasium teacher and head of the thinly disguised Nazi "Henleinist" party, began vigorously protesting Czech "oppression," demanding "freedom" to Nazify Sudeten areas; simultaneously he pledged loyalty to the Czech government. Despite their danger the Czechs were calm. They depended on their allies. They were prepared for their enemies, but not, as it later turned out, for their friends.

WELL-ARMED, DEMOCRATIC CZECHOSLOVAKIA was a dagger pointed at the heart of Nazism. Shaded areas show the troublesome Sudetenland which had been included within Czech border because its industries would provide the economic balance needed by the country. As the keystone of the Little Entente, the Czechs were a formidable barrier to Nazi expansion through the Balkans and the last bastion of democracy in Central Europe. Across her northern frontier stretched a line of fortifications comparable to the French Maginot Line. But her main defense was a pact of mutual assistance with France and the Soviet Union. England, in turn, was bound by pact to France's defense. With these three great powers on her side the Czechs felt secure.

"WE SHALL NEVER BE AN AUSTRIA," said Dr. Eduard Beneš, Czech president, as he inspected the country's $400,000,000 defense fortifications, built largely with British and French help to hold off Nazis until Russian and French aid could arrive.

NAZI TROOP MOVEMENTS NEAR THE CZECH BORDER increased the tension as Henlein increased the tempo of his campaign. Two million Czechs awaited the call to arms. Nazi prospects darkened when, on Mar. 24, Chamberlain said a Central European war might well involve England. The demand for collective security was rising and the statement was taken to mean England would resist.

BUT CHAMBERLAIN HAD QUIETLY MADE UP HIS MIND not to defend the Czechs, dreaming of an Anglo-French-Nazi-Fascist pact to dominate Europe. On May 10, at Lady Astor's Cliveden estate, he told American newsmen of these plans. But the Czechs knew nothing of this. During May they calmly endured grave provocations staged to give Hitler an excuse for invasion.

ON JULY 25 LORD RUNCIMAN entered the scene when Chamberlain announced he had asked Runciman, a member of the pro-Nazi Anglo-German Fellowship, to go to Prague as an unofficial "adviser and mediator." He is shown here returning the Nazi salute to the Henleinists, who greeted him as a savior. His meetings with the opposing sides followed this pattern: short, formal with the Czechs; long, informal with the Henleinists.

MEANWHILE SIR NEVILE HENDERSON, British Ambassador to Nazi Germany, spent his week ends hunting with Goering, who laughed at British-French threats to mobilize. Henderson, who had gone to Germany determined "to do my utmost to see the good side of the Nazi regime as well as the bad," was already convinced that European peace could be secured by an "understanding between Germany and England."

LITVINOV DRAMATIZED RUSSIAN BACKING OF CZECHS by seeking passage for the Red army through Rumania and bringing a score of high Red army officers to Geneva ready to begin talks with French and English. Meanwhile, on May 21, when the Nazis concentrated their armies near the Czech border, the Czechs mobilized 400,000 men. The Nazis quickly withdrew.

DALADIER, HARD-PRESSED BY CONNIVERY within his cabinet, slowly let all the initiative in negotiations slip into the hands of Chamberlain, although France—not Britain—was pledged to come to Czech aid. Daladier's indecisiveness permitted his pro-Nazi Foreign Minister Georges Bonnet to stack the cards; in reading General Gamelin's report on the army he read only the bad points.

On Sept. 12 Hitler threatened war if the Czechs did not submit to his demand for "freedom" for Sudetens.

Hitler Defies the World...

SPEAKING before thousands of massed, *sieg-heiling* storm troopers at the Nazi Nuremberg rally in September, Hitler lashed away at Beneš and Czechoslovakia, gave the signal to revolt to the Henleinists. Six days before Beneš had told his Cabinet it was impossible to hold out against increasing Anglo-French pressure any longer; he offered a new plan, virtually an unconditional surrender granting nearly all of Henlein's demands. But Henlein was ordered to break off negotiations. For four tense days Europe awaited Hitler's speech, almost certain it would mean war. But Hitler was not prepared to go to war for what he was certain he could bully Chamberlain and Daladier into giving him. Though he defied the world to stop him, he "assured" the people of France and Britain the Nazi war machine would not be thrown against them if only they would let him finish with these "criminal Czech torturers, these Bolsheviks, these liars." He had hardly finished speaking when Henleinists began murdering Czechs, storming trade-union halls, looting and wrecking homes of Czechs and Jews. The next day Henlein called for a return of Sudetenland to the Reich, whence he had fled, and the Czechs, ordering the dissolution of the Henleinist party, calmly prepared to fight.

THE NEXT DAY, SEPT. 14, CHAMBERLAIN FLEW to Berchtesgaden to see the Fuehrer. Greeted by the wily Von Ribbentrop, Chamberlain met with Hitler to discuss "(1) liquidation of the Sudeten problem on the basis of a plebiscite, (2) more general problems concerning Europe and the Third Reich." Strangely enough, Czech integrity was not even considered. Chamberlain brought Hitler's demands home, secured Daladier's agreement to accede to them, and returned to see Hitler at Godesberg. But Hitler now had new demands: seizure of all Czech strategic points, rail system, and munitions plants. Even Chamberlain could not accept these—immediately—and negotiations broke off. Meanwhile, the British and French ministers in Prague called on Beneš and told him he must immediately accept their plan for settlement of the Sudeten problem. Under this pressure the Beneš Cabinet resigned.

THEN THE CZECHS, UNDER GENERAL SIROVY, mobilized their spirited, magnificently armed troops. Previously the British and French had applied tremendous pressure to prevent mobilization lest it upset their diplomatic applecart. Britain and France also mobilized. The Czechs, now that it looked as though they were not going to be betrayed, carried out their mobilization speedily and with great enthusiasm. But Chamberlain had not yet given up hope of appeasing Hitler. Noting that Hitler had promised this would be his last territorial demand, he said: "How horrible . . . how fantastic . . . that we should be digging trenches and trying on gas masks because of a quarrel in a faraway country between people of whom we know nothing." Meanwhile, Russia had informed Benes that she would come to the aid of Czechoslovakia even if France did not, providing no fortification was yielded voluntarily.

Appeasement's most vigorous critic, Winston Churchill, leaves the House of Commons during the Czech crisis he had foretold

"LOOK AT THE DANGER IN WHICH WE STAND"

Anti-Chamberlain riots broke out at 10 Downing Street when it became known that Chamberlain had not defied Hitler at Berchtesgaden. Public indignation boiled over. Mass opposition to the Chamberlain policy of appeasing the dictators had been growing since 1933 and now it had as its spokesmen Winston Churchill, who had been First Lord of the British Admiralty during World War I, and Sir Stafford Cripps, wealthy lawyer and Laborite. Of the two, Churchill was the more popular. His tempestuous political career had been at its lowest ebb in 1933 when he began his outspoken criticism of Nazism, of which he said: ". . . All these bands of sturdy Teutonic youths, marching the streets and roads of Germany, with the light of desire in their eyes to suffer for their Fatherland, are not looking for status. They are looking for weapons, and, when they have the weapons, believe me they will then ask for the return of lost territories and lost colonies, and when

that demand is made it cannot fail to shake and possibly shatter to their foundations every one of the countries" of Europe. He led in the revelation of secret German rearmament, fought in vain for greater defenses, particularly aircraft, for England. Always championing a strong England, he had felt sanctions against Mussolini had thrown Il Duce into Hitler's arms, and for a time he favored "non-intervention" in Spain, later denouncing it as a "deceitful masquerade." By 1938 his dominant theme had become "collective security" through a strong League of Nations and a pact of mutual assistance with the Soviet Union, the very thing Chamberlain abhorred most. He said about Russia: ". . . how improvidently foolish we should be, when dangers are so great, to put needless barriers in the way of the general association of the great Russian mass with resistance to an act of Nazi aggression." But the voice of Churchill was heard only by the English people.

Chamberlain greeted Hitler warmly at Munich. Within a few hours Chamberlain and Daladier signed the pact of betrayal.

THEN CAME ROOSEVELT'S DRAMATIC PLEA for continuance of the negotiations. But he proposed a conference of all countries concerned. This seemed "too democratic," since that would include the Czechs and Russians—something Hitler would never agree to. And so Daladier instigated diplomatic moves to have Benito Mussolini intervene as the savior of peace. Chamberlain in a startling interruption before Parliament announced he had just been invited to a Four-Power Munich conference by Herr Hitler to "save peace."

The next day, Sept. 29, the Munich conferees quickly found themselves in agreement. While they drew up their final maps, cut up Czech territory, destroyed her fortifications, gave away her great industries, and planned the evacuation of her undefeated army, the Czech delegates, Dr. Hubert Masaryk and M. Mastiny, were allowed to cool their heels in the outside hall. Finally, at 1:30 A.M., they were curtly handed the plans for the emasculation of their country, and told it was to be occupied by German troops on October 1.

Symbolic of the Czechs, this housewife met the German troops with the Nazi salute and the tears of a broken heart.

"UNDER PROTEST TO THE WORLD" began the Czech proclamation of Oct. 1 yielding to the decision of the men of Munich. It ordered the undefeated army to retire, leaving intact every fortification, plant, and railway. In London Chamberlain, stepping from his plane, announced, ". . . peace was saved . . . peace with honor . . . *peace in our time* . . . . To accuse us of having betrayed Czechoslovakia is simply preposterous. What we did was to save her from annihilation and give her a chance for a new life." The "new life"

began with Nazi storm troopers brutally attacking Czechs, Jews, Sudeten democrats—robbing, murdering, wrecking. Poland and Hungary seized areas that contained their minorities. The "new life" ended March 15, less than six months later, when Hitler, the man who wanted no more territory, seized what was left of Czechoslovakia. And in less than a year Hitler's troops, using cannon and shells from the famed Skoda works which Chamberlain and Daladier had given him, were unleashing their attack on Britain and France.

Gaunt, austere, unimaginative, colorless, Sir Neville Chamberlain was simultaneously the symbol of appeasement and one of its master minds. Unlike so many British statesmen, he was neither thinker, writer, nor soldier. He was a businessman and he tried to do business with Hitler. His father, Joseph, and his half-brother, Austen, had also been famous politicians. Yet neither became Prime Minister and Neville, born in 1869 and trained for business, entered politics late in life and won that post. Like most men of his age, class, and outlook, he was obsessed with a fear of Soviet Russia which made him easy prey for the ranting anti-Soviet Hitler. His foreign policy was more pro-peace than anti-Hitler and more anti-Soviet than pro-British. Most of his friends were pro-Nazi in their views. At every step along the road to war where he might have made a stand he refused. He maintained with steadfast vigor the hypocrisy of "non-intervention" in Spain even after the open intervention of the Fascist powers. Over the vehement protests of Lloyd George, Winston Churchill, Sir Stafford Cripps, a great majority of the British people and many others he insisted on appeasing the dictators, dreaming of a huge Nazi-Fascist-Anglo-French alliance. After Munich, termed by Churchill "an unmitigated defeat," his biggest task was to rearm Britain as quickly as possible. In this, too, he failed for he placed it in the hands of men like Sir Kingsley Wood and Captain Lyttelton, who for one reason or another were neither energetic enough nor vigorously anti-Hitler. The results were tragic for England.

Cold, legalistic, scholarly Sir Samuel Hoare was the brain and engineer behind Neville Chamberlain. A member of Britain's oldest banking family, he represented Toryism at its worst. His India bill, intended to grant "home rule," only tightened British control. With Laval he wrote the Hoare-Laval pact to give Il Duce Ethiopia. Favoring an Anglo-Nazi-Fascist-French pact but the worst speaker in Parliament, he did most of his work over the luncheon table or while week-ending in the country.

Appeasement

Sly, unscrupulous, avaricious Pierre Laval was the brain of French appeasement. A "corridor" politician, Laval worked in the shadows with Otto von Abetz, Hitler's special agent. Long contemptuous of democracy, as Premier he ruled by decree; secretly dealt with Goering and Mussolini. The mouthpiece of the pro-Nazi Comité des Forges industrialists, he whispered promises of power and property to jittery, balky senators, paving the way for Nazism in France. The French underworld knew him as its most powerful protector.

Tall, elegant, hard-boiled, and bony, Georges Bonnet was the most energetic of the Munich plotters. In 1934 his career as Finance Minister had been checked by his connection with the Stavisky scandals. Returning to politics in 1936, he worked with Flandin, who had become so pro-Nazi as to openly prefer "Hitler rather than the Fronte Populaire." Finance Minister of the second Popular Front, Bonnet provoked the financial crisis which left France without a government when Hitler seized Austria. He entered Daladier's government as Foreign Minister. He and his wife frequently entertained Nazi agents: Baroness von Einem, Elizabeth Buttiner, Nazi financier Hirsch, and Otto Abetz, then head of Nazi fifth column in France. When suspicious Daladier finally declared "The traitors must go." Bonnet replied: ". . . it's not a question of traitors, nor of spies. . . . After all, why shouldn't there be German agents here? They represent the interests of their country, which is their legal right. We . . . represent the legal interests of France. If that leads to our having something in common, that is neither treason nor anything else—except patriotic action." Daladier, for some unaccountable reason, accepted this amazing explanation. In the last pre-Munich days he told the British the French would not march, told the French not to rely on the British, told everyone the Russians had been weakened by the "purge." To Daladier he gave only the weak points of Gamelin's report on the army and omitted his conclusion—that the defense of Czechoslovakia was vital to the defense of France.

The Sinking of the *U.S.S. Panay*

THE Munich betrayal created hardly a ripple in the United States. Yet within three months America was subjected to an outrageous assault that had its beginnings in the loss of prestige sustained by the democracies at Munich. On Dec. 11, 1937, Japanese land forces fired on British gunboats in the Yangtze River near Nanking. On the following day, at 1:38 P.M., Japanese planes began bombing the U.S. gunboat *Panay*. Just two hours before the attack Admiral Yarnell had notified the Japanese exactly where the *Panay* was so that she would not be mistaken for a Chinese craft. The American seamen attempted to fight off the bombers with machine guns, but at 3:45 P.M. the *Panay*, riddled with holes, sank. The survivors were machine-gunned as they put off in small boats and even after they reached shore. The Japanese attack was ordered by Colonel Hashimoto, a Black Dragon leader, to show the Chinese Japan was not afraid of the United States or Britain who he felt had demonstrated their weakness at Munich. Afterward the Japanese apologized profusely, but President Roosevelt wrote a sharp letter demanding an explanation and damages. Terrified, the Japanese paid the $2,000,000 damages and contritely explained that the entire incident had been due to a grave error.

THE *PANAY* WAS CLEARLY MARKED with American flags, including some pinned down on canvas awnings over her decks.

ONLY AFTER JAPANESE BOMBS began tearing through the *Panay's* plates did her men realize they were being attacked.

FIGHTING BACK WITH MACHINE-GUNS, the Americans sustained many casualties, including Capt. J. J. Hughes and Lieut. A. F. Anders, who wrote his orders in chalk after he was shot in the throat. After two hours of bombing the *Panay* began sinking rapidly.

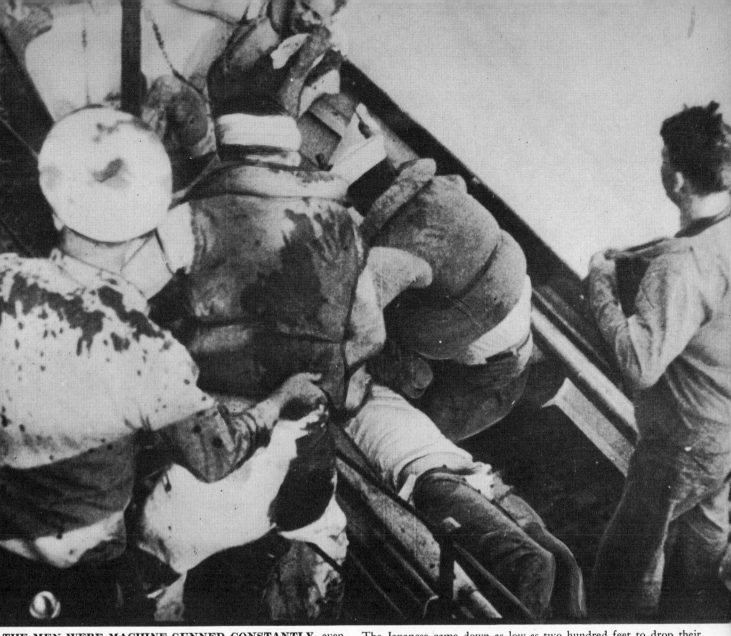

THE MEN WERE MACHINE-GUNNED CONSTANTLY, even as they loaded their wounded into small boats and made for shore.

The Japanese came down as low as two hundred feet to drop their final bombs and spray the survivors' boats with their machine guns.

CHINESE PEASANTS HID THEM in the marshes and helped carry wounded to Hanshan as the Japanese continued their attack.

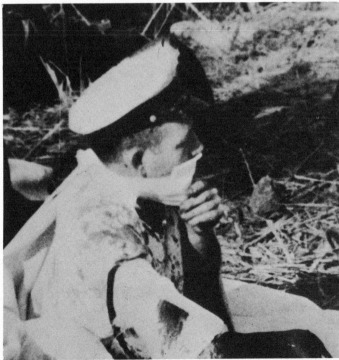

HIS WOUNDS BANDAGED, this U.S. officer was struck by flying shell splinters and now awaits help for the long trek to Hanshan.

HITLER DEMANDS DANZIG

AFTER Munich Nazi pressure on remnant Czechoslovakia increased. On March 10 Stalin, warning that Soviet Russia did not intend to be caught in any new Munich trap, declared Russia would strengthen her relations with *all* countries. Of Chamberlain he said: "The big and dangerous political game started by the supporters of non-intervention may end in a serious fiasco for them." Events moved swiftly. On March 14 Nazi troops moved on what was left of Czechoslovakia, and a few weeks later Chamberlain dutifully and legally turned over to Hitler $6,000,000 in Czech gold stored in London. New evidence that Chamberlain was still trying to do business with Hitler cropped up when British

Overseas Minister Hudson proposed a $5,000,000,000 loan to Nazi Germany. On March 18 the British asked Russia what she would do if Rumania, then under Nazi pressure, were attacked. The Russians suggested an immediate conference to consider the question of Nazi aggression, but this, Chamberlain said, was "premature." On March 21 Hitler seized Memel from Lithuania and Chamberlain said with masterful understatement: "These recent happenings have, rightly or wrongly, made every state which lies adjacent to Germany unhappy, anxious, and uncertain about Germany's future intention." Immediately after his seizure of Bohemia, Moravia, and Memel, Hitler demanded the Free City of Danzig

ALBERT FOERSTER, DANZIG NAZI LEADER, held constant demonstrations after Hitler seized Memel. He shuttled back and forth between Berlin and Danzig in a manner reminiscent of Konrad Henlein during the Czech crisis. Danzig had been established as a free city by the Versailles Treaty for a sea outlet for Poland.

CHAMBERLAIN'S FOREIGN MINISTER HALIFAX (right) signed a pact of mutual assistance with Col. Joseph Beck (left) and Count Raczynski (center) of Poland when Hitler demanded Danzig although there was no way for Britain to aid Poland directly. Russia, which was in a position to aid Poland was ignored. It was, as Raymond Gram Swing had said, "Chamberlain's fatal blunder."

and the right to build a road across the Polish Corridor. Meanwhile, Mussolini seized Albania as his share of the Munich loot. The Poles rejected Hitler's demands, notified France—with whom she was allied—and England. Chamberlain immediately guaranteed Polish borders, although there was no way of giving Poland direct aid. Russia, the only country in a position to render aid to Poland, was left out of Anglo-French-Polish pacts of mutual assistance. On April 28, Hitler repudiated the Anglo-German friendship pact for which Chamberlain had sacrificed Czechoslovakia, and denounced the German-Polish non-aggression treaty. Public pressure on Chamberlain to bring Russia into a mutual-assistance pact, reached tremendous proportions, and finally talks with the Russians began. They hit an immediate snag

in the British-French refusal to guarantee the Baltic States from indirect as well as overt aggression. The Baltic States, notoriously anti-Soviet, had declared they would rather have Hitler than be defended by Voroshilov and in this Chamberlain and Daladier backed them up. Churchill bellicosely asked if England would let Belgium fall to Hitler because the Belgians didn't want the English to defend them. But it was of no avail. Significantly, Litvinov, who had been Russia's spokesman for collective security, resigned and was replaced by Premier Molotov. Finally, on June 12, Mr. William Strang, a minor British official, left for Moscow with new proposals. Negotiations broke down immediately because the British were not authorized to conclude any kind of a pact.

ON MAY 27 CHURCHILL SAID: "If His Majesty's government, having neglected our defenses, having thrown away Czechoslovakia with all that Czechoslovakia means in military power, having committed us to the defense of Poland and Rumania, now rejects and casts away the indispensable aid of Russia, and so leads in the worst of ways into the worst of wars, they will have ill-deserved the generosity with which they have been treated by their fellow countrymen."

ON MAY 31 MOLOTOV WARNED: "We stand for peace and for preventing the further development of aggression. But we must remember Comrade Stalin's precept to be cautious and not allow our country to be drawn into conflicts by warmongers who are accustomed to have others pull the chestnuts out of the fire for them." Significantly, he reviewed trade relations between the Soviets and Italy and Germany, pointing out that trade negotiations with Germany might be resumed.

ON July 29 Lloyd George declared: "Negotiations have been going on for four months with Russia, and no one knows how things stand today. You are dealing with the greatest military power in the world; you are asking them to come to your help; you are not negotiating terms with an enemy but with a friendly people whose aid you want. Mr. Chamberlain negotiated directly with Hitler. He went to Germany to see him. He and Lord Halifax made visits to Rome. They went to Rome, drank Mussolini's health, and told him what a fine fellow he was. But whom have they sent to Russia? They have not even sent the lowest in rank of a Cabinet minister; they have sent a clerk in the Foreign Office. It is an insult. Yet the government wants the help of their gigantic army and air force, and of this very brave people—no braver on earth—who are working their way through great difficulties to the emancipation of their people. If you want their help you ought to send somebody there who is worthy of our dignity and of theirs. Meanwhile, Hitler is fortifying Danzig. Danzig is becoming a fortress, and before that treaty is signed Danzig will be as much a city of the German Empire as Breslau or Berlin. They (Chamberlain government) have no sense of proportion or of the gravity of the whole situation when the world is trembling on the brink of a great precipice and when liberty is challenged."

Molotov signed the Non-Aggression Pact when Von Ribbentrop offered it on Aug. 23, 1939.

THE NAZI-SOVIET NON-AGGRESSION PACT

Russian suspicions that Chamberlain was plotting a new Munich which would bring Nazi Germany to their borders grew hourly as the approach of war became more imminent. On July 23, though political negotiations had not yet been concluded, the Soviets asked Britain and France to send military missions to Moscow to begin staff talks immediately. This was, for the Russians, the acid test of the sincerity of Chamberlain and Daladier. The Russians expected Lord Gort and Gen. Gamelin to arrive by air within a few days. Instead it was ten days before the Anglo-French mission left London by slow boat and six more before they reached Moscow; almost wholly unknown staff officers were sent, not Lord Gort and Gen. Gamelin. The joint mission was met by the highest Soviet military officials, headed by War Commissar Voroshilov. He promptly proposed that if Hitler should invade Poland, the Russians would send two armies against him, one against East Prussia and the other against central Germany through southern Poland. Voroshilov then asked what the British and French would do and learned no one there had the authority to say. The final test came when Col. Beck, encouraged by Chamberlain, announced Poland would never permit Red troops to cross its borders and neither needed nor wanted them. That ended the talks as far as the Russians were con-

cerned. After having exerted every possible effort to achieve collective security for almost a decade and seen every one of them fail because of the appeasement efforts of Chamberlain, Daladier, and Bonnet, the Russians decided that it was time for them to look out for themselves as Stalin had warned they would do in March. When a Nazi trade delegation then in Moscow asked if Russia would be interested in a non-aggression pact, the Russians said yes, and on Aug. 23 Von Ribbentrop flew to Moscow. After three hours of conversation he signed an iron-bound ten-year non-aggression pact. News of the pact stunned the world which had been lulled by Chamberlain's assurances that negotiations were proceeding. It was the most crushing defeat British diplomacy had suffered in a century. Meanwhile, the Nazis, overjoyed at having neutralized the menace of powerful Russia, intimated that Russia had secretly signed a military alliance with them. This Nazi propaganda was widely believed, and Russia was denounced in most countries for having betrayed the democracies. But Russia made it clear in the ensuing months that she desired strict neutrality and, having little faith in Hitler's promises, she set about redoubling her military might in preparation for the day when Hitler might turn toward her. That her premise was correct was clearly affirmed less than two years later.

THE INVASION
OF POLAND

On the 25th Hitler promised Chamberlain that when he had settled Poland and received some colonies he would guarantee the British Empire. On the 29th Hitler announced a mobilization but agreed to accept the British offer to have Poland send an emissary to Berlin with "full powers." He insisted that he arrive the next day —a virtual impossibility. Britain put pressure on Poland the next day, but at midnight Sir Nevile Henderson told Ribbentrop the entire procedure was unreasonable. Ribbentrop's reply was the rapid reading of a 16-point proposal for a settlement. When Henderson asked for the text Ribbentrop answered that it was now too late, since the Poles had not sent an envoy to Berlin. Thus the alleged offer of a settlement was never presented to Poland. At dawn Hitler went before a hysterical, sieg-heiling puppet Reichstag to announce German troops were invading Poland.

NINETEEN DAY BLITZ

THE men on whom fell the duty of leading the defense of Poland were disciples of Pilsudski from the army he led against the Russians in 1914. All rabid Polish nationalists, they were known as the "Colonels." The Versailles Treaty, recognizing Poland as a nation, made Danzig a free city and gave Poland access to the sea through the "Corridor" which was taken from Germany. In 1926 Pilsudski seized power with his "Colonels." The most important "Colonels" were Gen. Edward Smigly-Rydz, chief of the

army, and Col. Josef Beck, Foreign M ister. They inherited Pilsudski's conten for democracy, banned all political p ties except their own, and oppressed Jewish minority and outlawed lab unions. Their only important opposit came from General Sikorski, who posed Pilsudski's 1926 *putsch*. Their f eign policy was greedy and opportunis They played the French against the G mans until 1934, when Beck and Hit signed a non-aggression pact which w potentially an anti-Soviet pact. Dur

Poland's best units were cavalry. Her air force was negligible.

Hitler's march into Austria and Czechoslovakia they worked with him, receiving Teschen as their share of the loot. Their refusal to permit the Red army to cross Poland in case of Nazi aggression sounded the death knell for collective security. The Polish army numbered 350,000 men, chiefly infantry, while it had 1,645,000 trained reserves. Although 40% of the national budget went into armament, Poland had only a handful of tank divisions, a negligible 800 planes, very little heavy artillery, a large cavalry.

Polish Army Chief Edward Smigly-Rydz, shown reviewing bicycle troops en route to the front, learned his war under Pilsudski.

Poland's People and Resources

THIS PEASANT GIRL is typical of the agrarian folk who comprise 75% of Poland's 32,000,000 people. Like 70% of them, she is of Polish stock. Included within Poland's borders were a large Ukrainian and Ruthenian minority comprising 15% of the population. The peasants' living standards were among the lowest in Europe due to the poverty of the land.

THIS ENORMOUS SLAG PILE IS RESIDUE from Poland's great steel center at Trzyniec, within a stone's throw of the German frontier. Before the war Poland produced 1,556,000 metric tons of steel a year, 46,700,000 metric tons of coal. She had vast mineral deposits. Textiles were her main manufacturing product.

Poland's Exports: Oil and Ham

SOUTHEAST POLAND'S 3,000 OIL WELLS produced over five million barrels of crude oil annually, most of which was exported to more highly industrialized European states. Her natural·gas was virtually untapped.

POLAND BUILT MODERN GDYNIA because Danzig was not capable of handling all her export trade and because she feared Danzig might be returned to Germany. Over 3,000,000 tons of shipping went through Gdynia yearly.

HAMS FROM POLISH PIGS, dairy products, coal, sugar, barley, timber, textiles, and oil were Poland's chief exports. Most of these went to Germany, although there was considerable trade with the United States.

Simultaneously Nazi mechanized columns drove deep into Poland at sever points. They swept around Polish armies instead of fighting.

urtling out of the gray dawn of Sept. 1, dive-bombing Nazi Stukas destroyed the bulk of the Polish air force while it was still on the ground. Meanwhile, heavier planes bombed railroads, harbors, munitions, supplies and fortifications.

NAZI BOMBS SET AFIRE nearly every city and village. Outnumbered by the fires, Poland's ill-equipped fire brigades battled the flames with the spontaneous but poorly organized help of civilians. Poland had no civilian defense corps. Meanwhile, the Polish General Staff strove to complete their general mobilization which had been delayed until August 31, although the Nazis were fully mobilized.

BY THE END OF THE FIRST DAY'S FIGHTING Nazi mechanized columns were recklessly plunging ahead of their main infantry support to encircle and pinch off Polish defense positions for the infantry to mop up. That night President Roosevelt, declaring United States was neutral, told Americans that he would do everything to prevent a "black-out of peace" but warned we must prepare.

THESE POLISH CIVILIANS have been rounded up as hostages to be shot in reprisal for guerrilla activities. Thousands of Poles were later shipped off to Germany and East Prussia as slave labor. Rather than face the Nazi terror, many Jews killed themselves. Others fled eastward ahead of Nazis to Soviet Union. Ribbentrop delighted in showing movies of the Nazi ruthlessness to Balkan diplomats.

THIS PICTURE, SMUGGLED OUT OF POLAND, shows Nazi soldiers who have just desecrated the Catholic church in the background wearing the priest's robes and holding a mock religious service. This was part of the Nazi pagan creed. The Nazis destroyed many churches because in Germany the churches had become centers of resistance to the Nazi regime.

NAZIS PUT TO DEATH AS SNIPERS THOUSANDS OF civilians. This woman has just seen her loved ones shot. By Sept. 3 the Germans had virtually cut off the Polish Corridor and nearly completed the capture of the industrial southeast surrounding Cracow. These pincer movements cut communications and allowed the Nazis to reach Lodz by Sept. 7, driving the Poles toward Warsaw.

HITLER FLEW TO THE FRONT to congratulate his men as they entered the outskirts of Warsaw on Sept. 15. Meanwhile, England and France, which had waited until two days after the invasion to enter the war, found it impossible to render Poland direct aid. On Sept. 5 French troops "contacted the enemy" and cautiously advanced until they faced the main Nazi fortifications, then stopped.

NAZI PANZER TROOPS POURED INTO WARSAW from all sides as the Polish army crumpled and the Polish government fled; Smigley-Rydz himself was captured by the Nazis as he attempted to escape into Rumania. Fighting continued in the areas encircled by the Nazis, but the main strategic points were all in the hands of Germany. On the 17th Warsaw defied the Nazi demand for surrender.

ON September 17 Moscow announced that since the Polish government had collapsed, its armies were crossing the Polish border to protect their blood brothers in Byelo-Russia, western Ukraine, and Galicia, and to safeguard the Soviet frontier. This new Soviet act was termed a "stab in the back," but nowhere were the Reds-being resisted and in many places they were being welcomed by the Poles. Berlin quickly announced the Red army had moved with its full knowledge, but there is no evidence of it. Advancing with great speed, the Soviet troops passed Lwow within two days, cutting Hitler off from the Galician oil wells and direct contact with Rumania. On the third day they reached Brest Litovsk, the Nazi armies retreating before them. The Red troops reached the 1918 Soviet border, recovering territory Pilsudski had wrested from the ragged Red armies. Thousands of Jews and Poles, seeking escape from Nazi terrorism, fled into Russian-occupied territory. Winston Churchill, broadcasting in London, hailed the march of the Red army: ". . . that the Russian armies should stand on this line was clearly necessary for the safety of Russia against the Nazi menace . . . an Eastern Front has been created. When Herr von Ribbentrop was summoned to Moscow it was to learn the fact, . . . that Nazi designs upon the Baltic States and upon the Ukraine must come to a dead stop."

The Red Army Marches Into Poland

Red army tank corps commanders were given the Moscow order to advance immediately into eastern Poland on Sept. 17.

Meeting with no resistance, the highly mechanized Soviet army raced across almost half of Poland in only two days.

Nazi troops crossing the San River to capture the Galician oil wells were turned back by the Red army.

ON SEPT. 27 THE HEROIC DEFENDERS OF WARSAW, abandoned by their own government and under constant bombardment from German artillery and dive bombers, surrendered to Nazi General von Blaskowitz in a railway car. The fortress of Modlin on the Vistula River held out until Sept. 29 and fighting continued on the Hela Peninsula until Oct. 2, near Lubin until Oct. 5.

The Heroes of Westerplatte

For five days a handful of Polish soldiers held the tiny island fortress in the mouth of the Danzig fortress against the point-blank shelling of the Nazi battleship *Schleswig-Holstein* and the 500-pound bombs of Nazi Stukas (below). Their heroic commander (above) was allowed to keep his sword by the Nazis.

POUNDING ON MEDIEVAL DRUMS, TRIUMPHANT NAZIS PARADED THROUGH POLAND, THEIR NEW SLAVE STATE.

BALTIC SEA

MEMEL

LITHU

KÖENIGSBERG

EAST
PRUSSIA

ELBING

ALLENSTEIN

LYCK

BIALY

NAZI

TORUN

MLAWA

VISTULA
RIVER

PULTUSK

POSEN

WARSAW

GERMANY

LODZ

P O L

LUBLIN

BRESLAU

Final
Russian-Ger
Border

OPPELN

GLEIWITZ

VISTULA
RIVER

CRACOW

PRZEMYSL

BRUNN

ZILINA

CZECHOSLOVAKIA

SAN
RIVER

USTRIA

ERNEST CABAT

HUNGARY

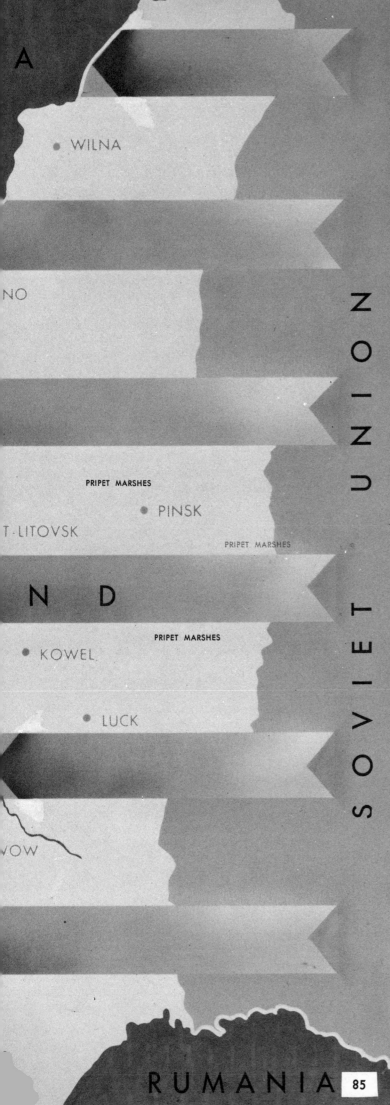

NAZI CAMPAIGN IN POLAND

EXCEPT for mopping up isolated pickets of resistance, the Nazis conquered Poland in exactly nineteen days, adding a new word to the American vocabulary—*blitzkrieg*, lightning war. On the adjacent map are shown the main Nazi mechanized thrusts and the westward push of the Red army (gray). The Nazi blitz plan called for a heavy thrust across the corridor meeting a similar thrust from East Prussia. But the main attacking forces started from Breslau and headed southeast. One of these columns split off and, encircling Lodz, pushed onto Warsaw to meet another column moving on Warsaw from East Prussia. Another raced on to Cracow, where it split into two columns, one heading northward to join the forces converging on Warsaw while the second attempted to reach Lwów and establish a frontier with Rumania. This last drive was stopped by the speed with which the Red army advanced across the Galician plain. The Poles had planned delaying resistance to the Nazi attack, slowly falling back to their main defenses on the interior river line of the Narew—Bug—Vistula—San, protecting Warsaw and the industrial triangle of the southeast. However, because they were not fully mobilized when the Nazis struck, they were not able to put this defensive plan into operation. By the end of the second day the Nazi air force had completely wiped out the Polish air force, disrupted its already chaotic rail system, disorganized the military command. Nor had the Poles counted on the speed and recklessness of the German mechanized forces which often ran as far as 100 miles ahead of their main infantry support. Instead they had counted on mud and rains to slow the Nazi advance, and the rains never came. By a series of enveloping attacks the Nazis were able to chop the main Polish forces into small bands, wholly out of touch with one another, which could be easily annihilated or captured. The Polish cavalry, main mobile force of the Poles, was so lightly armed that its mobility only carried it into defeat; its raids on the Nazi flanks only resulted in its being mowed down because the cavalry had no anti-tank guns—indeed, the entire Polish army had only a few hundred. The Nazi blitz was carried out by seventy youthful divisions, including eleven armored divisions, while twenty older divisions manned the Siegfried Line to stop any possible English-French attack to relieve pressure on Poland.

IN THE UNITED STATES PRESIDENT ROOSEVELT established the War Resources Board, headed by Edward J. Stettinius, Jr., center, as the first step toward safeguarding America.

THE WAR OF NERVES

DALADIER AND CHAMBERLAIN HAD DONE VIRTUALLY NOTHING to aid Poland. After Poland's fall the French troops which had advanced to face the German Westwall were withdrawn as the twenty Nazi divisions manning the Nazi forts were supplemented with the seventy divisions that had conquered Poland. Military operations were reduced to patrol clashes and artillery duels. The United States neutrality law was amended to permit "cash-and-carry" sales to belligerents.

FOLLOWING the collapse of Poland Hitler made a ridiculous peace bid which was firmly turned down by Chamberlain on Oct. 12. A month before Britain announced plans were being laid on the assumption the war would last three years or more and passed the Emergency Powers bill granting the government the right to impose extensive regulations. In France Daladier was given power to rule by decree. Meanwhile, the complexion of the British War Cabinet was altered considerably by the inclusion of Churchill and Eden, outspoken opponents of Chamberlain's appeasement policy. The Labor and Liberal parties, however, refused to join the government because its leading members were "men of Munich." In France Daladier made few shifts, none of which altered the character of his Cabinet; his most notable change was to shift the insidious Bonnet from the Foreign Ministry to that of Justice. Intended to cut Bonnet's influence, the move put Bonnet in a position to rack France with internal strife. His chief instrument for this was a gigantic "Red" hunt. Bonnet hated the Communists because in Oct. 1938 a Communist editor, Gabriel Peri, had exposed his ties with Otto Abetz, Hitler's special contact man for France. Some sixty Communist deputies were jailed on charges of treason and Communists everywhere were hunted down and thrown into concentration camps. Coupled with this was the wiping out of the social reforms of the Popular Front, and many labor leaders who opposed these decrees were jailed as "Reds." In normal times Bonnet would never have been able to carry this out, but due to the confusion over the Soviet-Nazi non-aggression pact, the "Communazi" myth, the dual position of the Communist view which called for the defense of France but the end of the war, he had little opposition. Even Gamelin's protest that Bonnet's activities were demoralizing the army was ignored. Meanwhile, mainly because of the inactivity on the Western Front, the war became popularly known as the "silent war" and the "phony" war. Actually, it was a war of nerves conducted by such fifth columnists as Bonnet who created suspicion, distrust, and disunity. There were also moves on the diplomatic front, the Soviet Union signing treaties of mutual assistance with Estonia, Latvia, and Lithuania in early October which gave the USSR military, naval, and air bases in those countries and wiped out German influence in the Baltic.

French troops withdrew from Germany after Poland fell.

Englische Arbeiter
an ihre deutschen Brüder

Der Nationalrat der englischen Arbeiterpartei, die über fünf Millionen Mitglieder zählt und damit die grösste, geschlossene Vereinigung Englands ist, hat in ihrer letzten Sitzung einen Appell an das deutsche Volk beschlossen, aus dem wir nachstehend die Hauptpartien Wieder gebruck:

«Wer ist schuld an der schändlichen Lage, in der wir uns heute befinden? Manche von Euch mögen sagen, dass der Friede Europas bedroht ist, weil Deutschland von Feinden eingekreist werde, die es zerstören und das wirtschaftliche Leben des deutschen Volkes unmöglich machen wollen. Dies ist eine böswillige Entstellung der Wahrheit. Niemand weiss dies besser als Euer Propagandaminister.

Hitler, Mussolini und die Ereignisse, für die diese beiden Männer verantwortlich sind, sind die Hauptfaktoren, die das englische Volk zu dieser Politik bestimmt haben. Die Kriegs- und Drohreden Hitlers, Mussolinis und ihrer Mitarbeiter haben andere Nationen in Furcht versetzen müssen. Und in Wirklichkeit war dies auch der Zweck Ihrer Reden. Die Diktatoren hofften, sie könnten andere Völker ebenso in Schrecken jagen, wie Ihr eigenes Volk und sie zwingen, sich ihnen zu unterwerfen.

Eure Regierung hat sich immer wieder geweigert, die Methoden friedlicher Verhandlungen anzuwenden, um Ihr Ziel zu erreichen. Sie hat es vorgezogen, zu drohen, um zu pressen, Gewalt zu üben. Die Ereignisse, deren Abschluss am 15. März der brutale Einfall in die Tschechoslowakei war, haben uns davon überzeugt, dass das, was Eure Regierung will, nicht weniger ist als die Unterwerfung und Versklavung ganz Europas.

Und jetzt wieder, Polen gegenüber, in der Sache Danzig, wendet Eure Regierung die Methoden an, die uns bereits vertraut sind: militärische Vorbereitungen, Lügenpropaganda, provozierte Unruhen. Wenn dies so weiter geht, ist das der Krieg.

Das britische Volk ist zu dem Schluss gelangt, dass seine eigene Sicherheit ihm verbietet, sich mit der grösstmöglichsten Zahl von Völkern zu verbinden, um den Frieden aufrecht zu erhalten und gegen den Angriff Widerstand zu leisten. Nicht nur das englische Volk hat empfunden, dass seine Sicherheit erweitert werden müssten. Das gleiche gilt für Frankreich, Polen, die Türkei, Rumänien und Griechenland, und wir sind glücklich darüber, dass Grossbritannien jetzt Defensivpakte mit diesen Ländern besitzt. Wir hoffen stark, dass ein ähnliches Abkommen auch zwischen der britischen und der russischen Regierung geschlossen werden wird. Die britische Arbeiterbewegung hat ihren ganzen Einfluss dafür eingesetzt. Die letzte Botschaft des Präsidenten Roosevelt an Hitler und Mussolini hat unzweideutig bewiesen, dass auch die Vereinigten Staaten von Amerika, diese grosse und mächtige Nation, angesichts der beunruhigenden europäischen Lage nicht gleichgültig bleiben wollen.

Wir sprechen offen mit Euch! Wir wollen Euch begreiflich machen, dass niemand gegen Deutschland Krieg zu führen wünscht, und es ist von unendlicher Bedeutung, dass Ihr dies begreift. Wir sind Eure Freunde. Die Kriegsgefahr, die Euch bedroht, liegt innerhalb der deutschen Grenzen, nirgends sonst. Und verantwortlich für diese Gefahr sind Hitler und seine Regierung. Hitler kreist sich selber ein und übt so perverse, so unnütze Zeit. Alles dies ist so wahnsinnig, so pervers, so unnütz. Euer Land, unser Land, und noch andere Länder, unerwünschen Mittel, die die in harter Arbeit erworben, um Werkzeuge des Todes und der Zerstörung aufzuspeichern. Die Intelligenz, die Mühe und das Geld, die so vergeudet werden, könnten die soziale und wirtschaftliche Lage der Völker verbessern. Uns ist Butter lieber als Kanonen...

Ihr, wie die Arbeiter aller Länder, müssen

darauf dringen, dass bestehende Streitpunkte vernünftig geregelt werden, nicht durch Krieg. Abzu die entscheidende Situation, in der wir uns heute befinden, ohne Lage, die weder Friede noch Krieg ist, kann nicht unendlich dauern. Wir können nicht fortfahren, den Diktatoren unter der Drohung der Gewalt Konzessionen zu machen. Denn wir wissen aus Erfahrung, dass jede Konzession sie nur noch unvernünftiger macht.

Um eine glückliche, sichere und blühende Welt aufzubauen, ist friedliche Zusammenarbeit das einzige Mittel.

Wir kennen Eure Schwierigkeiten. Wir wissen, dass die Diktatoren in Eurem Lande und in Italien Furcht vor ihren Völkern haben und dass sie Euch deshalb verbieten, frei zu sprechen und zu diskutieren. Man hat Euch das Recht genommen, die Gedanken anderer Völker kennen zu lernen und zu erfahren, was in anderen Ländern geschieht. Man sagt Euch nicht, wie überlegen die militärischen und ökonomischen Kräfte wären, mit denen Euer Land im Kriegsfall zu tun haben würde. Aber wir bitten Euch: tut alles, was Ihr könnt, um Eurer Regierung begreiflich zu machen, dass Ihr den Frieden wollt und nicht den Krieg.

Sobald Eure Regierung zu Verstand kommt, sobald sie die Methoden des Friedens und nicht mehr die der Gewalt anwenden will, werden Verhandlungen auf der Basis der Gleichheit stattfinden können. Nichts liegt uns ferner, als Euer Land einkreisen und vernichten zu wollen: wir fordern Euch auf, selber in den Kreis einzutreten! Wir wollen, dass Ihr Euch einer Weltgemeinschaft anschliesst, dass das deutsche Volk, mit seinen grossen Qualitäten mitwirkt bei dem Aufbau einer Welt, in der die Menschheit gedeihen kann. Wir wollen kein Massaker der Völker. Wir wollen ein Zusammenleben in Frieden und Freundschaft.»

THE INCLUSION OF CHURCHILL AND EDEN in the British War Cabinet reassured the British people that Chamberlain was at last ready to fight Hitler. Churchill, a vigorous critic of Chamberlain in the past, now became First Lord of the Admiralty, and Eden, who had once resigned from the Cabinet because he disagreed with appeasement, now became Dominions Secretary. Churchill vigorously applied a sea blockade to Germany and organized the convoy plan for English shipping.

ENGLISH PROPAGANDA LEAFLETS such as this, addressed to Germans, nightly were showered by the ton on the German troops and cities by the R.A.F. during the early months of the war. The propaganda war on both sides was intense. The Nazis installed strong loud speakers opposite the Maginot Line for a "peace" offensive. Allied propaganda warned of disasters.

88

THE SUDDEN RESIGNATION OF HORE-BELISHA on Jan. 5, 1940, took the British people by surprise. He had energetically shaken up the army High Command, done much to democratize it and better the lot of the common soldier. The only hint as to the cause lay in his cryptic remark that he had not thought the army could be made "too democratic to fight for democracy." Stiff criticism as a result of his ouster brought several Cabinet changes with Churchill in charge of the fighting services.

OVER 158,000 BRITISH SOLDIERS WERE IN FRANCE by Oct. 1 and they continued to come in a steady stream. In December they occupied a section of the Maginot Line. But there was no fighting, and both the French and British armies spent most of their time drilling and engaging in sports. Neither the Allies nor the Nazis showed any inclination to attack.

The Struggle for Control of the Seas

BUT if all was quiet on the Western Front, the war at sea was waged ruthlessly from the first day when the American-bound passenger ship *Athenia* was sunk without warning. Together the Allied fleets totaled nearly two million tons while the German naval strength totaled only 235,000. The Allied fleets swept Nazi merchant shipping from the seas, Nazi crews scuttling 200,000 tons of shipping to prevent its falling into British hands. By the end of December nearly eight per cent of German shipping had been sunk while the rest was tied up in neutral ports and at home. Britain started the war with 21,000,000 tons of shipping. By the end of 1939 her losses totaled 460,000 tons. However, her seizures of Nazi ships, transfers from neutrals, and new construction made up for five sixths of her losses. Britain's very life depended on what she could import and Churchill's speedy, capable organization of convoys to protect the 2,000 ships she had at sea daily, rapidly cut her losses to one fourth of those in September. The chief Nazi sea weapon was the submarine, of which she had 65 when the war started. Nazi Admiral Raeder effectively made up for his lack of destroyers and raiders with Stuka bombers until the British equipped all their boats with anti-aircraft guns. Another weapon the Nazis used in their attack on British shipping was the magnetic mine. These were dropped by the hundred from Nazi planes along the English Channel and wreaked havoc on Channel shipping until December, when British engineers developed an electrical detecting device which cut losses sharply. Submarine warfare on both sides was extensive and daring. On Sept. 18 a Nazi sub sank the *Courageous*, an old battleship which had been converted into an aircraft carrier. On Oct. 1 another Nazi sub made its way through the mine fields and submarine nets outside the British naval base of Scapa Flow, sank the anchored *Royal Oak*, a heavy battleship, with a loss of 812 men and then escaped. This feat forced the British to make a less accessible base their main anchorage. The British warfare against the Nazi U-boats was ceaseless and relentless. By the end of Dec. 1939 the British had destroyed 36 Nazi submarines and British U-boats had torpedoed the Nazi cruiser *Leipzig*, a heavy cruiser, possibly the *Blücher* and a 6,000-ton cruiser of the Köln class.

With the coming of February the Nazis unleashed the fury of their U-boat warfare on neutral shipping. By the end of March they had destroyed nearly 200 neutral ships. It was but a forerunner of what was to come later on.

A rare picture taken from a Nazi sub which has torpedoed a British ship and has begun shelling it.

British, Americans, Chinese, and Malayans, both crew and passengers, crowd into the Sirdhana's lifeboats after hitting an enemy mine off Singapore just a few weeks after war began. The initial victim of the sea war was the Athenia, sunk first day of the war.

A FEW MOMENTS AFTER THIS PICTURE was taken this British Channel steamer was sinking. Nazi planes made up for the German lack of a navy, sinking much necessary coastal shipping, damaging even more.

ON DEC. 13 the *Admiral Graf Sp* a Nazi pocket battleship raiding Sou Atlantic shipping, was sighted by t British heavy cruiser, *Exeter*, off t Uruguayan coast. The *Spee* imm diately offered battle. The Brit light cruisers, *Ajax* and *Achilles*, ca to the *Exeter's* aid. The *Spee's* 11-in guns were far heavier than the *E eter's* 8-inch guns. The *Ajax* a *Achilles* had only 6-inch guns. Aft four hours the *Exeter's* steering ge

HIT BY A NAZI MAGNETIC MINE, the *Dunbar Castle* slides under the waves. Below a Nazi airman, shot down by British fishermen, is helped aboard their boat and his wounds dressed. Many downed Nazi flyers were rescued.

d heavy guns were out of order.
t by mid-afternoon the brilliant sea-
anship of the speedier British had
sulted in putting the *Spee*'s fire-
ntrol tower out of action. Hits on
e *Spee* bow practically sank her,
d as night fell she stole away to the
ontevideo harbor. After a diplo-
atic wrangle over how long she
ight stay there, the *Spee* was scuttled
 her own crew on Dec. 17 in the
ver Plate on Hitler's direct orders.

The British destroyer Ardent slips by a near hit in the Harstad Fjord off the coast of Norway. Two daring raids by British destroyers, aided by the battleship Warspite, wiped out fourteen Nazi destroyers in the narrow, hemmed in confines of the Narvik fiords.

8

This unusual picture was made through the range-finder of one of the Nazi warships that sank the British destroyer Glowworm in the North Atlantic during the month of April. Note the sailors desperately clinging to the sunken ship's hull

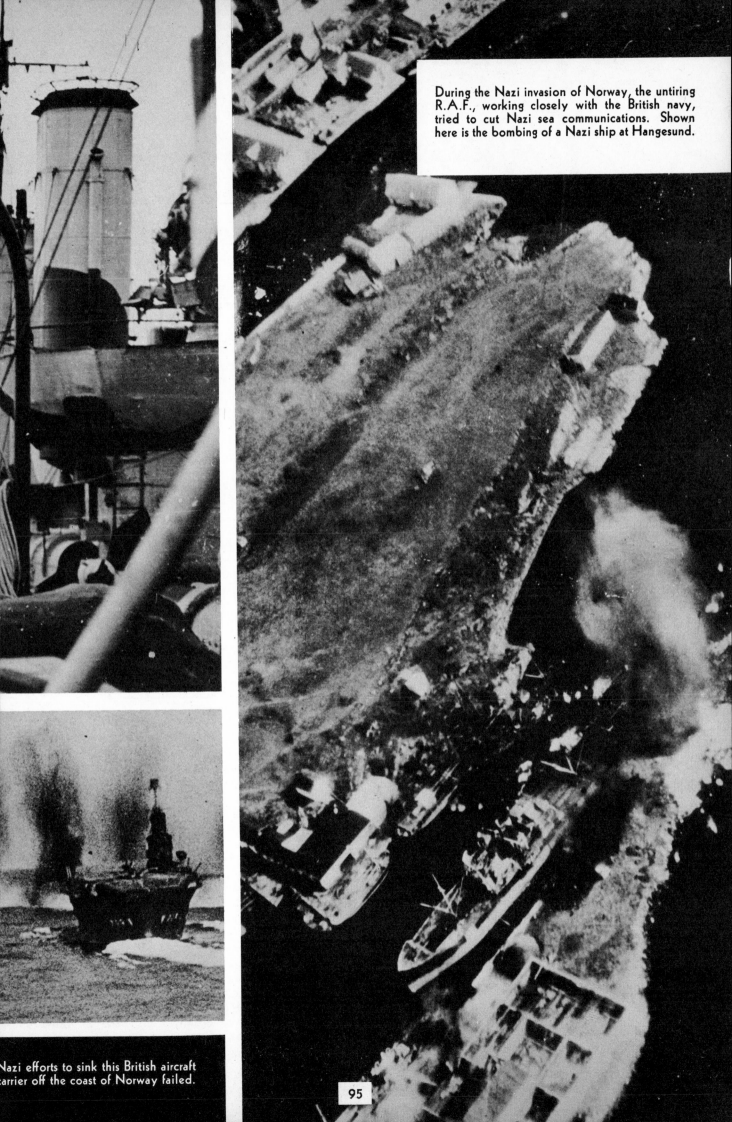

During the Nazi invasion of Norway, the untiring R.A.F., working closely with the British navy, tried to cut Nazi sea communications. Shown here is the bombing of a Nazi ship at Hangesund.

Nazi efforts to sink this British aircraft carrier off the coast of Norway failed.

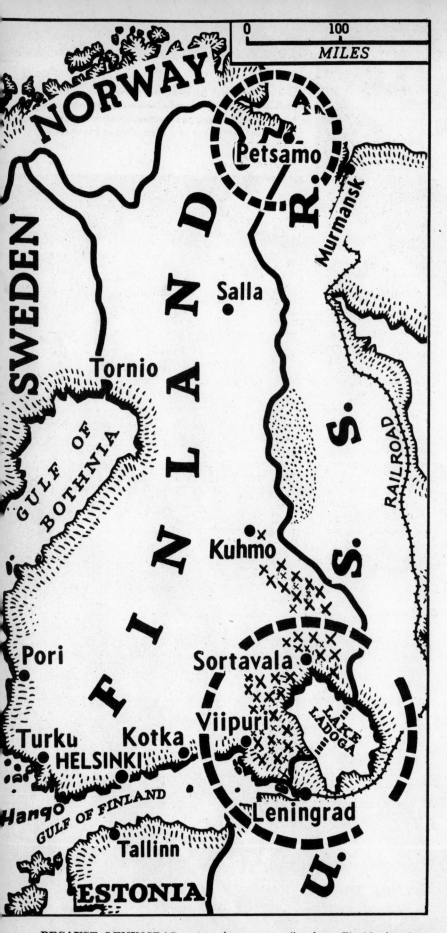

BECAUSE LENINGRAD was only twenty miles from Finnish frontier, Russia asked Finland to cede enough territory along the Karelian isthmus to put the city out of range of guns on the Mannerheim Line. They also asked to lease Hangö as a naval base. In return they offered twice the amount of land ceded. But Finland refused. Her fortifications built over a long period of time were among the best in the world.

WAR IN FINLAND

Having completed mutual defense treaties with the other Baltic States, Russia opened negotiations on Oct. 9, 1939, with Finnish Negotiator Passikivi to safeguard the western approaches of Leningrad. Its chief industrial and second largest city, Leningrad lay only twenty miles from the Finnish Karelian frontier—easy artillery range. Ever since 1918–20, when Finland was used as a base for military intervention against the Soviet government, Russian leaders had been extremely sensitive to the vulnerability of Leningrad. In fact, Soviet policy was based on the assumption that sooner or later their country would be invaded again through Finland. The construction of the Mannerheim Line with its numerous airports equipped to handle air fleets ten times the size of Finland's and the obvious anti-Soviet basis of the appeasement policy of Chemberlain and the Bonnet-Laval clique tended to confirm the Soviet view that a major attack was being planned on the U.S.S.R. Therefore, Stalin, always with an eye on the possibility that Hitler might turn on Russia next, acted quickly to remove the threat to Leningrad. The Soviets asked Finland to cede enough territory on the Karelian isthmus so that Leningrad would be out of artillery range of the Finnish border, certain small islands commanding the Gulf of Leningrad, and to give Russia the right to lease Hangö as a naval base. In return the Russians offered to cede twice the amount of territory asked from Finland along the non-strategic central Russo-Finnish border. They also offered a substantial trade agreement. At the opening of negotiations Finnish Premier Cajander issued a public statement declaring the Soviet proposals did not compromise Finnish integrity or independence. But following a conference of the Scandinavian countries and marked diplomatic intervention on the part of Chamberlain and Daladier, Passikivi, who was willing to accept the Soviet proposals, was replaced by Väinö Tanner, long hostile to Russia. The Finnish army was mobilized. Negotiations deadlocked over the leasing of Hangö as a naval base. Then the Russians modified their original proposal, reducing the size of the base and the term of the lease from thirty years to the duration of the war between the Allies and Germany. On Nov. 26 the Soviets protested against Finnish shooting of Red army soldiers and asked the Finnish government to move its troops back twenty miles from the border to prevent repetition of such incidents. The Finns' reply was to suggest that the troops of both countries be removed twenty miles from the border. Since this would put the Soviet troops into Leningrad proper, giving Finland a military advantage, the Soviets took the view that the Finnish reply presumed a hostile attitude and broke off relations. The Cajander government fell and was succeeded by one headed by Tanner. On Nov. 30 Molotov denounced these "Finnish provocations" and the Red army marched into Finland.

96

WEARING WHITE CAMOUFLAGE, the highly mechanized Red Army advanced at five points and within a week had seized Petsamo, reached the outer forts of the Mannerheim Line, and north of Lake Ladoga swept some eighty miles toward Uleaborg in an attempt to cut Finland's waist. Note that Red soldier in the center foreground of the above picture has just been shot and is falling. In the picture below a Red flame-throwing tank is shown advancing toward the Mannerheim Line where the Reds put great pressure but attempted no break-through. A world-wide campaign to aid Finland began. Meeting with unusual speed, the League expelled Russia.

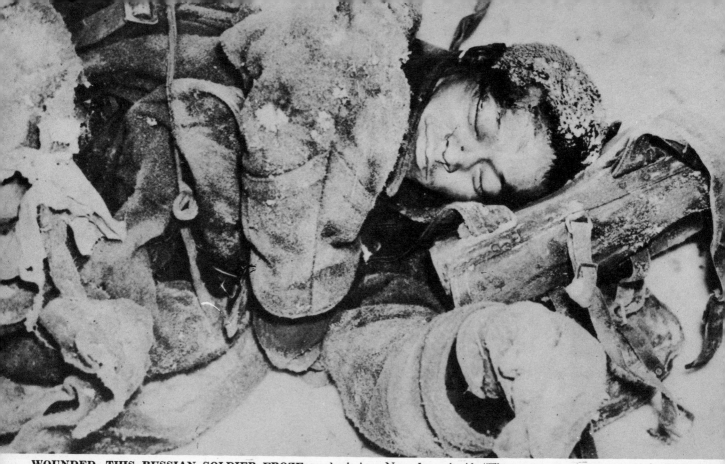

WOUNDED, THIS RUSSIAN SOLDIER FROZE to death in the sub-Arctic temperatures in which the war was fought; often it dropped to 60 degrees below zero. The weather plus the rugged terrain held up the Red advance until mid-February. Commenting on newspaper stories of that period which told of faulty Red equipment, lack of clothing, fantastic Russian losses, the U.S. Army and Navy *Journal* said: "There appears to be no ground for large numbers of reports . . . that the Russians are inadequately equipped and fed and that many are freezing to death due to lack of clothing and shelter. As a matter of fact, it is quite likely that the losses have been considerably less than contended in dispatches. As a matter of fact, the entire Russian invading forces number only 200,000 men."

ON FEB. 11 RED ARTILLERY BEGAN POUNDING THE FORTS of the Mannerheim Line as the Reds abandoned their earlier strategy of cutting Finland's waist to attempt to break through the Mannerheim Line. Under the incessant hammering of the big guns, the forts were uprooted one by one, throwing their fire out of line. Relentlessly the Reds advanced through the supposedly impregnable series of fortifications. After only a fortnight Summa was captured, Koivisto falling on Feb. 26.

FINNISH LOSSES MOUNTED RAPIDLY as the Russian attack moved forward. As the military analyst Max Werner later said, "with the precision of a machine, without reverses or failures." Red airmen, meanwhile, smashed Finn supply lines, depots, concentrations.

BARON CARL VON MANNERHEIM, an old Tsarist general, headed Finnish forces. He was friendly to Finnish Nazis. Toward the end of the war he quarreled violently with Generals Osterman and Wallenius, his chief aides, who had been trained by Germans.

FINLAND WAS NOW RECEIVING AID from Chamberlain, Daladier, and Mussolini. An Allied expedition of 50,000 men was organized but Norway and Sweden refused permission for Allied troops to cross their borders en route to Finland. Meanwhile, the Finn army collapsed.

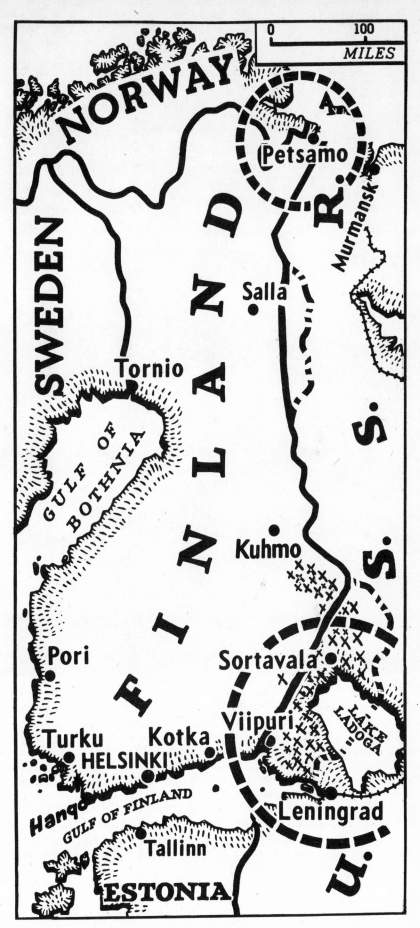

UNDER THE PEACE TREATY SIGNED BY THE FINNS ON MAR. 12 Russia got only a strategic peninsula commanding Petsamo, a strip of wasteland near the vital Murmansk railway, and enough territory on both sides of Lake Ladoga, including Viborg, to put Leningrad well out of the range of artillery. Hangö was leased to Russia for 30 years. But the Russians returned Petsamo and its rich nickel mines with all damage repaired. The defenses thus secured saved Leningrad two years later.

WITH the end of winter the Allies applied their blockade of Germany more strenuously in the hope of provoking her into attack, thinking such an attack could be easily overcome and the Nazis put on the defensive. Meanwhile, early in March the Nazis had secretly set about preparing the seizure of Norway which would accordingly safeguard the iron they were receiving from Narvik and Sweden. With their plans all laid, the Nazis offered to buy 30,000 tons of frozen fish from Norway which, determined to maintain strict neutrality, queried the Allies, offering them half their fish supply. The Allies turned down the offer but said they needed whale oil and iron and would send boats for it. Norway, meanwhile, told the Nazis they could have the fish which was stored at Narvik, Bergen, and Trondheim. The Nazis then sent Norway a list of ships, adding that the deckhand complement of them had been doubled to facilitate the rapid handling of the fish, which might rot. The list seemed large, but the Norwegians, checking up, found the refrigeration needed would take up considerable space and concluded the German ships were approximately the number needed. The Nazi ships landed in Norway April 6, 7, 8, while the Allies paid little attention to the deal except to mine Norwegian

waters at three points to discourage similar expeditions. O the night of April 8 survivors of a boat which had struck mine were picked up and found to be Nazi troops who sa they had been en route to Norway to protect her from invasion by Britain. This incident was ignored by the Briti but they passed the information on to the Norwegian Cal net, which decided that since the British were not going do anything, they wouldn't either. At dawn Nazi nav forces steamed into six Norwegian ports and out of the s called "fish" boats streamed thousands of Nazis, who seiz control of the ports before the surprised Norwegians cou understand what was happening. They were aided I traitors in the coast forts who refused to fire on the Naz At Trondheim the Nazi warships surrounded themselv with Norwegian craft which deterred Norwegian fire. Oslo energetic fifth columnists seized the town, held it un Nazis arrived; the only fighting took place at the airpo Meanwhile, the British attempted to cut Nazi sea commur cations and successfully sank 50 per cent of the Nazi capit ships, 33 per cent of their heavy cruisers, and 45 per cent their destroyers. But the Nazis continued to get throug and the British rushed an expeditionary force to Narvik.

NORWAY BETRAYED

Above: Thousands of German troops and many tanks, hidden in the holds of Nazi freighters tied to Norwegian docks, poured forth to aid the invading Nazi naval craft. Fifth columnists in coastal ports issued rehearsed false commands, refused to fire on Hitler's forces.

Right: Covered by the menacing guns of Nazi battleships that slipped into fjords a snowstorm, Nazi troops poured into Norway at six different points. Nazi air superiority drove off British Naval Attempts to cut German sea communication lines.

ABOVE: NAZI TROOPS were ferried in by air when the British blows at their sea lines began to have a telling effect. Norwegian forces attempted to block the Nazi advance from Oslo toward Sweden. However, the Nazis landing troops southeast of Oslo, fought their way inland, overcoming the improvised defenses of the Norwegian people. By April 15 the Nazis reached the Swedish frontier.

BELOW: RAPIDLY ADVANCING Nazis moved North along the main railroads toward Trondheim. Meanwhile, British forces landed at the northern port of Namsos and at Andalsnes. The British aim

The Norwegians Are Seafarers

was to seize Trondheim before the Nazis, since it offered a base from which to wage a campaign. But they could not land heavy equipment at Namsos, which was rapidly being devastated by Nazi bombers.

THIS NORWEGIAN HUNTER is typical of Norway's 2,814,775 people. Because their land is barren, the Norse have been seafarers, hunters, and fishers for centuries. Their ancestors came to America before Columbus.

THIS POWER DAM AT VAMMA IS ONLY ONE of Norway's numerous water-power projects. They make electricity so cheap it is used extensively for heating; may some day make Norway an industrial country.

Quisling Organized the Betrayal of His Country

His name has become synonymous with traitor.

THE ALLIED FORCES WHICH RACED INLAND lacked heavy artillery and mechanized equipment because the Namsos and Andalsnes docks had no cranes for unloading such material. Worst of all, they lacked anti-aircraft weapons and had no supporting planes. All efforts to achieve Norwegian air bases failed. Their only air support had to come from Britain and offered no real protection.

THE man who organized the betrayal of Norway to the Nazi invaders was Major Vidkun Abraham Lauritz Quisling, who was born in 1887 and trained for a diplomatic and military career from youth. The height of his career was reached—in free Norway, that is—in 1931, when he became Minister of Defense. His anti-labor attitude won him the support of Norway's industrialists, and in 1932 he resigned from the progressive Farmer party to form his own party, *Nasjonal Samling*, on a platform calling for suppression of the "revolutionary" parties and the "freeing" of labor from the trade unions. However, this Hitlerlike party met with no success and never elected a member to the Norwegian Storting or parliament. However, it did find support among Quisling's powerful friends in the Norwegian army and navy. In July 1937 Quisling represented Norwegian Nazis at a conference of Nazi emissaries at Riga to discuss General Haushofer's favorite theory of Nazi domination of the Baltic. It was at this meeting that he was promised the premiership of Nazi Norway by his close friend, Alfred Rosenberg, the "philosopher" of Nazism. On the night of April 5, 1940, Quisling was in Berlin getting his final orders on the betrayal of Norway. Three days later the Nazi warships successfully ran the gantlet of Norse forts commanded by Quislingites who either gave no orders to fire on the Nazis or delayed their orders until the Nazis had passed. A few days later Quisling proclaimed himself Premier. The Nazis removed him from this post but in August 1940 they named him Norway's sole political leader, which crystallized Norwegian anti-Nazi sentiment into violent action.

THIS BRIDGE WAS BLOWN UP by Norwegian populace which sought to impede the Nazi advance by sabotaging their communication lines. But the Nazi air superiority had already reduced the Allied expedition to a holding operation. By April 25 the Nazis were in a position to launch an attack between Dombaas and Storen, which threatened to split the Allied forces.

MEANWHILE KING HAAKON FLED FROM NAZI BOMBS, moving from town to town. It was part of the Nazi strategy of terror to bomb the king in the hope of killing him. They chased him from Oslo, to Hamar, to Elvrum, to Nybersund, where the above picture was taken as Haakon fled into the woods with his aides to escape raiding Nazi planes. Later, when Norway was completely lost, he escaped to England to direct the fight of Norwegian forces. Nazis outnumbered the Allies by ten to one toward the end of April, and on May 1 Allied troops were evacuated from Andalsnes and Namsos to save them from useless destruction. Nazi planes, which more than anything else had accounted for the defeat of the Allied expedition, sank three protecting destroyers.

THE NAZIS WERE IN COMPLETE CONTROL of all southern Norway after the evacuation of the Allied forces. British troops had landed outside Narvik, held by a Nazi force supplied by planes via parachutes. On May 28 the British attacked and after a day's battle seized it only to find the Nazis had slipped out of town and fallen back to prepared positions. To avoid dissipation of strength needed on the Western Front, the British withdrew altogether from Norway. This left the Nazis free to exploit the Narvik mines, consolidate their control of the country, cart back to Berlin some $75,000,000 in gold found in Oslo and Copenhagen, quantities of motor tires found in Danish warehouses, and some 500,000 tons of oil. More important was the Danish food supply.

THE FALL OF CHAMBERLAIN

THE fall of Norway brought the fall of Chamberlain. When the Nazi invasion began Chamberlain had encouraged the British public to believe Hitler had at last made a reckless move which would recoil on him. "Hitler has missed the bus," he declared. The storm of angry criticism that followed the British defeat was not over Norway alone, but was the cumulative effect of discontent which had begun to grow when Ethiopia was sacrificed. This discontent had grown with each new appeasement of the dictators—China, Spain, Austria, Czechoslovakia, Albania. It was crowned with Chamberlain's failure to draw Russia into a mutual-assistance pact, his refusal to take counsel, his anemic prosecution of the war. In rebuttal Chamberlain was defiant, unrepentant, and implied that he was sorry that he had opposed Hitler's invasion of Norway. He seemed to regret criticism of himself more than the failure of the British expedition. He once again refused to consider any Cabinet changes. Until now Chamberlain had maintained himself in office through the solid support of the Conservative party. But now he was no longer able to control it. Chamberlain was sustained by Commons on May 8, 1940, by a vote of 281 to 200. But the Conservative party in the House numbered 365 and only 252 voted for the government. The bulk of the 65 absentee Conservatives had deliberately abstained from voting, and they included such prominent conservatives as Duff Cooper, Hore-Belisha, Amery, and Lord Winterton. Every Conservative member of the fighting services voted against Chamberlain. Thus while Chamberlain had won a majority, the vote was an outright condemnation of his leadership. Chamberlain, realizing his control over the Conservative party was shattered, nevertheless still believed he could remain Prime Minister by broadening the basis of his government. He asked the Labor party, headed by Herbert Morrison, Clement Attlee, and Ernest Bevin, to join his government. But the Laborites refused, although they had endorsed his policy of appeasement and anti-Soviet maneuvering to the point of expelling Sir Stafford Cripps, who opposed them. Their refusal settled Chamberlain's fate. There was nothing for him to do but resign immediately or await the next disaster and be voted out. He therefore resigned on May 9 and Winston Churchill, pugnacious, rhetorical, impetuous, succeeded him on May 10. Churchill's Cabinet included the Labor party leaders.

Churchill broadened the government, brought to it vigor, imagination, and determination to fight.

THE RISE OF CHURCHILL

WINSTON CHURCHILL was the one man who at that time ould unite England, guide her through the desperate days hat lay ahead. With his accession to office a new spirit f confidence and determination swept England. The son f Lord Randolph Churchill and an American girl named ennie Jerome, Churchill had long been the most unpre- lictable leader in British politics. On numerous occasions is career was said to have been ended. Yet on each occasion e rose to new heights. Trained as a soldier, he became reporter. A Conservative when he entered Parliament, he oon became a Liberal. His political unorthodoxy shocked nglish politicians. As First Lord of the Admiralty in 1914 e mobilized the fleet on his own responsibility although ngland was not yet at war with Germany. His disastrous ttempt at invasion at Gallipoli forced him out of the dmiralty in 1915. As Secretary of War in 1919 he sent an xpeditionary force to northern Russia to assist the White Russian forces in their counterrevolution against Lenin nd Stalin. This, too, ended in disaster for Churchill, for it vas much against the will of the British people and Churchill ost his seat in Parliament. He did not regain it until 1924.

He was not affiliated with any party but voted with the Conservatives, who eventually made him Chancellor of the Exchequer. The Labor government in 1929 ended this, and for the next eleven years Churchill wrote books and became the outstanding critic of the government. Throughout the years of Hitler's rise he warned of the growing danger, beseeched Baldwin and Chamberlain to build up England's strength. But it was to no avail. His attacks on Chamberlain increased as the Prime Minister's policy of appeasement increased England's danger. Especially did he denounce Chamberlain's ignoring of Russia in the days when collective security was the hope of the world. His bold, vigorous speeches were in startling contrast to the inept, laconic understatement of Chamberlain. Most Englishmen believed, with Sir Archibald Sinclair, that "six months of Winston Churchill before the war started would have been six nails in Hitler's coffin," and they were heartened by his return to the Admiralty. After the disaster in Norway they were sure he was the man England needed at the helm. He promised only "blood, toil, tears, and sweat."

A RARE PICTURE of Churchill at the age of twelve when he was a student in the famous public school, Harrow. He was born in 1874, the son of Lord Randolph Churchill, the seventh Duke of Marlborough and a young American girl named Jennie Jerome.

AS A LIEUTENANT in the Spanish army, he served in Cuba. His military career began at Sandhurst, British West Point. During the Boer War he first became known to the public as a war correspondent. He was captured by the Boers but escaped.

CHURCHILL WAS ONE of the first flyers in England, shown here at the controls of a rickety biplane in 1913. He had entered politics in 1900 as a Conservative, shifted to the Liberal party in 1906, appointed Undersecretary of Colonies in 1908.

CHURCHILL BECAME FIRST LORD of the Admiralty in 1911 after serving for a short time as president of the Board of Trade. When England went into the war in 1914 he amazed the Cabinet by telling them he had already mobilized the fleet. But his attempt to invade Germany through Gallipoli was one of the bloodiest disasters in military history and caused the fall of the Asquith government.

IN 1915 CHURCHILL resumed his military career. He is shown here going to the front with his commanding officers. By this time his political career was virtually a wreck and he had sunk to the minor office of Chancellor of the Duchy of Lancaster. At the front he narrowly escaped death when a German shell obliterated his dugout. He commanded a Scottish regiment with bravery.

CHURCHILL, SHOWN HERE WITH HIS WIFE, after a visit to Buckingham Palace, found his stock rising again toward the end of 1916 as the demand for a rapid conclusion of the war grew. Churchill symbolized vigorous, daring, offensive action. But at the same time the disaster of Gallipoli created much distrust of him.

IN 1917 PRIME MINISTER LLOYD GEORGE returned Churchill to public life, making him Minister of Munitions. He tackled the problems of production with vigor and imagination, slashed red tape, and increased production tremendously within a few months. Shown here making a speech to munition workers in a Middlesex factory, Churchill was one of the first war leaders to recognize the importance of the industrial front in modern war.

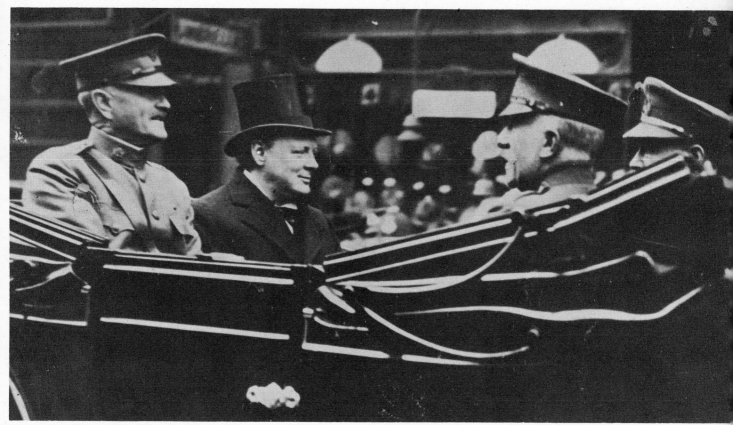

GEN. JOHN J. PERSHING, chief of the first A. E. F., was welcomed to London in 1919 on his return from France by Churchill, who was then Secretary for War and Air. That year Churchill sent an expeditionary force to Archangel in northern Russia to assist the White Russian armies in their counter-revolutionary war on the young Soviet Union. Though decidedly not Communist, the British people did not share Churchill's enthusiasm for an anti-Soviet war and, led by labor leaders such as Ernest Bevin, demanded a policy of "Hands Off Russia." Churchill was forced to withdraw the troops, but before he did so they were badly mauled by the ragged Red army. Public fury against Churchill now reached new heights. Everywhere it was said that Churchill's career was ended.

AFTER THE WAR Churchill was called before various investigating bodies to defend decisions he had made as Secretary of Munitions. He is shown here justifying the awards he made to inventors of tanks. He had done much to encourage the development of tanks. But the political stock of the Lloyd George government and of Churchill personally was now on the downgrade.

THIS RARE PICTURE SHOWS CHURCHILL when he was at the bottom of his career. In 1921 he had lost his Parliament seat, largely because of his preoccupation with the "Red Menace." He tried unsuccessfully for many years to regain his seat in several constituencies. But in 1924, when this picture was made, he managed to win in Epping and since then has represented that district.

THE PRINCE OF WALES (Edward Windsor) and Churchill became close friends in the early twenties and spent much time playing polo together. Years later, in 1936, Churchill was to savagely attack Prime Minister Baldwin for forcing the Prince, then King George VII, to abdicate because he wanted to marry Mrs. Simpson. During the years Churchill was out of Parliament he wrote prolifically and began his history of World War I, the *World Crisis*.

OFFICIALLY INDEPENDENT, Churchill voted with the Conservatives who rewarded him with the Chancellorship of the Exchequer. One of the most important offices in postwar Europe, it involved working out new settlements of reparations and debts. Advent of the Labor government in 1929 removed him from this post.

CHURCHILL WAS HIT BY A TAXI when he visited United States on a lecture tour in Dec. 1931. Americans greatly enjoyed his paying all hospital expenses by writing an article on how it feels to be hit by a car. At home Churchill devoted most of his time to writing. He was kept out of government posts because he refused to endorse the Conservative policies and fought its India Bill.

CHURCHILL'S PET HOBBY for years was bricklaying, but with the rise of Hitler he devoted more and more of his time trying to warn Britain of her danger. He blasted the meager defense measure of Prime Ministers Baldwin and Chamberlain. Much to the discomfort of the Chamberlain clique, he conducted a vigorous campaign against the policy of appeasing Hitler and not rearming.

POPULAR DEMAND forced Chamberlain to make Churchill First Lord of the Admiralty again when Poland was invaded in Sept. 1939. By his long but unsuccessful campaign for new defenses and against the appeasement policies of Chamberlain, Churchill had become the symbol of anti-Nazism for the British people. In April 1940 he was named head of all Britain's armed services. It was a popular choice.

AS PRIME MINISTER Churchill immediately succeeded, through vigorous efforts, frankness, and courage, in uniting all Britain as it had never been united. He called for "victory . . . at all costs . . . in spite of all the terror . . . however long and hard the road; for without victory there is no survival."

PEACEFUL HOLLAND HAD EVERY DESIRE TO REMAIN at peace. But at the same time she was not without her defenses. Twice within a year she had opened her dykes when the Nazi blow seemed imminent. When, on May 7, Nazi troops were reported concentrating at key points along the frontier she again flooded her fields and called up her 450,000 troops. Belgium canceled all army leaves and manned her fortifications. Both small countries lacked anti-aircraft, heavy artillery, and planes; Holland, for instance, had only 400 planes, most of them obsolete. Neither Holland nor Belgium had defensive pacts with Britain and France; they did not even have them with each other for fear of provoking Hitler. Even after the fall of Norway they refused defensive alliances.

DEFENSES OF THE LOWLANDS

Holland's chief defenses were flooded fields. The Dutch had no heavy artillery and only 44 pillbox forts on the border.

HE DUTCH NAVY WAS MODERN AND WELL TRAINED. consisted of six cruisers, sixteen destroyers, and twenty-two sub-arines. But it could not defend the border. Worse, between Bel-um and Holland lay an unguarded corridor forty miles wide rough which the Nazis, after taking one Belgian fort, could split e two countries. The Belgian defenses were the Albert Canal on

the north and in the center the series of forts around Liége, all modernized. For the rest they depended on their armies to fight a delaying action until help could arrive. At 5:30 A.M., May 10, as if it were timed to coincide with the fall of Chamberlain, the Dutch Minister was handed an insulting memorandum, told to study it for a half-hour, and phone his government to surrender or be invaded.

The Belgian fortifications were modern but not elaborate. Newest of them was the Fort Eben Emael at the Meuse River.

LARGE NUMBER OF NAZI PARACHUTISTS descended on the airports at Rotterdam and Waalhaven within an hour after the assault upon the Dutch frontier, taking the Dutch by surprise. Assault units in air transports followed.

LANDING AT A DOZEN DIFFERENT POINTS, Nazi paratroops raced to their specific objective, usually a key strategic point in the Dutch defense system. Some 3,000 troops were flown in wearing Allied police uniforms, women's dresses.

THIS UNUSUAL PICTURE TAKEN FROM AN R.A.F. PLANE as it bombed the Nazi-held Rotterdam airport shows the ruined hangars and, in the upper left corner, a German Dornier transport used to fly troops. Captured Nazi parachutists had lists of Dutch anti-Nazis, political leaders, and unionists whom they were to shoot on sight. The Nazis knew the location of every telephone bureau, power plant, and railroad bottlenecks, so completely had the fifth columnists done their work. The Dutch attempted to round up the 3,000 German tourists in Rotterdam but could locate only 700. The others had gone to a small island the night before the invasion and remained there. When the Nazis found they could not hold the airport, they began the massed bombing of Rotterdam itself.

WHILE ROTTERDAM'S PEOPLE TOOK TO THE ROAD or sought the bodies of their loved ones, the Dutch army courageously tried to stem the mechanized might of the Nazis. Part of the Nazi strategy was to capture Queen Wilhelmina and the royal family, Nazi parachutists having been landed with that specific objective. But the royal family escaped, to be followed relentlessly by Nazi bombers from village to village. On May 13 the Queen asked the British, who had been rushing aid to Holland within an hour after the attack, to evacuate her and the family. Meanwhile, the Dutch fired the oil tanks of Amsterdam, sank an ore steamer in the harbor to block it, and shipped their precious machine-tool diamonds to England. British navy aided refugees and neutral ships to escape.

THIS FAMOUS PHOTOGRAPH OF A SHELL-SHOCKED father gazing at the broken body of his daughter on a Rotterdam corner shows the utter ruthlessness with which the Nazis destroyed that city and its people. Virtually the only anti-aircraft protection the city had came from the Dutch ships stationed in the harbor and which were soon sunk. Meanwhile, British marines and army troops had landed near Rotterdam and plunged into the fight against overwhelming odds. But Nazi parachutists had seized and successfully held the Moerdijk Bridge, preventing its demolition, which enabled the Nazi panzer divisions to outflank the whole of the Dutch water defenses. On the fourth day the Nazis were able to extend this column, cutting off the bulk of Holland from help from the south.

Dutch Fifth Columnists Gave Nazis Detailed Defense Plans

Von Mussert organized the betrayal of Holland.

THE NAZI fifth column in Holland did its treacherous job with even more thoroughness than its Norwegian counterpart. The Nazi movement was organized in Holland at the time Hitler achieved prominence in Germany by Von Mussert and Major von Kruyt. In 1934 Hess was personally assigned to the job of development of Nazism among the Dutch. The Dutch Nazis were financed by Von Beuringen, Dutch-German munitions king. By 1935 they controlled ten per cent of the Dutch vote. The picture below, found on the body of a dead parachutist, shows a Dutch fifth columnist meeting parachutists to direct them to bridges and strategic points.

BEGINNING WITH THE THIRD DAY, British ships began evacuating Dutch soldiers, especially the wounded. Everywhere the courageous Dutch were collapsing under the pounding of Stukas and tanks. The entire Dutch air force was destroyed the first day.

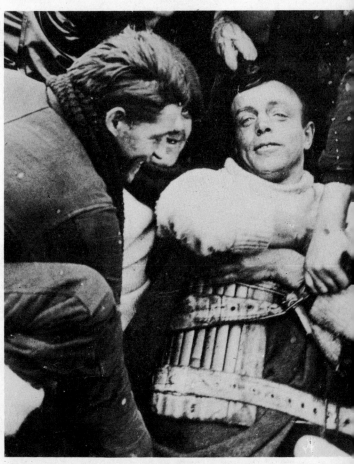

THIS WOUNDED DUTCH FISHERMAN WAS severely hurt when his boat was suddenly attacked by a Stuka dive bomber which machine-gunned the survivors. Such attacks on larger Dutch naval forces paved the way for Nazi troop transports from Wilhelmshaven.

WHEREVER THEY HAD NOT BEEN ABLE TO OUTFLANK the water defenses via bridges protected by fifth columnists and parachutists, the Nazis quickly pumped up rubber boats, paddled their way across under the protection of an artillery barrage. Fifth columnists had supplied the Nazis with exact measurements of many of the important bridges. From these measurements the Nazis built exact replicas which they brought with them in sections and ready to be quickly erected when needed.

NAZI CAVALRY HUNTED DOWN and raided Dutch forces off the main roads which the Nazis were using for their big units. By the end of the third day the Dutch had lost 200,000 men of their original 450,000 and it became impossible for them to continue fighting. They hung on for one more day and on May 14 General Winkelman surrendered. Fighting continued until the 17th, but British troops were evacuated on the 14th. After a fortnight of military rule Holland was placed under Dr. Seyss-Inquart of Austria.

NAZI BREAK-THROUGH IN BELGIUM

THE violence and speed of the surprise Nazi blow which broke the Dutch defenses also carried the Nazis through tiny, defenseless Luxembourg and through the first Belgian defense lines without loss of speed. Maastricht, the key fortress of the defenses built around the Albert Canal, was captured immediately, and on the second day the strategic and modernized fortress of Eben Emael fell, the victim of what the Nazi High Command called "a secret weapon," probably flame-throwing tanks. The fall of Eben Emael opened a gap which allowed the Nazi motorized divisions to sweep around the fortresses of Liége which were left for infantry to mop up. Meanwhile, another Nazi mechanized column swept through southern Holland and northern Belgium toward Antwerp. To meet it British and French forces rushed up. But the Allied High Command had not yet studied the lessons of Poland sufficiently to know how to stop the Nazi panzer divisions. The Nazi pattern of operation followed these procedures: reconnaissance cars, radio-equipped, rushed miles ahead of the main Nazi forces. They were followed by motorcyclists armed with rapid-fire machine guns. If they met with resistance, Stuka dive bombers were radioed for support and scout cars moved up. If the resistance continued, light tanks, then medium tanks joined the original forces. As the tanks broke through, motorized infantry was rushed up. The arrival of the infantry signaled the withdrawal of the tanks, which were raced around the enemy's flanks while Stuka dive bombers pounded the center. Under this type of attack the Belgians rapidly fell back to the fortifications of the Rheims line, where they were joined by the Allied forces. When the Allies advanced from their prepared positions in France to aid the Belgians they carried out a right wheel with its pivot at Sedan. In the process they shifted a number of troops from this sector, leaving it weak. But the British and French counted on the rocky, wooded terrain of the Belgian Ardennes Forest to hold off the German attack until they could strengthen that sector. Meanwhile, they took up positions along the Meuse River, which were already under Nazi air attack.

Fast-moving Nazi tanks poured through road barriers left open by ever-present fifth columnists in the hilly Ardennes Forest.

The main Nazi force included 8 panzer divisions. It raced around town after town, bypassing nearly every fortification.

Not until May 15, after Namur was encircled, did the Allies realize the main Nazi forces were crossing the Meuse to flank them

Attacked by dive bombers, these terror-stricken Belgian soldiers have thrown away their guns to run for their lives. Note the look of anguish on the face of the soldier on the extreme right.

Attacking incessantly, Nazi bombers functioned as artillery, blasted Belgian strong points. Sirens terrorized troops and civilians.

THE ruthless Nazi bombing of cities and towns filled Belgian roads with hundreds of thousands of refugees, choking roads and bridges and delaying Allied forces moving toward the front. Leaving their ruined home, the widow on the left is setting off for France with her only possessions, her babies. The others await evacuation to England. Note the British soldier giving a drink to a Belgian baby.

FRENCH TANKS, CHEERED BY THE BELGIAN populace, were still moving into position when the Nazis broke through at Sedan, threatening to outflank the entire French system of fortifications. Nazis had 12 armored divisions in Belgium, eight of them at Sedan. Against this the French had five and the British only one. Nazi air superiority was never threatened by the Allied forces, although their pilots often outfought the Nazis. When the breakthrough between Sedan and Maubeuge occurred, General Gamelin, head of the French armies, took little cognizance of the "bulge." When pressed to retreat in the north, he sided with King Leopold of Belgium, who protested against the surrender of Brussels and Antwerp. By May 17, however, the "bulge" forced a retreat.

WHILE BELGIAN ARMIES RESTED AT THE ROADSIDE in some sectors, British troops replaced them at the front. But they were unable to halt the Nazi armies, which entered Antwerp May 18, forcing the Allies to withdraw. Meanwhile, the "bulge" in the south was being rapidly broadened and deepened by the Nazis, who captured General Giraud in charge of the French armies in that sector. A new "secret Nazi weapon"—a heavily armored 70-ton tank—rolled right through French lines. By now the situation of the Allied forces had become extremely precarious and the French began firing their famous 75-millimeter guns at the giant Nazi tanks to stop the Nazi drive. They failed, however, and on May 21 the Nazis reached Abbeville, cutting off the Allied forces from France itself.

THE FALL OF THE BELGIAN FORTS

THIS dramatic picture shows the surrender of Fort Boucelles, one of the forts outside Liége. On these forts the Belgians and Allies hung their hopes that the Nazis' attack could be delayed. The main defenses of Belgium, they were also the last fortifications the Nazis had to pass to outflank the French Maginot Line, excepting a series of pillboxes hastily erected by the French in Sept. 1939. The two key Belgian forts were Maastricht and Eben Emael. The Nazis took both fortresses within two days. First, the forts were hammered by low-diving Stukas. Then the Nazis advanced at dusk with heavy flame-throwing tanks, capable of shooting a scorching, terrifying stream of flame 75 feet. These were accompanied by special assault troops on foot, armed with automatic rifles, grenades, and flame-throwers. Slipping through the dusk until they were so close to the forts that the Belgian guns could not be depressed enough to fire on them, the tanks let go with their terrible boiling flames and rushed forward. They were followed closely by the assault units whose job it was to lob grenades through portholes and stick the nozzles of their flame-throwers into ventilators, ports, and doors. Note the scorching the fort below received. Then, blasting and shooting their way in, the Nazis seized the forts. With Maastricht and Eben Emael out of commission, the Nazis by-passed the other fortifications to strike deep into Belgium.

This strategy was based on the simple logic that the forts could not carry the fight to them, that by-passing isolated them for later troops to seize and did not impede the conquering of the country as a whole. Blitz strategy reduced even the strongest Allied fortifications to traps, to be mopped up later.

OVERCOMING EVERY OBSTACLE placed in their path, the Nazis in northern Belgium had swept through Louvain, Antwerp, Brussels, and Ghent with incredible speed. Meanwhile, the Nazis who had reached the channel at Abbeville turned northward up the coast, threatening to cut off the Channel ports which were the Allies' sole source of supply and only hope of escape from what was rapidly becoming a hopeless situation. As the Nazis turned northward on the Channel the Nazi air force unleashed violent attacks on all the Channel ports in an attempt to destroy the ports themselves. By May 23 the Nazi panzers had reached Boulogne despite the fierce resistance of the Allied forces. After two days the Boulogne garrison was evacuated by destroyers which fought off the Nazi heavy tanks.

Declarq headed the Belgian fifth columnists.

NAZI FIFTH-COLUMN work in Belgium was directed by the Nazi Consuls Klee and Hellwig. When the Nazi blitzkrieg struck, its members seized important bridges until the Nazi troops reached them, failed to set off mined roads, created panic among the civilians. The two leaders of the Belgian Nazis, Degrelle and De Clarq, called Rexists in pre war years, made no secret of their sympathies for Nazism. Their propaganda, directed from Berlin, "Belgium wants peace. The war had always been between France and Germany. We must break our alliances with France and Britain lest we offend Hitler." Leopold was influenced by Henri DeMann, Social Democratic leader, whom Jules Romain later revealed as a Nazi agent. In 1937 Leopold abandoned the alliance with France and Britain.

Belgian Nazi youth organizations parading in 1939.

ALLIED FORCES RESCUED CIVILIAN VICTIMS of the ruthless Nazi air attack when they could. The Nazis reduced town after town to ruins, regardless of its military importance.

THE NAZI ADVANCE ROLLED INTO CALAIS from the south and to the approaches of Ostend from the north, narrowing the corridor of escape to the port of Dunkerque, already under Nazi fire.

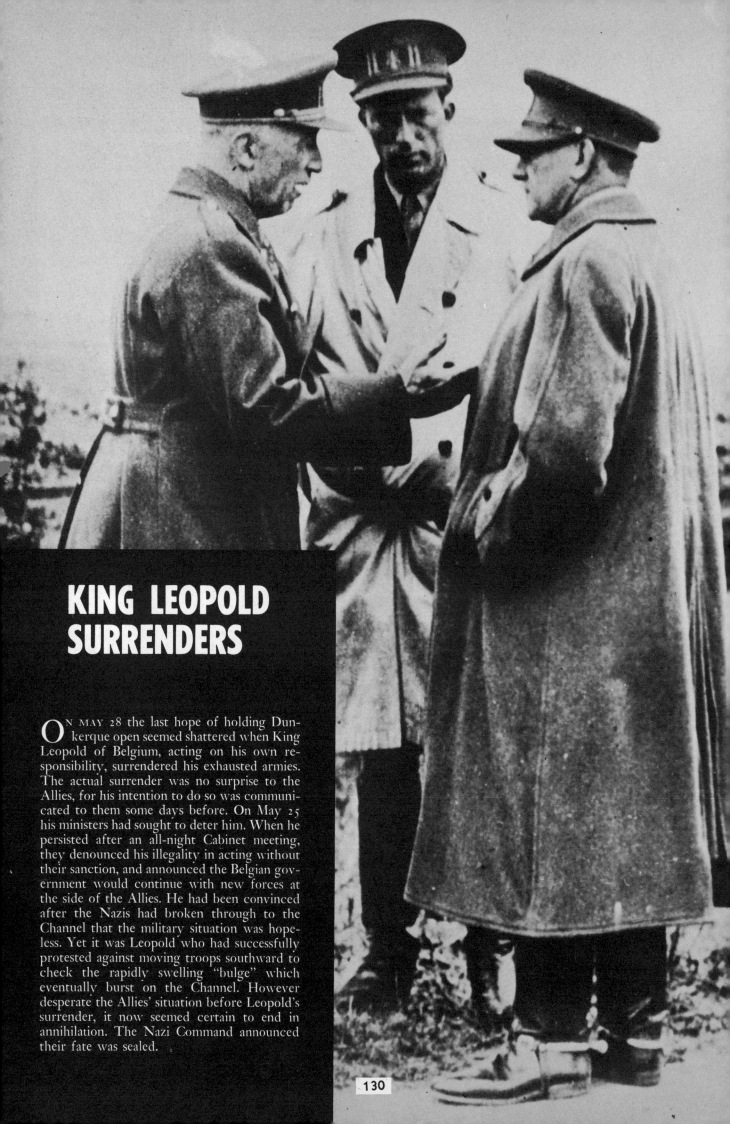

KING LEOPOLD SURRENDERS

ON MAY 28 the last hope of holding Dunkerque open seemed shattered when King Leopold of Belgium, acting on his own responsibility, surrendered his exhausted armies. The actual surrender was no surprise to the Allies, for his intention to do so was communicated to them some days before. On May 25 his ministers had sought to deter him. When he persisted after an all-night Cabinet meeting, they denounced his illegality in acting without their sanction, and announced the Belgian government would continue with new forces at the side of the Allies. He had been convinced after the Nazis had broken through to the Channel that the military situation was hopeless. Yet it was Leopold who had successfully protested against moving troops southward to check the rapidly swelling "bulge" which eventually burst on the Channel. However desperate the Allies' situation before Leopold's surrender, it now seemed certain to end in annihilation. The Nazi Command announced their fate was sealed.

BRITISH SOLDIERS BEGAN FILING INTO DUNKERQUE despite the incessant air attack of the Nazi dive bombers. Immediately after Leopold's surrender, the Allied troops had quickly organized the exposed front created by the surrender and begun their slow but steady withdrawal in the face of an enemy exerting his full might to crush them. The area around Dunkerque was flooded to afford extra protection against Nazi tanks pushing up from the south. The French tank corps fought a brilliant rearguard action around Lille under General Prioux, checking the advance of a far superior foe by a series of counterattacks that often cut them off from the main body of troops. The morale and the discipline of the troops were superb. Gradually they abandoned their heavy equipment.

EVACUATION OF DUNKERQUE

ON THE BEACHES OF DUNKERQUE they waited in thin, winding, but disciplined lines for the small boats to take them to the transports and warships which lay off shore. Overhead the R.A.F. fought valiantly against the numerically superior Nazi air force and managed to completely nullify the Nazi air raids during most of the evacuation. The evacuation fleet consisted of practically every boat England and France had which could cross the Channel. It varied between ferryboats and small fishing trawlers to transports and warships. A vast flotilla of small boats shuttled between the beaches and the big ships off shore. Day and night, for five days, the evacuation went on while the Nazis pushed the heroic rear guard closer and closer to the ruined port of Dunkerque.

Above: In the final desperate hours daring R.A.F. strafing held the Nazis back until the main British forces could be evacuated.

Below: The white beaches were black with war-weary men who looked anxiously to the sea, their last and only hope of escape.

The last men of the 335,000 to leave waded out into the sea to meet the battered fleet. More than 30,000 were lost at D

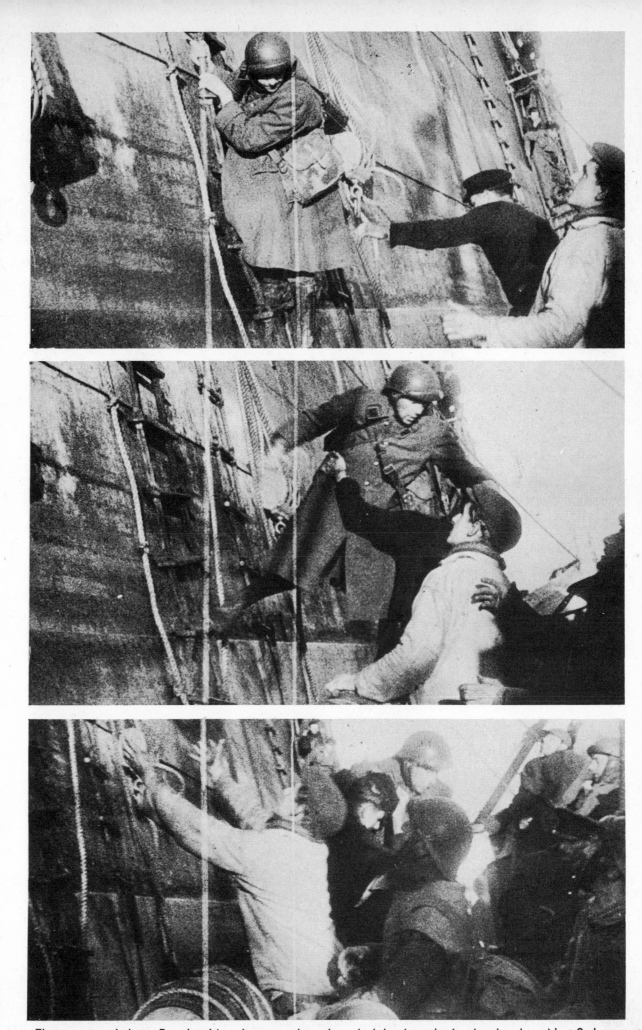

These men are helping French soldiers leave a sinking ship which has been hit by dive bombing Nazi Stukas.

Sunken ships, battered tanks, blasted ammunition dumps, broken trucks, debris were all the Nazis found in Dunkerque.

BATTERED, BUT UNBROKEN IN SPIRIT, these British soldiers were typical of the 350,000 men who were so heroically evacuated. But though the army had escaped with only some 30,000 casualties, their losses in matériel included practically all Britain's mechanized equipment and 1,000 heavy guns. Few of the men had either rifles or helmets. Of the 1,000 ships which evacuated the men, the British lost six destroyers, twenty-four small craft, and 24,000 tons of merchant shipping. The French lost seven destroyers and one supply ship. The equipment loss set Britain back many months, and for the first time since Napoleon's day England faced the possibility of an invasion. Nazi planes were only an hour from the industrial heart of Britain and the Nazi push into France had already begun.

A LARGE PART OF THE FRENCH AIR FLEET was destroyed by Nazi raids at dawn on French airports even before the evacuation from Dunkerque. On June 1 the Nazis raided the industrial plants of the Rhone Valley, particularly around Lyons, and on June 3 they struck the Paris airports where the French had left many planes on the field just because they did not expect the Nazis to penetrate so deeply into France. French air strength amounted to some 3,000 planes. Both in quality and quantity it was inferior to the Nazis'.

Gen. Ironside and Gen. Gamelin headed Allied defenses.

THE BATTLE

Time, which Britain and France had so often acclaimed as being on their side, had become a fickle ally. Taking full advantage of the evacuation of the British, the Nazi armies speedily reorganized, and at dawn on June 5 struck at France with all their might along the Somme and Aisne. The French position, though difficult, was not hopeless from a military point of view. Though the Nazi breakthrough at Sedan had permitted the outflanking of the Maginot Line, the French still possessed a series of modern, defense-in-depth fortifications along the northern front, behind which they might hold out for some time. Their armies were intact, well equipped, although lacking in mechanized equipment. On May 18 Paul Reynaud, who had succeeded Daladier as Premier on Mar. 20 but kept him as War Minister, dropped Daladier and took over the job of War Minister himself. Simultaneously he took into the Cabinet aging Marshal Pétain, who had the special task of advising Reynaud on the conduct of the war. Pétain, whose Fascist sympathies

NAZI STUKAS LED THE DRIVE INTO FRANCE on June 5 with a dawn attack on a 150-mile front along the Somme and Aisne rivers. While they blasted French lines, German infantry struck along the entire front. The Nazi tank force, which in Poland, Holland, and Belgium had preceded the infantry, was now held in reserve to exploit such breaches in the French defenses as the infantry might effect. Meanwhile, Nazi pressure on the outflanked Maginot Line was increased to prevent the shifting of troops to northern France.

FOR FRANCE

were well known, was somehow expected to rally the French people to the defense of their land against Fascism. The marshal's price for entering the Reynaud Cabinet was the removal of General Gamelin from command of the French armies and his replacement by General Weygand, who had been removed from the French High Command in 1935 for his connections with the pro-Nazi Croix de Feu and Cagoulards. Like Pétain he secretly believed the battle was already lost. Their first move was to dismiss 15 generals from their commands, striking a heavy blow to the morale of the army. Not until June 5, the day the Nazis unleashed their drive, did Weygand and Pétain permit General de Gaulle to become one of Reynaud's military advisers. This they did only because Reynaud insisted upon it. Though they stated they had mobilized six million men, it was later revealed that Pétain and Weygand had actually mobilized only three million. This put only 60 French divisions along the Somme line to oppose at least 150 Nazi divisions.

General Wilhelm Keitel and Hitler planned the Nazi drive.

ALL ATTEMPTS OF FRENCH INFANTRY to recapture bridge-heads along the Somme, which had been seized by the Nazis in their break-through to the Channel, failed. Weygand and Pétain had re-fused to attempt a major counteroffensive against the Nazis to dis-rupt their organization of a drive into France before that drive had begun. These bridgeheads became main avenues for the Nazi assault.

INSIDE THE MAGINOT LINE on France's eastern front were kept thousands of reserves with the result that the forces along the Somme and Aisne had no reserve troops while the Nazis constantly replaced their blitz corps with fresh men. Nazi superiority in man power was heightened by the fact that the Nazi firepower was at least four times that of the French.

THE NAZI MOTORIZED INFANTRY WAS DISMOUNTED temporarily in the assault on the Somme line and advanced on foot in mass formations. The main attacks were delivered on the lower Somme and along the Ailette Canal between the Aisne and the Oise. Wherever a breach occurred the Nazi tanks rushed in in an attempt to break through. The first day they penetrated the outer defenses.

MEANWHILE FRENCH RAILWAY GUNS ALONG THE Maginot Line opened up against the German Westwall, now manned by comparatively few men. However, no large counteroffensive was attempted and instead the Nazis began an attack on the Maginot Line to prevent reinforcements from being sent to the Somme front where the Nazi attack was increasing by the hour.

ONE OF THE GREAT PHOTOGRAPHS OF THE WAR, this picture shows a Nazi motorized gun crew crouching as a French shell bursts just ahead of them in a northern French town shortly after their break-through. In the east the Nazis had reached Chemin-des-Dames by the second day, while in the west the fast-moving Nazi blitz, often passing the retreating French, reached the Seine River

Rouen on June 9. The Aisne was crossed at two points and advance units of the Nazi drive were within thirty-five miles of Paris. "The objective," said the Nazi High Command later, "was to break through the northern front, forcing a split up of French army units toward the southwest and southeast. . . ." Disintegration of the French armies began as the government left Paris on June 10.

AMERICAN-MADE CURTISS P-40's now made up the backbone of the French air fleet, but they were so outnumbered they could not check the constant Nazi bombing. In leaving Paris Reynaud appealed to President Roosevelt for "new and ever larger assistance." Roosevelt's reply was to release almost 100 Army and Navy planes which were returned to factories and resold to France. While they awaited shipment to France, the intensity of the Nazi attack increased, and the brunt of the Allied air burden fell on the R.A.F. which attempted to hamper the Nazi advance by bombing communication lines and oil stores such as that at Dunkerque (below).

SAVAGE COUNTERATTACKS BY FRENCH TANKS checked the Nazi progress in the east at Rethel and Reims. However, after three days of continuous fighting, the French tankmen (below) were so weakened from the heat and fumes that they collapsed. They had no reserves and their tanks lacked the speed, firepower, and armor of the Nazis. Worse than this, however, was the behavior of the French officers. Soldiers later revealed that many of the officers, most of whom had pro-Nazi sympathies, fled when the Nazis approached, leaving their units without direction and ammunition locked in forts. With few exceptions, the remaining officers ordered only retreats.

ON THE AGED AND CRIPPLED THE NAZI BLOW FELL
hardest. Confused and often hysterical, they were swallowed up by
the hurrying mobs of refugees, separated from their relatives.

Refugees Clogged the Roads of France

As the Nazi blitzkrieg swept on toward Paris thousands of French families, their homes in northern France destroyed by the Nazis, fled in a desperate attempt to escape. By June 9 the roads north of Paris were choked with refugees. Some rode bicycles, others ox carts and wagons, a few drove automobiles, but most of them made their way south on foot. Little girls pushed their grandfather's wheel chair while their mother carried the baby and the rest of the family a few possessions. Soon there were so many of them that those in vehicles were unable to move faster than those who walked. Hundreds of cars were abandoned when they ran out of gas. Time and again retreating French army units were swallowed up and carried with the steady push of the refugees. Topping the confusion, the heat, the dust of thousands of tramping feet, was the racing Nazi motorized attack, which repeatedly swept ahead of the refugees and the retreating French army. The Nazi air force attempted, by strafing and bombing, to clear the roads for the advance of the Nazi infantry. Thousands of small, hungry children were separated from their parents, thousands of aged and crippled were abandoned as the refugees scattered to escape. Refugee agencies completely broke down under the impact. With the decision of Weygand and Pétain not to defend Paris, nearly a million new refugees joined the flight southward. This completely disrupted the French army's withdrawal to the Loire, where it was expected to make a stand.

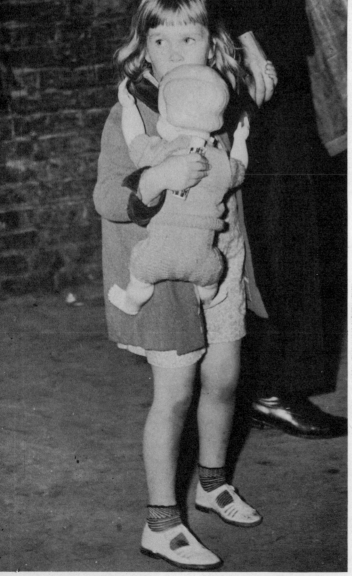

Thousands of bewildered children were shipped to England.

146

THIS UNUSUAL PHOTOGRAPH shows an aged woman, driven hysterical by Nazi strafing, and bombing of the refugee-filled roads, being aided to safety by other refugees and French soldiers. In many instances the French reinforcements found they could not get through to the front because so many civilians clogged the roads. The French retreat to the Loire was completely upset by refugees.

At designated refugee centers lost children were collected.

The horrors of war were written on their frightened faces.

PARIS FALLS WITHOUT A FIGHT

WEYGAND, BAUDOIN, REYNAUD, PÉTAIN, and the rest of the French Cabinet fled to Tours as the Nazis neared Paris. Baudoin, thought to be anti-Nazi by Reynaud, soon revealed he was one of Laval's most ardent disciples. From Tours they went to Bordeaux.

B Y June 10 the western arm of the giant Nazi pincer into France had crossed the river Seine at several points and moved toward Paris while the eastern arm, driving through Rheims, struck toward the Marne where the French armies had turned back the Germans in 1914. No effort was made to prepare defenses for Paris, and before nightfall the government, declaring it an "open city," fled to Tours. It is ironic that the French declaration said Paris was being abandoned to the Nazis to "save" it. Thus Paris became the first great national capital anywhere in the world to be given up to the Nazis without a fight. More than half the French Cabinet were, by now, ready to "save" all France by abandoning it to the Nazis. Their next move was to attempt to get Britain to release France from her pledge of "no separate peace." On June 13 Churchill, Lord Halifax, and Lord Beaverbrook flew to Tours where Reynaud requested the release of France. The British ministers refused, promising all available help. They agreed, however, that Reynaud should make a fresh appeal to the United States for help and if that failed the situation should be again reviewed.

ON JUNE 14 THE NAZIS ROLLED INTO PARIS. The eastern arm of the Nazi pincer was given the honor of occupying the city which was virtually deserted. It was estimated that between two and four million people, most of whom awaited the call to defend the city, fled Paris when the government announced its abandonment. The French left the city's administration to U. S. Ambassador Bullitt.

WHILE THE NAZIS PARADED past the Arc de Triumphe, Weygand and Pétain were campaigning for an armistice. Obsessed with the possibility of revolution Weygand attempted to frighten patriots within the Cabinet with stories of Communist uprisings. On June 13 Reynaud again appealed to U. S. for "clouds of airplanes." President Roosevelt promised aid.

In a triumphant visit to Paris Hitler toured the once gay capital, visited the Eiffel Tower, and swaggered down the Champs Elysees, but he made his longest stop at the marble tomb of Napoleon Bonaparte.

This Frenchman, his eyes filled with tears, is watching France's famous battle flags being carried off to North Africa for safe-keeping. For their betrayers the French reserved their greatest hatred.

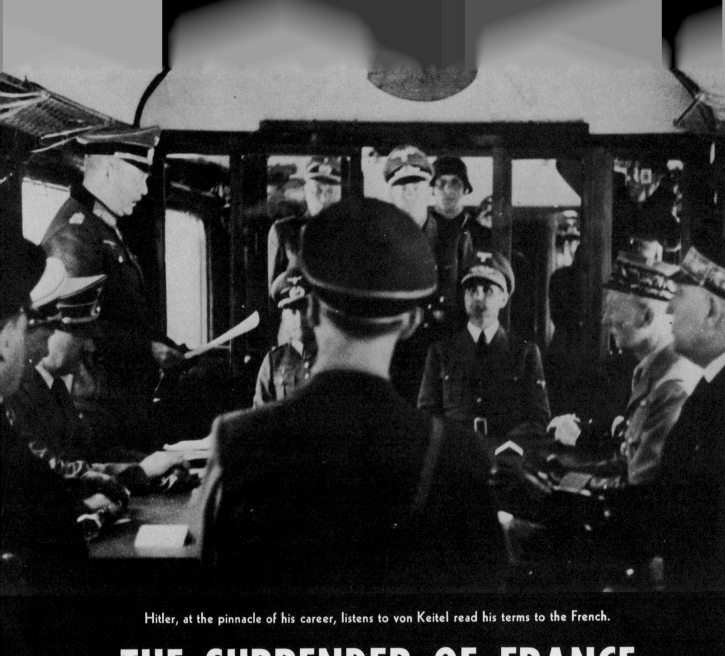

Hitler, at the pinnacle of his career, listens to von Keitel read his terms to the French.

THE SURRENDER OF FRANCE

Gen. Huntziger signed for France.

ON JUNE 21 GENERAL WILHELM KEITEL READ TO A FRENCH DELEGATION THE terms on which the Nazis would stop fighting. The scene: the very railway car in which Foch had dictated the armistice terms to the Germans in 1918 at the exact spot in Compiègne Forest where the car stood on that date. Seated in the car were Hitler, who occupied Foch's old chair, Nazi General von Brauchitsch, Goering, Hess, Admiral Raeder, Ribbentrop, and the French headed by Generals Huntziger and Bergeret. On June 14 the French government had moved to Bordeaux from whence it might embark to carry on the fight from Africa as Reynaud had pledged it would. But Pierre Laval, who followed every shift of the Cabinet, was busy buttonholing the few members of Cabinet Weygand and Pétain had not been able to win over to their plan for capitulation. Within two days, faced with constant defections to the Laval clique, Reynaud was forced to resign. President Lebrun, long under Laval's influence, turned the ministry over to Pétain on June 17 and the Marshal immediately announced he would seek an armistice. On June 18 Hitler and Il Duce, who had entered the war June 10, discussed terms, and the French were reminded to request the Italians for an armistice also. On June 21 the Nazi terms were read, and signed the following day. Then a French delegation flew to Italy and an armistice was signed on June 24. Meanwhile, the fighting continued until 1:35 A.M. on June 25.

ITALY WAS IN THE WAR ON FRANCE ONLY 15 DAYS

ONLY WHEN THE FALL OF PARIS WAS IMMINENT did Mussolini send his troops rolling against France. Despite Il Duce's bombast the Italians were easily checked by the twenty French divisions along the border until Pétain's capitulation. Then, as French morale cracked and Mussolini threw the entire weight of Italy into the fight, the Italians made some gains. Under the armistice Italy was to occupy the land she had won and was given full rights to Djibouti and the French section of the Djibouti—Addis Ababa railroad in Africa.

THE TREATY THE FRENCH TOOK HOME gave the Nazis the right to occupy the richest, most highly industrialized two thirds of France at French expense. This included the entire Atlantic coast, which the Nazis had not conquered, putting them in direct contact with Fascist Spain. The French army was to be demobilized with all equipment going to the Nazis. Captured Nazis were to be released —but not French. Germany and Italy reserved the right to cancel the terms if they felt the French had failed to live up to them.

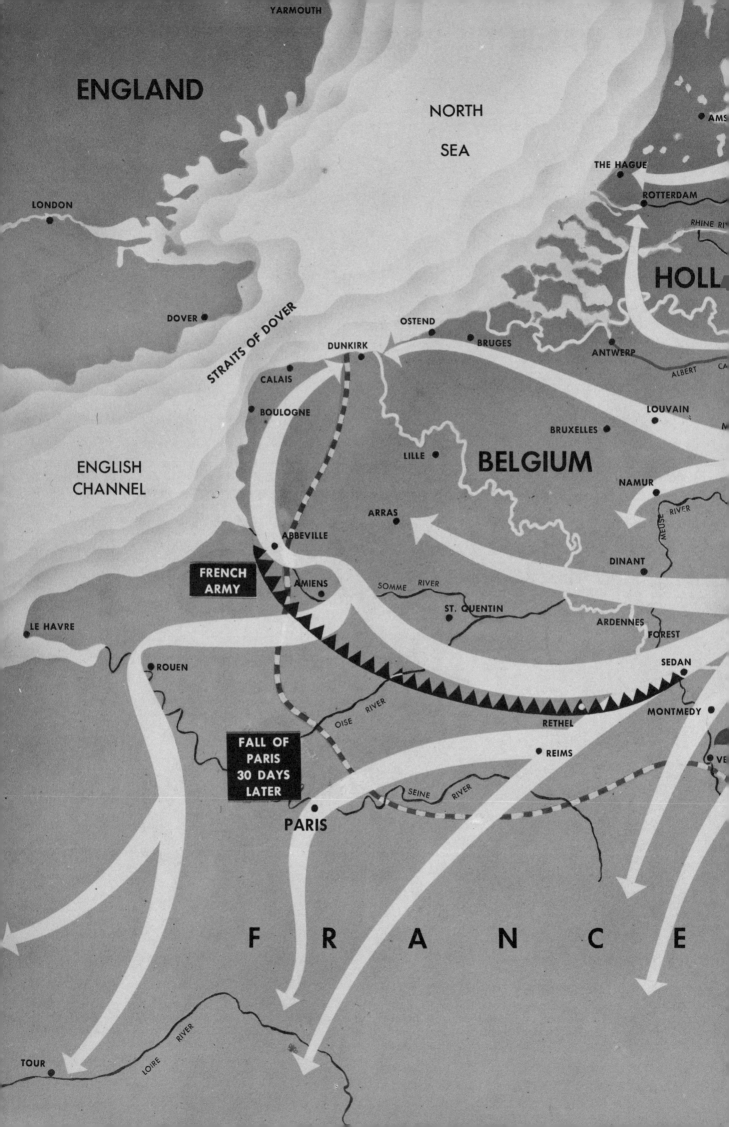

Nazi Conquest of Lowlands, France

Map labels:

YESSEI

RIVER

RIVER

GERMAN DRIVE ISOLATING HOLLAND AND BELGIUM

ESSEN

DUSSELDORF

COLOGNE

GERMANY

COBLENZ

START OF GERMAN DRIVE MAY 10, 1940

MAINZ

UXEM BOURG

METZ

MAGINOT LINE

RHINE RIVER

STRASBOURG

GERMAN CE IN RLD WAR

THE Nazi blow which struck simultaneously at Holland and Belgium on May 10 found the Allies wholly unprepared for blitzkreig warfare and revealed incredible blunders in strategy and traitors in the French High Command. The weight of the initial Nazi drive fell on Holland when the Nazis, crossing the undestroyed Maastricht Bridge, outflanked Holland's water defenses and pushed down the unguarded corridor along the Albert Canal, isolating the country. Parachutists seized strong points along the Maas, the Rotterdam airport, while Stukas bombed the Hague, Amsterdam, and Rotterdam. On May 16 the exhausted Dutch surrendered. Meanwhile, a simultaneous drive took Maastricht and Eben Emael, then split, one column racing westward to Louvain while the other circled the Liébe fortresses, reaching Namur in three days. As the Allies, who had been manning the Somme line, pivoted on Sedan to move to aid Belgium the main Nazi thrust broke through the Ardennes to attack the new French positions along the Meuse. Gen. André Corap, whose forces were nearest the strategic Sedan pivot and had the shortest distance to go, moved so slowly that less than half his troops were in position by May 14 when the Nazis crossed the undestroyed bridges of the Meuse between Namur and Sedan. The Nazis immediately broke through the thin French lines; outflanking the Maginot Line. Gen. Giraud, who replaced Corap, was captured. Gamelin failed to consider the break-through dangerous until the Nazis had almost reached the coast. At times the Nazi corridor splitting Belgium and France was only 12 miles wide, but the traitorous Weygand and Pétain refused to throw the main French armies on the Somme against it. The Nazis reached Abbeville on May 24, turned northward to attempt to trap the Belgian and British armies which were now being hard pushed from the north by the Nazis who had taken Bruges, Brussels, and Ostend. Evacuation from Dunkirk became the only hope of the British when Leopold surrendered on May 27. It took the Nazis until June 4 to reach Dunkirk but the next day they launched their drive into France. Its western column broke through and reached Rouen while the eastern column cut through Reims, then split to take Paris on June 14. With the failure of the French armies to make a stand on the Loire, Pétain sued for peace on June 17.

ERNEST CABAT

Already decidedly pro-Fascist, Pierre Laval met Goering in 1935 at Pilsudski's funeral, became an ardent Nazi collaborationist.

THE FRENCH FIFTH COLUMN

BEHIND the French military collapse lay the work of the most powerful Nazi fifth column in the world, headed by Laval and Bonnet, subtly directed by the clever personal emissary of Von Ribbentrop, Otto Abetz. It had its birth in the determination of French industrialists and financiers to resist the demands of the French people for more democratic control of their government and much-needed social reforms. Chief of these industrialists was François de Wendel, who headed the powerful federation of French Comité des Forges; he had many financial ties with Nazi Germany and carried card No. 13 in the Fascist Croix de Feu which he supplied with funds. His political spokesman and personal attorney was oily, scheming, Fascist Pierre Laval, who had long admired Italian Fascism. As Premier from 1934 to 1936 Laval laid the foundations for the betrayal of France. Immediately after assuming office he sent out feelers to Rome and Berlin, suggesting formation of an alliance. Berlin sent Von Ribbentrop and Otto Abetz to Paris, where on Dec. 2, 1934, they met privately with Laval, receiving assurances from him that he would not interfere in the coming Saar plebiscite. This was Laval's first known contact with the Nazis. A short time later he had a two-hour private meeting with Goering in the Hotel Europe, Warsaw, when both attended the funeral of Pilsudski. Pétain, who likewise attended the funeral, also had a private session with Goering and shortly thereafter became a violent objector to the Franco-Soviet pact, the basis of France's de-

fensive alliances. On his return to Paris Laval alienated Britain and helped Hitler's advance tremendously by refusing to move when Hitler, violating the Versailles Treaty, began rearming and introduced conscription in Germany. At the same time he set to work to smash the League of Nations, making a secret arrangement for Mussolini to invade Ethiopia. In October 1935 he completed plans with Colonel de la Rocque for a Fascist *putsch* on Nov. 11, but lost his nerve when reports showed that any attempt at a *putsch* would be met by a solid general strike by French labor. He secretly helped finance the purchase of arms and planes for the militarized Fascist Croix de Feu from government funds. When Laval was forced from office by the Popular Front in 1936, his work within the government of strengthening the Axis while weakening France was carried on by Flandin and Bonnet. Meanwhile, industrialists such as Ernest Mercier, the electrical magnate; Eugene Schneider, the French munition king; and Alexander Dreux, vice-president of Comité des Forges, poured money into the hands of De la Rocque and Ybarnegaray, Laval's accomplices. When Hitler seized the Rhineland, Flandin refused to mobilize the army to resist this violation of the Locarno Pact; a year later, after a mysterious trip to Berlin, Flandin began preaching the value of an alliance with the Nazis. It was the surrender of Czechoslovakia, France's ally and a bulwark in the defenses of France, that awoke many people to the fact that Bonnet and Laval were actually working for the betrayal of France

François de Wendel financed the Fascist Croix de Feu.

Nazi agent Otto Abetz directed fifth column's work.

INTRODUCED to rich, decadent Parisian society by Count Ferdinand de Brinon, Otto Abetz had in the meantime become the darling of the fashionable salons of the Marquise de Crussols, the "lady friend" of Edouard Daladier, and Countess Hélène des Portes, the "lady friend" of Paul Reynaud. Through these influential ladies and the ambitious wife of Bonnet, who frequently entertained him, Abetz reached the most powerful men in France. Abetz told the French Fascist-minded industrialists and financiers what they wanted to hear most: that Hitler wanted peace with France to attack Soviet Russia. Bonnet conferred with Abetz frequently, made his "suggestions" official French policy. Abetz poured out $10,000,000 in bribes to the corrupt French press to adopt his "peace" line. In this Count de Brinon proved a valuable aid. The leading journalist of the Right, Count de Brinon had been pleading for a powerful Franco-German alliance and the crushing of French democracy for many years. He was constantly in secret communication with Nazis.

Flandin was openly pro-Nazi after a 1937 Berlin trip.

Bonnet carried out the "suggestions" of Herr Abetz.

Col. de La Rocque headed the Fascist Croix de Feu.

Fascist-minded Pétain was a "front" for Laval's bloc.

THE French fifth column included most ranking officers in the army. Pétain and Weygand were leading spirits of the Croix de Feu and the secret Fascist "hooded men," the Cagoulards. When the Cagoulard plot for armed revolt was exposed in 1937, Bonnet and Chautemps prevented the exposure from reaching Pétain, who was named in Cagoulard plans as the possible dictator. Laval, meanwhile, had begun backing Jacques Doriot and Marcel Déat, renegade labor leaders and Trotskyites, whose job it was to split and divert anti-Fascist French labor with "neo-socialism" and anti-Semitism. After Munich, Bonnet promised the Nazis (Document 149, official French *Yellow Book*): ". . . elections would be suspended; public meetings would be stopped. . . ." When the suspicious but weak Daladier moved Bonnet from the Foreign Ministry to the Ministry of Justice, Bonnet made good his promise to choke off all public expression and anti-Nazism. Though France was at war with Nazism, he persecuted everyone even faintly tinged with anti-Nazism while

Count de Brinon was the foremost Nazi propagandist.

Weygand never gave the army a chance to defend Fran

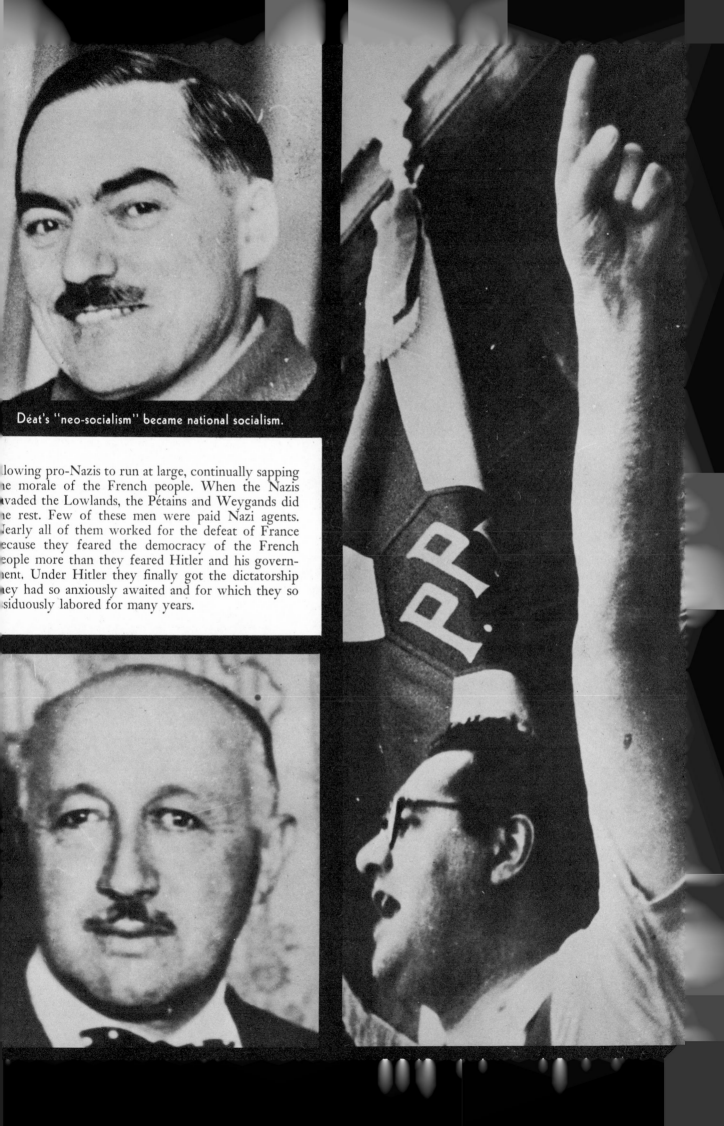

Déat's "neo-socialism" became national socialism.

lowing pro-Nazis to run at large, continually sapping
he morale of the French people. When the Nazis
waded the Lowlands, the Pétains and Weygands did
he rest. Few of these men were paid Nazi agents.
Nearly all of them worked for the defeat of France
ecause they feared the democracy of the French
eople more than they feared Hitler and his govern-
hent. Under Hitler they finally got the dictatorship
hey had so anxiously awaited and for which they so
siduously labored for many years.

FREE FRANCE

O N JUNE 17, when Marshal Pétain asked fo
an armistice, Gen. Charles de Gaulle, one o
the few anti-Nazi generals in the French army
fled to London where he called upon Frenchme
all over the world to join with him and fight t
free France. First reports from Morocco, Syri
and Indo-China indicated they intended to figh
on. Then the Nazis cracked down on Pétain an
Laval, who dispatched Weygand to Syria wher
he persuaded Gen. Mittelhausser to accept th
armistice. Morocco was brought into line. Th
governor of Indo-China was replaced. Meanwhil
Britain, whose vital Mediterranean life line wa
endangered, recognized the "Free French" an
pledged full economic and military support t
any colony that would join the common caus
Chad, French Equatorial, and West Africa joine
De Gaulle. So did thousands of French soldier
who deserted from Vichy-held areas. So did Ge
George Catroux, Admiral Emile Muselier, Ge
Edouard de Larminat, Gen. Paul de Genti
homme. On Sept. 22 De Gaulle led a joint ex
pedition against Vichy-held Dakar, which faile
because of lack of co-ordination. Yet by De
1940 the Free French had some 35,000 arme
troops, 20 warships, 1,000 airmen, and some sixt
merchant ships, besides many followers.

ABOVE, SOME FRENCH NAVAL UNITS cor
tinued to fight against Nazism, sailing into British por
to place themselves at the disposal of the British. But th
bulk of the French fleet did not, becoming a potentia
weapon for Hitler and the Nazis.

LEFT, GEN. CHARLES DE GAULLE was pract
cally the only French general to recognize that Franc
was vulnerable to mechanized attack. He shocked Frenc
General Staff with his demands for mechanization.

Top left: Free French troops inspected by De Gaulle. Right: the famous Spahis, many French colonial infantrymen (bottom left), deserted Vichy-held Syria. Bottom right: De Gaulle's airmen numbered over 1,000.

The Battle of Oran

On June 14, when it became clear that the French would probably make a separate peace with Hitler, Churchill had them promise to send the French fleet into British ports if they should give up the fight. However, the armistice stipulated the fleet should return to French ports to be demilitarized under joint Nazi-Italian control. While the Axis Powers promised the French they would not use the fleet against Britain, the British decided they had had enough promises. With the French ships in Axis hands Britain would face an enemy with nineteen battleships to her fourteen. Therefore, on July 3 a British squadron appeared off Oran, Africa, where the bulk of the best ships of the French lay anchored. The British commander presented an ultimatum to the French Admiral Gensoul which included alternatives to prevent the ships from falling into belligerent hands. The French commander refused, and the British fired.

THE BRITISH FIRE WAS CONCENTRATED on the French battleship *Bretagne*, which caught fire after the first broadside. The French returned fire, but the narrow harbor hampered operations.

HARD HIT AND SINKING, THE *BRETAGNE* was soon disabled. Behind her lies the aircraft carrier *Commandant Teste*, which was sunk a short time later. The *Bretagne* was extremely powerful.

WITH THE *BRETAGNE'S* **STERN NEARLY UNDER** water, the British concentrated their fire on the new, fast *Dunkerque* and on the light cruisers and destroyers trying to escape.

WITH FIRES RAGING THROUGH HER superstructure, the *Bretagne* rolled over on her side. Meanwhile, the heavy cruiser *Strasbourg* eluded the British along with some smaller ships.

WHILE SURVIVORS OF THE *BRETAGNE* swam toward the British squadron, the British guns hammered at the *Dunkerque*. Aircraft pursuing the *Strasbourg* scored a hit but did not sink her.

FINALLY THE BRITISH HIT THE *DUNKERQUE*'S powder magazine, which disabled her guns and wrecked her fire control. The French drove the wrecked ship onto the shore.

BRITISH FIRE LEFT GAPING HOLES in the *Dunkerque's* armor. This picture, made after the battle, shows some of the damage inflicted by the British broadsides.

AFTER THE SMOKE OF BATTLE HAD CLEARED the bodies of these dead French seamen were found on the main deck of the *Dunkerque*. Within a few days the British smashed the new, almost complete, French battleship *Richelieu* as she lay in the Dakar harbor, and the French squadron based at Alexandria agreed to surrender. By July 8 most of the French fleet had been put out of action.

THE BATTLE OF BRITAIN

"What has happened in France makes no difference to British faith and purpose. We have become the sole champions now in arms to defend the world cause. We shall do our best to be worthy of that high honor."
—Winston Churchill, June 17, 1940.

This unusual picture was taken during the height of one of the Nazi raids on London. Through the smoke may be seen famous St. Paul's Cathedral, lighted by fires set by Nazi incendiary bombs.

Nazi invasion barges were concentrated at Dunkirk's docks. This picture was taken just before the R.A.F. bombed barges.

ENGLAND FACES THE THREAT OF NAZI INVASION

AFTER DUNKIRK the Nazis boasted they would be in London no later than September 15. Britain prepared in grim earnestness and with desperate speed. By September 1 the Nazis were concentrating self-propelled invasion barges all along the French and Belgian Channel coast. The R.A.F. and the Royal Navy unleashed smashing and damaging attacks on the barge centers while every man, woman, and child throughout the country prepared to fight "on the beaches . . . the landing grounds . . . on the fields . . . in the hills . . . and never surrender. . . ."

BRITAIN'S CHANNEL BEACHES were patrolled constantly by the British army. Large contingents of Canadians, Australians, Indians arrived to bolster England's rearming fighting services.

SEA FORTS WERE BUILT some distance out in the Channel to serve as strong advance posts to smash the Nazi invasion armada. Channel fortifications were built by men working day and night.

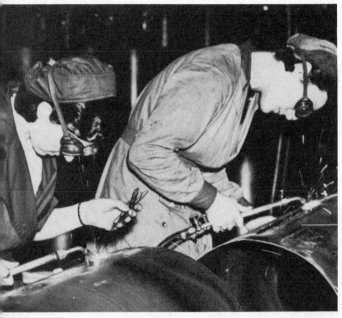

TO RELIEVE MEN for the armed forces, British women took over multitude of jobs, carrying mail, welding, delivering, driving busses, riveting. Production of tanks went up 125%.

THOUSANDS JOINED the women's auxiliary services, uniformed military organizations. Of the 1,517,000 registered in the first women's conscription, only 650,000 were not in war work.

EVEN MINISTERS JOINED the home guard, learning how to use rifles for the first time in their lives. During June and July many of the Home Guards were armed with only pitchforks and clubs.

England's Air Defenses

CIVILIAN PLANE SPOTTERS, THE EYES OF BRITAIN'S air defenses, never ceased their vigilant watch for Nazi planes. They reported the speed, height, number of planes.

BRITAIN had not waited for Nazi raids on England to begin bombing Germany. With the invasion of Holland she struck at industrial areas such as the Ruhr, submarine bases, oil depots, and munition plants. But with the arrival of the Nazis on the Channel coast the principal task of the R.A.F. was the air defense of England. Without air superiority Germany could never attempt an invasion. The Nazis set out to obtain that superiority in a series of raids on R.A.F. bases in July, which sought to knock out the R.A.F. while it was still on the ground. A parallel Nazi objective was to smash the ports of southern England to obtain control of the Channel. Beginning on Aug. 8, the Nazi raids increased in intensity and the number of raiders from hundreds to well over a thousand. Britain's air defenses were built around balloon barrages, anti-aircraft guns, and fighter planes. Their valiant work made it impossible for the Nazis to prevent the British fighters from taking to the air. Once in the air, the Nazis were unable to drive the British Spitfires and Hurricanes off and suffered mounting losses.

ENGLAND'S INTERCEPTOR SYSTEM DEFEATED the Nazi plans. All England was divided into sectors directed by an interceptor controller working in a room like that above. As Nazi planes were spotted, their speed, direction, number, height were relayed to him and symbols for them put on the map table. As the Nazis roared inland the girls at the map pushed the symbols along their course. The controller's job was to so calculate the strength and speed of the Nazis that the planes working on his orders could intercept and drive them off. A difficult assignment, it required him to analyze the main raid (often the Nazis sent over false raiders to draw British fighters away from their real raiders) and take into consideration such factors as wind, rate of climb of British fighters.

A BALLOON BARRAGE WAS SENT UP AROUND LONDON
immediately upon the approach of Nazi planes. The balloons, from
which hung heavy steel cables capable of fouling a plane, drove the
Nazis so high their bombing was inaccurate. But the cables caught
almost as many R.A.F. planes as Nazi and cannot be counted a complete success. Right, a downed Nazi bomber with a cable "cutter."

SENT INTO THE AIR INSTANTLY upon the controller's command, British Hurricanes and Spitfires sped toward the calculated point of interception. All sector commands were linked in groups and were in constant communication by telephone and radio with each other. When the interceptor commands were set up a controller who could accurately calculate the point of interception 30% of the time was considered good. But by the summer of 1940 Britain's system was functioning so well that 90% was not unusual. The result showed in ever-mounting Nazi losses, which reached their peak on Aug. 15, when 180 Nazi planes were downed. Nazi August losses totaled 957, the British toll averaging over 15% of the raiders, and by Sept. 1 the Nazis gave up trying to knock out the R.A.F.

HUNDREDS OF LONDONERS WATCHED the interceptors fight off the attack of 350 Nazi bombers and pursuit ships on the city Sept. 7 when the Nazis made their first mass assault on London. Nazi bombs battered the docks and turned the East End into a sea of flame, but not before the R.A.F. had downed 108 planes while its losses amounted to only 18. With invasion weather growing short, the Nazis launched a supreme effort to smash London on Sept. 15 consisting of two waves of 250 planes each. Both waves broke through the interceptors, but their losses for the day totaled 185. That marked the turning point in the daylight assaults. Instead the Nazis began mass night raids which offered some relief from the interceptors but made bombing inaccurate.

THE NAZI MASS DAYLIGHT RAIDS THAT FOLLOWED Sept. 15 lost as high a percentage of planes as those which had preceded it. Between Sept. 6 and Oct. 5 a minimum of 883 Nazi planes, chiefly bombers, were lost over Britain. A large percentage of the downed raiders was accounted for by the English anti-aircraft defenses. London was surrounded by a ring of numerous anti-aircraft emplacements which were capable of throwing a solid wall of fire around the entire city as high as 15,000 feet. Like the balloon barrage, the effect of the ack-ack fire (so called because of the peculiar bark of the anti-aircraft guns) was to drive the Nazis so high their bombing was inaccurate. Soon the Nazi daylight raids fell off to small groups of "nuisance raiders," which dropped their bombs and fled.

172

Concentrated anti-aircraft fire at "Hell's Corner" on the Straits of Dover was especially effective because the Nazi bombers had not yet attained much altitude. Nazi attempts to destroy these guns failed.

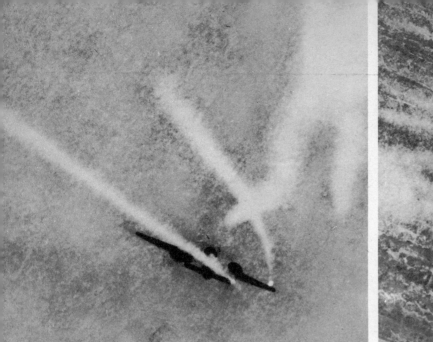

Pouring tracer bullets into a Messerschmitt 110, an R.A.F. Pilot keeps right on its tail until it finally falls into the sea.

UNDER STRONG ESCORT, THE FIVE-MAN CREW of a Heinkel 111 is marched off to a prison camp for the duration of the war. High loss of expert pilots and bombardiers was the most serious blow suffered by the Nazi air force. The Nazi loss of an estimated 1,800 planes in August and September was made up by Germany's production during a single month. But pilots, radio men, navigators, and bombardiers could not be replaced that rapidly, even though the Nazi fliers were given much less and inferior training.

174

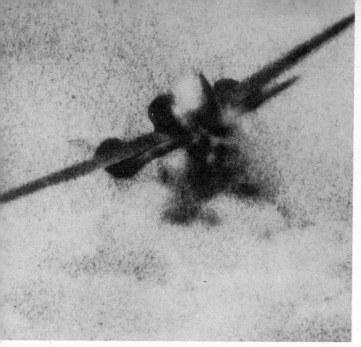

A Heinkel 111 has its tail shot off by an R.A.F. Pilot. Pictures were taken by a camera in the wings of the British plane.

THIS WOUNDED NAZI AIRMAN WAS RESCUED from the Channel by British fishing craft. So great were Nazi personnel losses and so undecisive were the effects of their raids that by Nov. 1 the Nazis abandoned their daylight raids in favor of night attacks.

THE MORE INEXPERIENCED NAZI PILOTS were easy prey for the R.A.F. Most of those captured by the British were young boys; many still in their teens. But neither inexperience nor capture diminished their arrogant confidence in a Hitler victory.

COVENTRY—SYMBOL OF NAZI RUTHLESSNESS.

THE night of Nov. 14 was clear and moonlit. There was no haze, and visibility from aloft was fifteen miles. Two days before the Royal Air Force had had the audacity to bomb distant Munich while Hitler was speaking to his old party members there on the anniversary of their unsuccessful 1923 beer-hall *putsch*. Suddenly wave after wave of Nazi planes, mostly bombers, roared over the eastern Channel coast and winged their way inland. A few minutes later they began bombing Coventry, a small but highly industrialized town near Manchester. Swooping low over the heart of the city, the first wave of bombers dropped thousands of incendiaries to guide succeeding waves which carried heavy demolition bombs. All night long over 500 planes battered the city, dropping some 400 tons of highly destructive bombs in a concentrated area in the crowded residential and business districts. The very character of the raid indicated a new change in Nazi air tactics. Heretofore night raids had been made at several locations by fairly large numbers of planes, but never by such masses of planes as bombed Coventry, and nearly always the main effort was at least near military objectives. But in the raids on Coventry the important airplane manufacturing and assemblying plants on the outskirts of the city were relatively undamaged; within a few days' time full production was resumed in every department.

he hardest blows had been endured by the civilian center
the city. It was evident that the Nazis, in their desperate,
utal total war, had attempted to exterminate the entire
o,ooo persons living in the area and to devastate the com-
inity as a whole; 600 were killed. Few homes still stood.
hole blocks of houses were completely leveled. Only a
ndful of buildings remained standing in the business dis-
ct and none of these were unscathed. Only a shell was
t of the city's fine old cathedral. Water and gas mains
re broken in numerous spots, disrupting all service, and,
orst of all, increasing the danger of fire and explosions
ile decreasing the means with which to fight such dan-

gers. Ravaged Coventry became a symbol to the entire world
of Nazi ruthlessness. Yet after all the horror the fact remained the Nazis had not been able to exterminate the brave
people of Coventry, who dug themselves out and went to
work to rebuild their city. That the mass night raid had
become a definite part of the Nazi technique was made certain the night after the bombing of Coventry, for London
underwent a similar raid of great destruction. Against the
night raiders the British were almost helpless, and so they
turned to an air counteroffensive, sending night raiders deep
into Germany to bomb munitions works and plane factories,
hoping to divert the enemy to the home front.

ST. PAUL'S CATHEDRAL.

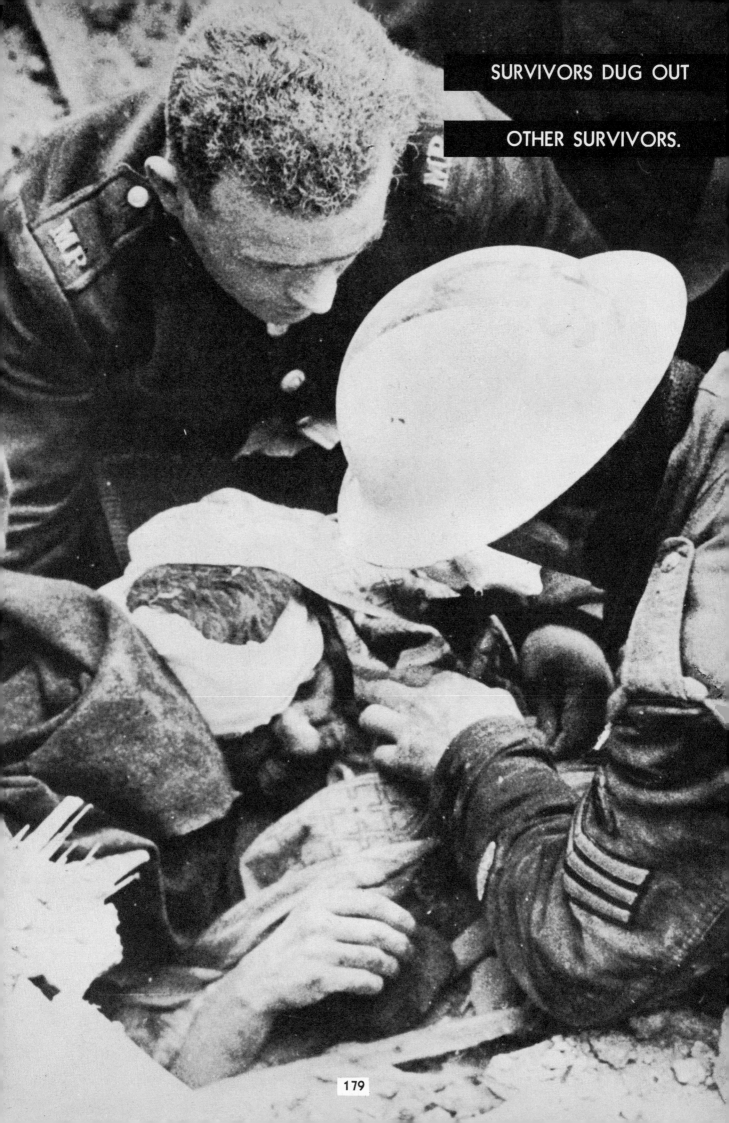

SURVIVORS DUG OUT

OTHER SURVIVORS.

BOMBED OUT OF THEIR HOME, THIS EAST END FAMILY WALKS TO THE BUS THAT WILL EVACUATE THEM. ON THEIR FACES IS WRITTEN THE HORROR OF WAR AND THE COURAGE OF A PEOPLE DETERMINED TO REMAIN FREE.

THIS WAS AN OFFICE BUILDING.

THIS WAS A HOME.

THESE LIVED THROUGH IT.

THE HOUSE OF COMMONS.
Ancient, Honorable, and Famous—the House of Commons.

AND BUCKINGHAM PALACE.
Royalty's Job—To Cheer England's Heroic People.

BLIND CHILDREN
IN A SHELTER
DURING A RAID.

A TERROR-SHAKEN MOTHER
AND HER SLEEPING CHILD
LEAVE THEIR RUINED HOME.

"SO HELP US GOD." —Westminster Abbey.

CIVILIAN FIREMEN BECAME FRONT-LINE FIGHTERS. OFTEN A NEW RAIN OF BOMBS REFIRED BUILDINGS THEY HAD JUST SAVED.

"HAVE A MATCH?"

UNDER NAZI BOMBS "JUDY Q'GRADY AND THE KING'S LADY ARE SISTERS UNDER THE SKIN."

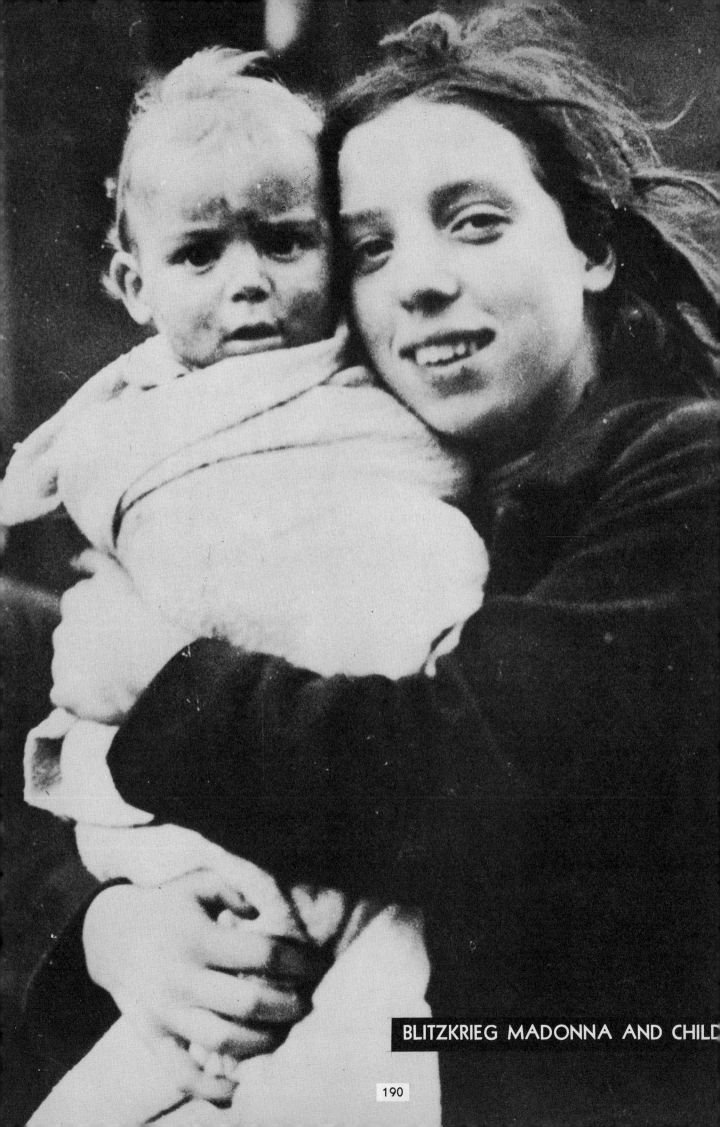

BLITZKRIEG MADONNA AND CHILD

THUMBS UP!

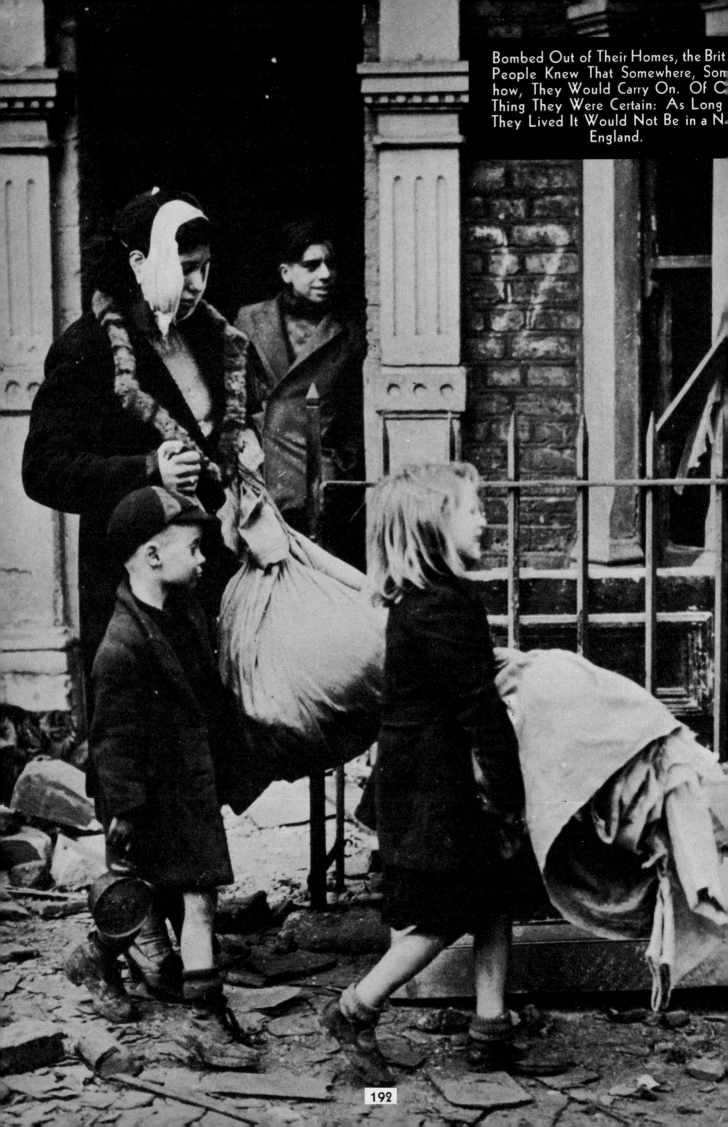

Bombed Out of Their Homes, the Brit
People Knew That Somewhere, Som
how, They Would Carry On. Of C
Thing They Were Certain: As Long
They Lived It Would Not Be in a N
England.

A DOG'S BEST FRIEND. A wounded man carries his injured, shell-shocked dog from their ruined home. Agencies were set up to evacuate pets, but this man did not avail himself of their service. Wild animals in zoos were either killed or shipped to America to prevent the possibility of their escape from a bomb-wrecked zoo. Below: a really dangerous job, the removal of unexploded bombs.

HIT BY BOMB FRAGMENTS, this woman is given first aid by an air-raid warden. Note lack of expression on the face of the dazed husband, who holds his stricken wife's hat and bag. By the end of Dec. 1940, 21,179 civilians had been killed, 6,965 of them in Sept. Below: With their only remaining possessions in their arms, a British family calls to their neighbors that they are still alive.

BOMBED-OUT FAMILIES WERE HELPED by their neighbors to move to the public rest centers where they received new clothing, food, and awaited assignment to new living quarters. As the intensity of Nazi raids increased, British morale stiffened. This was the very opposite of what the Nazis had expected. In one communiqué the Nazis complained of this "lack of co-operation."

THE EMBATTLED BRITISH PEOPLE STAGED impromptu celebrations after every raid to rejoice over their ability to survive the bombing. No amount of Nazi bombs could shatter their morale. But what did hurt their morale was the feeling that their own government was not doing everything it could to provide deeper shelters, more adequately equipped rest centers.

Britain's Shelters

WHILE the British government had made large-scale preparations for air raids before the war, they were carried out by Home Security Minister Sir John Anderson with little imagination about the character of such attacks and the needs arising from them. For instance, before they were reorganized, the rest centers for the bombed-out, usually schools, were looked upon as places where the homeless might go for a few hours until they found new quarters. But the raids made masses, sometimes half a town, homeless and in immediate need of food, clothing, and shelter. The schools were not equipped to feed, clothe, and house them. Worse, there was no organization to find new homes for them. Still worse, these centers were not in any way air-raid shelters. After the ghastly bombing of a center these muddles were corrected, and by October the situation was greatly improved, with a corresponding uplift in morale.

ONE OF BRITAIN'S BIG PROBLEMS was the "Anderson Shelter." Tiny and made of sheet iron, it failed to consider the possibility that raids might last for hours, offered little real protection.

LONDON MOVED INTO THE SUBWAYS with the coming of the mass raids, in September, sleeping on the station platforms and stairs, particularly at the Charing Cross and Piccadilly Circus stations, where the subways were deepest underground. The demand arose for the opening of deep warehouse basements as shelters. Sir John Anderson, whose sheet-iron surface shelters were widely criticized, made serious efforts to discourage the nightly movement into the subways, but in the face of determined public demand he was forced to yield. Yet he was slow to improve heating, ventilation, and lavatory facilities, and with the fall of the Chamberlain government he was replaced by Herbert Morrison, long an advocate of deep shelters, who set about increasing sleeping provisions.

NOT ONLY WAS LONDON THE TARGET for the Nazi mass raids, the great industrial and shipping centers of England, Birmingham, Liverpool, Plymouth, Manchester, Bristol, Worcester, Southampton, Sheffield, and Nottingham were subjected to repeated, although irregular, attacks. The Channel ports of Dover and Ramsgate were particularly hard hit because in "Hell's Corner," as the region soon became known, the British had concentrated many anti-aircraft guns which exacted a heavy toll from the Nazi raiders. Though over several thousand homes were completely destroyed in Ramsgate, casualties were low because the city fathers had had the foresight to dig into the near-by chalk cliffs when the prospects of war became serious. Women all over England spent much of their time in shelters knitting socks and sweaters for their soldier husbands.

CONSTRUCTION OF THIS TYPE OF BRICK SHELTER saved thousands of lives. Every house in this neighborhood was blasted, but there were no casualties. Although it could not with- stand the direct hit of a heavy demolition bomb, it was safer than the Anderson shelter, and more easily and speedily constructed than underground shelters which required tunneling.

LONDON COULD NOT RESIST COMING OUT of its shelters in the spring to watch the growing R.A.F. battle the Nazi raiders in dogfights over the city. A winter of mounting casualties, bombed-out homes, sleeplessness, unbelievable hardships, and unceasing tension had left England's people unbroken in their unity and determination to withstand the Nazis and win the war.

THE CIVILIAN HOME GUARD WAS JOINED by 2,000,000 men too old, too young, or not fit, for regular armed services. They were especially trained to capture parachutists.

Britain Emerges Stronger

THE coming of spring brought new heavy blows from the Nazi Luftwaffe as it sought to pave the way, in one final effort, for the long-heralded invasion, now seven months overdue. In Feb. 1941 only 793 were killed by Nazi bombs, but in March 4,298 died, and in April, 6,131, and in May, 5,520. But these casualties were suffered by a Britain far stronger than the Britain of June 1940. Six months had turned Britain into an armed fortress and made virtually every citizen a front-line fighter. The armed forces had been steadily reinforced by expeditionary forces from Australia, Canada, and New Zealand. The Home Guard now included nearly two million men. A twenty-mile defense-in-depth series of fortifications guarded her Channel shore. Over 3,000,000 women were serving in the armed forces and industry to release men for the actual fighting forces: they worked as firemen, messengers, dispatchers, drivers. Tank production was up 125%. Production of field guns had nearly doubled while the production of anti-tank guns was 600% better than in Sept. 1940. Aircraft production under Lord Beaverbrook's energetic direction was mounting steadily. Workers increased production by staying at their machines despite Nazi raids. The battle of Britain had been won, and Britain emerged stronger than ever, united by the magnificent courage, generosity, and suffering of her people.

ENGLAND'S COAST AND BEACHES WERE MADE special defense areas, strung with barbed wire and patrolled constantly after the fall of France. Sights like the one above were not uncommon. Eventually Britain's defenses consisted of a strip twenty miles deep along the entire coast line. Some coast areas were evacuated while fortifications, were completed.

VIRTUALLY ALL BRITAIN'S NUMEROUS FISHING BOATS were armed with anti-aircraft guns and equipped with radio transmitters, becoming the nation's first line of defense and her advanced raid spotters in the North Sea and Channel. So effectively did they serve as the "eyes" of British air defense that they were the object of incessant Nazi air attacks. Meanwhile, the regular British army strenuously prepared to fight off either a sea or air-borne invader. In the picture below British soldiers are shown approaching the rocky shore of a Channel inlet which they have just swam across with full packs. Hitler, it was felt, would certainly attempt invasion in (No Copy)

London, Dec. 30, 1940

On the night of Dec. 29 the Nazis resorted to mass incendiary bombing in an attempt to destroy London by fire. Previously the incendiary had been used to supplement the heavy demolition bombs; now the Nazis made it their chief weapon. In a night-long raid 500 Nazi planes dumped tons of incendiaries into the heart of London, the financial section known as "The City." It was the greatest disaster London had known since the Great Fire of 1666. The Guildhall, Old Bailey, and eight churches were destroyed. Whole blocks went up in flames. This picture of "The City" was made the morning after the raid. Compare it with the picture on pages 161-2 made from approximately the same position during the Nazi raid.

London Digs Itself Out

WITH the coming of spring 1941 England began to dig itself out of the debris of its shattered homes, stores, and public buildings. Throughout the worst raids of the winter demolition squads had been busy knocking down dangerous walls, the shells of famous and ancient buildings, while clean-up squads cleared streets and sidewalks and salvaged materials which could be used in Britain's war effort. Now that they had lived through them the British people, with their innate optimism, did not entirely regret the raids. For while some historical and beautiful buildings had been devastated, far greater numbers of wretched slums, narrow and crooked streets, and ancient eyesores had been demolished with them. The English looked forward to life in cities without slums, with parks and playgrounds, withou narrow and sunless streets. Among the other tasks Churchi assigned to Arthur Greenwood when he entered the Cab net in May 1940 was that of planning for the postwar recon struction of England. Greenwood, a Laborite, had devote most of his life to slum-clearance projects and to publi health measures. Working with him was Lord Reith, wh was directly in charge of all reconstruction work. Face with the task of rebuilding whole cities and the major po tions of many more, Greenwood and Reith laid down tw guiding principles for the reconstruction. First, there cou be no planning of isolated districts; cities must be planne as a complete and integrated unit. Second, there must be n

temporary reconstruction; this was designed to prevent the erection of makeshift, temporary buildings that might become permanent after the war. The price for land for new thoroughfares was set at its value in March 1939, a price which yielded the owner a fair return but prevented speculation. While temporary reconstruction was forbidden, "first aid" to bomb-splintered buildings was encouraged and the government allocated five million pounds for the purpose; "first aid" included such things as the replacing of a shattered door, a cracked chimney, repairing holes in roofs, removing dangerous cornices. By June 1941 over 90 per cent of the buildings which had been damaged by the raids had received "first aid." Typical of the plans for reconstruction

were those of Coventry, which was to be rebuilt around the hill on which its famous cathedral once stood and approached by a series of radial roads. Tall blocks of apartments were to be built in groups around its schools, community center, city hall, and stores, each being an integral part of the other. Between the buildings, which were to be tall to permit each family to receive a maximum amount of sunshine, would be pools, parks, and playgrounds. Out of these new cities will come a healthier, happier, and richer life. But, by Dec. 1941, when the above picture was made, plans were still in their preliminary stage. There was much more important work to be done—a war to be won before new construction could begin in earnest.

Kurusu, Ciano, Hitler listen to the formal reading of the Pact of Berlin. The new Axis pact was aimed directly at United States.

Matsuoka arrives in Berlin to get more of Indo-China in Mar. 1941

THE ROME--BERLIN--
TOKYO AXIS

ON Sept. 27, 1940, just thirteen months after the Na
Soviet Non-aggression Pact had shattered the An
Comintern Pact of 1936, Japan, Germany, and Italy sign
the Pact of Berlin. Japan, which had found herself da
gerously exposed by the Soviet Non-aggression Pact, h
been eager to resume her game of diplomatic blackm
with the Nazis since the fall of France. Collaboration b

Ribbentrop, Kurusu, Hitler, and Translator Schmidt plan new moves when the United States stiffens her attitude toward Japan.

ween the three major Fascist powers was nothing new. It had begun informally in 1935 and had been formalized by the Anti-Comintern Pact of 1936, which served as a device to win the support of the appeasers in the democracies and kept them from joint action against aggression. After the betrayal of France the Japanese saw—correctly, it may be added—that the Vichy government was a mere pawn in Hitler's hand and that the resumption of their mutual collaboration in diplomacy might swiftly and bloodlessly advance Japan's drive to conquer Asia. But Tokyo wanted Indo-China before signing any pact; Japan had been caught out on a limb by the Soviet Non-aggression Pact. Hitler agreed, and on Sept. 22 Pétain gave Japan garrison rights and air bases in Indo-China. Five days later the new Axis pact was signed. The *published text* differed from the old Anti-Comintern Pact greatly, specifically stating the sig-

natories' relations with the Soviets were in no way affected. Moreover, while the old pact had been ostensibly against the Soviets but in reality against the democracies, the new pact was directly aimed at the United States. The reason: Hitler wanted to divert U.S. attention from the European war and stop her aid to Britain by giving the Japanese an opportunity to move southward, threatening the Philippines and other U.S. possessions. All the signatories agreed to recognize Hitler's "New Order" in Europe and Japan's "New Order" in Asia, to go to war together if one signatory was attacked. The Japanese confidently expected the United States, already menaced on the Atlantic, to give in to blackmail on the Pacific. The United States' reply was to grant immediately a $100,000,000 credit to the hard-pressed Chinese, impose further restrictions on oil and scrap exports to Japan and increase her aid to Britain.

THE FALL OF THE BLACKSHIRT EMPIRE

British General Wavell directed the surprise blow.

SIMULTANEOUSLY with the Nazi mass air attacks on London in September Italian General Graziani struck out from Libya toward the Suez Canal. The British situation was precarious, for in Italian East Africa (Ethiopia) another Italian force was posed to thrust into Anglo-Egyptian Sudan. On Sept. 12, three days before the Nazis' heaviest daylight attack on London, Italian advance forces crossed the Libyan border. The British fell back, giving up Solum and concentrating on harassing the Italians. They planned to make their first serious stand at Matruh. On Sept. 17 Graziani took deserted Sidi Barani. There he stopped. Ahead lay 70 miles of scorching desert which he would have to cross to engage the main British forces and he had no intention of attempting it before completing campaign preparations. For three months he prepared, building water pipe lines, and several roads. Meanwhile, Britain rushed reinforcements and modern equipment to Wavell. Though the Greek campaign had started and the British were forced to divert much strength to that scene, Graziani made no effort to use it as a distraction. On Dec. 9 the British converted their raids into a heavy full-scale surprise attack on the stunned Italians at Sidi Barani. Graziani's defensive outposts fell before the Italians were awake to the fact that the British were bent on a major offensive.

ROARING THROUGH THE DESERT, Wavell's tanks led the coordinated attack on Sidi Barani. Outnumbered, Wavell outgeneraled Graziani with feints, broke through the town's defenses to trap two divisions. Meanwhile British mechanized units circled the town to cut off retreat. Italians made a stand at Solum and Fort Capuzzo but were overwhelmed Dec. 16, and fled to Bardia.

British Blenheim bombers blasted all Italian airfields on the African Coast to attain immediate air supremacy.

N CHRISTMAS DAY the British knelt to pray for victory before leashing a new attack on Bardia which they had had under siege ace Dec. 18. Within the town were three Italian divisions putting up desperate resistance to give Graziani, who had fled on to Tobruk, time to rally his routed forces. Bardia took a terrible pounding from British artillery, bombers, and Mediterranean fleet.

ON JAN. 3 THE BRITISH BROKE through Bardia's strong defenses. The Italians had worked for four years to make Bardia impregnable. It possessed a chain of fortifications, a ten-foot tank trap, and mine defenses. After an intense bombardment Australia infantrymen broke through the outer defenses in the southwes bridged it for the tanks which swept up from the rear.

ON JAN. 5 THE ITALIANS SURRENDERED. Expecting the main British drive from the southeast, they had been surprised by the southwest drive which deprived them of their artillery batteries. Thus in a month's time Wavell's army had captured 40,000 prison and suffered only 600 casualties. Almost from the start it had pended for water and gasoline on what could be captured.

R.A.F. Air Superiority Paved Way for Victories

INTENSE HEAT OF DESERT forced R.A.F. pilots, most of whom were British and Australian, to wear only helmets, shorts, and parachutes. Entire desert served as an airfield.

THESE UNUSUAL SEQUENCE PICTURES were taken from an R.A.F. bomber as it swooped low over a line of Italian oil trucks racing along a desert road. Air forces of both sides concentrated in trying to smash each other's communications. Below: a direct hit.

AMERICAN-BUILT "TOMAHAWKS" out-performed Italian Fiats. Most of General Wavell's planes were speedy Spitfires and Hurricanes, far superior to Mussolini's.

AN R.A.F. DESERT FIGHTER FIELD consisted of a kit rack for helmets and parachutes and an "ops" blackboard to list the flight pilots. These pilots are about to take off.

Gen. Graziani blamed lack of tanks for his defeat.

Captured Italians, shuffling across the desert sands toward prison camps in Egypt, numbered 133,000, included 19 generals, 1 admiral.

TOBRUK...
DERNA...
BENGHAZI...

With the fall of Bardia the British forces, which included some Free French units, concentrated on Tobruk, the main Italian base. Tobruk had been under the fire of British advance units since Jan. 6. Tanks were deployed to block the westward road to prevent retreat while air and land patrols reconnoitered carefully. Violent sandstorms, reaching hurricane proportions delayed the assault, but when the weather cleared on Jan. 21 the British hurled themselves on the town's defenses. As at Bardia the main attack came from the southeast,

once again surprising the Italians. The British broke through and overwhelmed the town after a day's fierce fighting. Meanwhile, British mechanized forces chased Graziani's escaping units westward to Derna where natural defenses made encirclement tactics impossible. On Jan. 24 the British began a strong frontal tank assault. By the 27th the main fort had been captured but on Jan. 30, when Australian infantrymen broke through their last defenses, the Italians escaped on the open road to the west. The British took Cyrene and Barce in quick succes-

British casualties: 438 killed, 1236 wounded.

...ion while a mechanized column which had previously taken Mekili raced westward to Soluch to cut off the Italians, who had now abandoned Benghazi. This column pushed 150 miles over unknown desert land in thirty-six hours to arrive just in time to block the Italian flight from Soluch. The Italians made an effort to break through, but on Feb. 7 they collapsed and the British victory was complete. Although Graziani still had 275,000 men, his mechanized forces were shattered and the threat to the Suez was removed for the moment.

"Violence is moral, when it is sudden as a storm. . . ."—Mussolini.

ITALIAN DEFEAT IN EAST AFRICA

WHEN, in Sept., 1940, Graziani pushed eastward towards the Suez and took Sidi Barrani, another Italian force swept out of Italian East Africa, consisting of Ethiopia, Eritrea, and Somaliland, and captured Gallabat and Kassala and threatened Khartoum. Wavell dealt with this move simultaneously with his attack in northern Africa and in much the same way. Throughout September British forces constantly harried the Italians with sudden raids and skirmishes, robbing them of the initiative. By Nov. 1 these raids had become so frequent and violent in their character that the Italians at Gallabat were forced to retreat to their base at Metemma across the border. Similar raids, ever increasing in their intensity, forced the Italians at Kassala to abandon the town on Jan. 18. Suffering and discontented Ethiopians, armed by the British and rallied by the once-ignored Haile Selassie, became an important part of the British drive. Immediately after the capture of Kassala the British took up the chase of the retreating Italians who fled toward Agordat and Barentu. Moving rapidly, the British cut the lateral road from Agordat to Barentu. This outflanked the Barentu force and on Feb. 2 they abandoned the town and headed for Asmara. In the meantime the other column, after the brief and unsuccessful attempt to stem the British at Biscia on Jan. 24, fled from Agordat to take advantage of the strong natural defenses of Keren. At Keren, situated among the peaks and forges leading to the Eritrean plateau, the British were unable to break through and began a slow encirclement toward the south. Simultaneously Ethiopian guerrilla bands and British mechanized units advanced from Metemma, which had fallen on Jan. 31, to attack Eritrea from the rear. Another British force drove into Somaliland, repeating Wavell's tactics in Libya, captured Afmadu on Feb. 12, Bulo Erillo, 130 miles from the frontier, on Feb. 13. On Feb. 14 Kismayu, second port of Somaliland, was taken with help from the British fleet. Advancing 70 miles in two days, the British reached the main Italian defenses on the Juba River, which were outflanked by a surprise crossing of the river to the north and on the south by the column which had captured Kismayu. The two British columns converged on the main Italian base, Gelib, overrunning it. On Feb. 23 the British took Brava and the following day the capital of the colony Mogadiscio. In two days this mechanized column had made a spectacular 220 mile advance and was now in a position to attack the Italian garrisons of Ethiopia.

NOW EQUIPPED WITH GUNS INSTEAD OF SPEARS, Ethiopian troops drove back the Italians, who had once gassed and bombed their helpless villages. Fighting with them were African natives from Sudan and the Gold Coast as well as Highlanders, Belgians, and Free French. Specializing in guerrilla tactics, the Ethiopians drove the Italians from Danghela and Burye in March.

HAILE SELASSIE, working with the British, directed the Ethiopians. The British drives converged on Addis Ababa after Keren fell.

MEANWHILE THE BRITISH crashed through the defenses of Marda Pass and the defenders of Keren at Asmara. It was expected that the Italians would make a serious stand at the Awash River. Instead they sent envoys to arrange the surrender of Addis Ababa.

ADDIS ABABA WAS OCCUPIED ON APRIL 6, the British capturing many rifles, munitions, and field guns. Though isolated Italian bands continued fighting until June, this marked the end of Musso-lini's costly East African Empire, the return of Haile Selassie to his throne, and the first territorial victory of the Democracies over the Axis since the war began in 1931.

BALKAN BLITZ

In the meanwhile Hitler, unable to knock out the R.A.F. and invade Britain, now turned to the Balkan countries, each of which was ruled by a native Fascist. The Nazis, with the support of fifth columnists, had already made great diplomatic advances in these countries. Until May, 1940, Fascist-minded King Carol of Rumania had been under strong Allied pressure not to release Rumanian oil to Hitler. But with the invasion of the Lowlands Carol immediately swung over to Hitler. On May 11 he proclaimed amnesty for pro-Nazi Iron Guardists whom he had imprisoned; on May 29 he demobilized his armies; pro-Nazi Girgutu was made Premier. The significance of the Nazi advance toward the Dardanelles and Black Sea was not lost in Moscow. On June 26, 1940, the Soviets countered with the demand that Rumania return oil-rich Bessarabia and northern Bukovina which had been taken from her at the end of World War I. Hitler refused to intercede and these provinces were immediately taken over by the Red Army.

HITLER AND HUNGARIAN DICTATOR Admiral Horthy had long been friendly. Hitler gave him a slice of Czechoslovakia, promised him Transylvania. Hungary became Hitler's Balkan pawn.

CAROL, SHOWN HERE WITH PRINCE MICHAEL, rushed frantically to Hitler when Russia demanded Bessarabia. But his new friend refused to risk war with Russia. The Red army immediately occupied their old territory. Hungary and Bulgaria then demanded Transylvania and south Dobruja, provinces taken from them in the last war. Hitler forced Carol to give these up in August.

IRON GUARDIST ANTONESCU, friend of Hitler, was then summoned by Carol to become Premier. On Sept. 5 Carol gave him sweeping powers in an effort to save his own neck. But the Iron Guardists were determined upon revenge for Carol's past coolness. On Sept. 6 Carol and Madame Lupescu fled. Antonescu put Prince Michael on the throne for the second time.

EARLY IN OCTOBER Nazi troops occupied Rumania to protect, said the Nazis in Berlin, the oil fields. To give the Allies the idea that the Russians were working with them Berlin announced that Russia had been informed of the Nazi occupation in advance. This, Moscow promptly and vigorously denied. Hungary formally joined the Axis on Nov. 20 and three days later Antonescu signed the Pact of Berlin.

KING BORIS OF BULGARIA, long a Nazi sympathizer, had no objections to joining the Axis, but his people, whose pan-Slavism affiliated them with Russia, protested violently. On Nov. 17 Boris made a trip to Berlin preparatory to joining the Axis. Russia immediately brought strong pressure to bear which temporarily kept Bulgaria out of the Axis and modified Hitler's Balkan success.

PRINCE PAUL, Regent of Yugoslavia, had many close ties with Nazi Germany. He is shown here lunching with the Goebbels family. In Oct., 1940 he signed a Nazi trade treaty making Yugoslavia dependent upon German trade. But few Yugoslavs liked the Axis. In Feb. 1941 Prince Paul was summoned to Berchtesgaden where the Nazis proposed an alliance. Fear of betrayal to the Nazis spread.

INVASION OF GREECE

FROM the start of the war Italy's role had been that of junior partner. In announcing his plans for Europe's "new order" Hitler made it plain by implication that Italy would continue in that role—hardly a glowing future in contrast with Mussolini's promises. When Hitler and Mussolini met at the Brenner Pass on Oct. 4, 1940, it was clear that Germany was making her diplomatic push in the Balkans alone, leaving Mussolini out of the picture. Mussolini decided he had better quickly establish a stake in the Balkans. At 3 A.M., on October 28, an ultimatum, based on charges of Greek attacks in Albania, was handed to the Greeks demanding certain strategic points be handed over to Albania. Asked what the points were, the Italian envoy was unable to say. This formality over with, the Italian invasion was launched from Albania at 5:30 A.M. It was "a striking lesson in how not to run a blitzkrieg." Italian air power, infinitely superior to the few planes of the Greeks, was little used. No parachutists appeared. No attempt was made to co-ordinate the navy with the army. Nor was there any co-ordination within the Axis; Germany did not even break off relations. In fact, according to Correspondent Winston Burdett, Hitler continued to supply the Greeks with ammunition for their German-made weapons. The Italians had counted on a quick Greek collapse. It was an almost fatal mistake for Il Duce. For his invading forces, whose lack of coordinated effort gave evidence of a hastily conceived and poorly prepared campaign, were met with the most ferocious kind of resistance from the Greeks.

THE MAIN ITALIAN FORCES ADVANCED toward Yanina in a two-pronged drive from Koritza. They progressed slowly, meeting with ferocious resistance from the ill-equipped Greeks. The Yanina drive met with disaster on Nov. 9 at the Oos River, when the Greeks descended on the Italian column from the mountain heights.

WHILE ITALIANS STRUGGLED up mountainous, icy roads, the Greeks seized the initiative. Never making a frontal attack, they carried out deadly assaults on the Italian flanks from the hilltops.

On Nov. 22 they took Koritza. Now in Albania they increased their fierce attack, taking Porto Edda, Premet, Argyrokastron, depriving the Italians of their main Albanian ports of entry.

TYPICAL OF MOST GREEK PATRIOTS, these Greek soldiers had practically no modern equipment. The British could divert little to them because most of their arms were tied up in Libya.

MUSSOLINI POURED NEW EQUIPMENT AND MEN into Albania, fired Gen. Soddu, replacing him with Gen. Cavallero. After his sea defeats, disasters in Africa, Il Duce needed a victory badly.

THIS ITALIAN COLONEL AND HIS AIDE were captured along with 20,000 others by the Greeks who took the strongly fortified peaks near Tepelini Feb. 13. An Italian counteroffensive failed. By

March British reinforcements and supplies were beginning to arrive. But in the meantime Germany had occupied Greece's neighbor, Bulgaria, which had rejected a Soviet mutual-assistance pact on Feb. 9.

The mass attack of Nazi dive bombers on airports at dawn, April 6, immediately wiped out the small Yugoslavian air fleet

THE NAZI INVASION OF YUGOSLAVIA AND GREECE

THE Nazi pressure on Yugoslavia for adherence to the Axis, begun in February, increased steadily. On Mar. Regent Prince Paul, long a pro-Nazi, presented a plan t the government calling for gradually increasing dependenc on Berlin. Army leaders allowed word to leak out tha Prince Paul was preparing to betray them as the French ha been betrayed. Determinedly anti-Nazi, the people poure protesting delegations into Belgrade. Prince Paul, in an effor

The Nazis used a fleet of 3,000 planes in their Balkan blitz.

Nazi troops are shown mopping up a small town near the border.

sweep the country into Hitler's lap before the people ould act, forced the cabinet to agree to his plan on Mar. . On Mar. 24 Premier Cvetkovitch hastened to Vienna here the agreement was signed. But what Cvetkovitch gned, the nation refused to ratify. The government collapsed. Great, spontaneous anti-Nazi demonstrations broke ut everywhere. Led by Air Chief Gen. Simovitch, the army nd Yugoslavian patriots seized the government. Traitorous

Prince Paul fled. 18-year-old King Peter assumed the throne and appointed Gen. Simovitch Premier. Simovitch refused Hitler's demands for immediate ratification of the pact and the signing of a non-agression treaty between Yugoslavia and Russia indicated that Russia might jeopardize his Balkan plans unless he acted at once. At dawn on April 6 the Nazi armies invaded Yugoslavia and Greece.

British Aid to the Balkan Countries

BRITISH VETERANS from Libya, arrived to meet the expected Nazi blow, began teaching Greeks how to operate their guns.

In January Gen. Wavell went to Athens to offer Greece military assistance, but the Greeks, fearing substantial aid would only provoke an early Nazi attack, declined. Meanwhile, Britain sought to stem the Nazi Balkan sweep by diplomacy. In this they were aided by the Soviets' startling announcement that they had not consented to the occupation of Bulgaria, a new sign that Moscow was viewing Hitler's march toward the Dardanelles with distrust. However, the British efforts met with success only in Turkey, where President Inönü, reversing previous steps toward acceptance of Nazi Balkan power, showed increasing coolness toward Hitler's approaches. By this time the Nazi armies were massing on the Greek-Bulgarian border and the Greeks now welcomed British military aid. While the African armies were reinforced by fresh troops from England, Anzac veterans of the Libyan campaign were shuttled to Greece as rapidly as possible. They brought with them an armored brigade and a tiny fleet of R.A.F. planes, all that could be spared from Africa. They faced overwhelming odds, for Hitler's armies included 40 divisions of his best troops, 5 mechanized divisions, and 3,000 planes. Nevertheless the British went to the immediate assistance of the Greeks. Churchill later revealed that the Cabinet had felt their forces doomed from the start, but felt world opinion would turn against England if they did not send aid.

GENERAL WAVELL HAD LANDED in Greece in January to see what help might be given. He returned again after his armies had taken Benghazi, but not until March did the Greeks ask for aid. The British had no force large enough to stop the Nazis available and lacked especially anti-tank and aircraft guns and planes. Most Greek guns came from Germany and British shells did not fit them.

The Nazi air fleet improvised airports such as this as soon as their parachutists had seized a likely plateau.

The Greek forces which had driven the Italians deep into the Albanian mountains were forced to retreat (below).

Two Yugoslavians look apprehensively behind them for Nazis as they flee past the ruins of the Royal Palace.

The Shelling of the Open City of Belgrade

WHEN Bulgaria was seized Prince Paul's traitorous government concentrated its troops in the north when it was obvious the main Nazi blow would come from Bulgaria on its eastern flank in an endeavor to effect a junction with the Italians in Albania, severing Yugoslavia from British and Greek aid. Before Simovitch could reform his forces, the Nazis struck, and by April 9 were astride the main communication lines with the south. A northern force moved slowly toward Belgrade, which was abandoned and declared an open city. Despite this, the city was subjected to a three-day artillery and aerial bombardment which matched in ferocity and ruthlessness the devastation of Warsaw and Rotterdam.

Rare Pictures of the Looting of Belgrade

Aт the war's outbreak the Yugoslav government hid its gold in a Serbian monastery. These pictures show its seizure by Nazis. Note dejection of priest. Mustached civilian in both pictures is probably a Yugoslavian traitor who revealed the hiding place. Below, gold is carried to trucks for removal to Berlin.

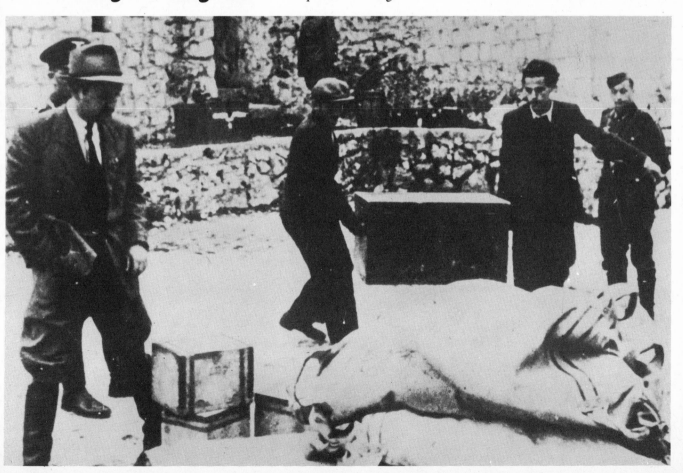

NAZI BOMBING OF CIVILIANS in Greece was carried out with the same ruthlessness that marked every Nazi campaign. With the collapse of the main Yugoslav armies on April 16 the Greek and British defense became desperate. The collapse of the Yugoslav resistance opened an unguarded avenue through which the Nazis advanced rapidly. The R.A.F. was overwhelmed by the clouds of Nazi planes. The Nazis quickly flanked the defenses at Olympus despite furious British resistance. Meanwhile, the Greeks had begun withdrawing from Albania to protect their rear. But a swift Nazi armored column beat its way to Yanina, cutting them off, and on April 20 Greek forces in that area were forced to surrender. Below, the Nazis are shown entering Salonika.

HARD-PRESSED ANZAC TROOPS began a slow withdrawal when Greek collapse appeared imminent on April 20. Despite the constant strafing and dive bombing, a rear guard held for three days against six Nazi divisions to permit withdrawal of the bulk of the troops to evacuation points. As at Dunkirk the men were evacuated from the beaches, but here they were without air protection. Some 45,000 of the original 57,000 troops were rescued by the navy which shuttled them to Crete, where they are seen landing below. Athens and Patras were taken on April 28 and on May 1, seven days after the Greek armies had been forced to surrender at Salonika, the evacuation ended. The Greek government under King George moved to Crete with the B.E.F.

WHILE Nazi bombers blasted British positions hundreds of Nazi parachutists and glider-borne soldiers floated down after dawn on May 20. These rare pictures show the downing of a Nazi transport after it had discharged its paratroops, and paratroops charging weakened British posts at the Maleme airport. Though aided by natives armed with pitchforks, the British were overwhelmed by the numbers of paratroops who were able to take cover in Crete's numerous gullies and valleys.

226

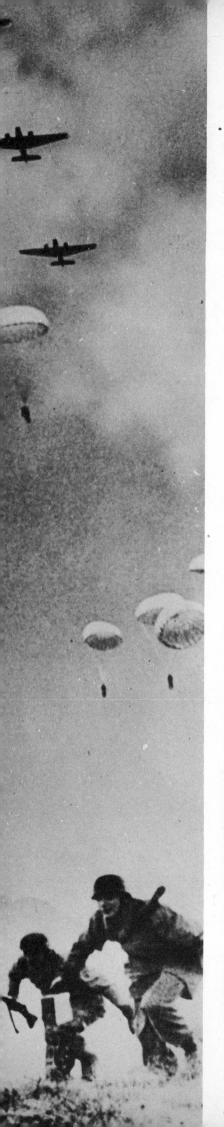

THE FALL OF CRETE

Most of the British troops evacuated from Greece were landed at Crete, from which the British hoped to raid Axis communications and bases. Moreover, the island was a strategically important defense base for the whole eastern Mediterranean including the Suez Canal. Nazi bombers began blasting the island's defenses as the British landed and meanwhile the Nazi command began concentrating its air force in Greece for a knock-out blow. By mid-May the Nazis were continuously raiding the main airports of Crete. Their surprise invasion came on the morning of May 20 when large flights of Nazi transport planes began dropping hundreds of parachutists. Simultaneously Nazi transports towed large gliders over Crete, each carrying twelve men equipped with trench mortars and machine guns and two-way radio sets, and released them to land in open fields. Nazi fighter planes beat off the skeleton R.A.F. and once the parachutists had landed they were able to seize strong defensive points for the rough terrain made it impossible to round them up. The primary objective of the air-borne troops was the important airport of Maleme near Canea. The British held the field until May 21 when the Nazis succeeded in landing mountain troops equipped with heavy guns. These troops captured the airport, repaired the runways for the landing of air-borne reinforcements. On the night of May 21 British naval forces smashed a sea-borne invasion force, consisting mainly of small boats, and another invasion fleet was destroyed the next morning. But the effort cost the British two destroyers sunk and four destroyers and two battleships severely damaged. On May 22 the shattered R.A.F. was withdrawn. Left without air protection, the British were slowly pushed to the island's westward end. By May 29 the Nazis had taken Suda Bay, Canea, and Heraclion. Evacuation became a necessity and, without air protection, a near disaster. Although 14,580 British troops were rescued, 13,000 were lost as well as 12,000 Greek troops.

NAZI PARACHUTISTS CAPTURE A BRITISH OUTPOST. In order to get the maximum number of men into Crete at the same time the Nazis recklessly crash-landed dozens of transport planes and transport gliders, which were directed by radio.

Rommel Revives the Axis Threat to Suez

To understand the fighting in Libya one must realize the sealike vastness of the desert permitted a war of movement closely resembling sea warfare. Tanks truly became land battleships. Like those of the sea they were accompanied by a speedy flotilla of destroyers in the shape of motorcyclists, scout cars, fighters and bombers, and motorized infantry. The aim of each belligerent was to trap and capture his enemy. Consequently, most activity in the desert consisted of racing columns trying to encircle or escape racing enemy columns. The fall of a strong point was usually a hollow victory, for generally the enemy escaped into the desert from which he might sally forth when reinforced and at the propitious time to fight again. Decisive victories without annihilating the enemy were virtually impossible.

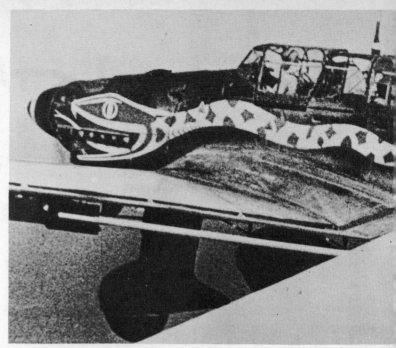

TO BOLSTER Graziani's shattered forces elite Nazi troops began arriving in Tripoli in Feb. 1941. Within a month they were joined by three Nazi panzer divisions headed by Gen. Rommel.

GEN. ERWIN ROMMEL, most daring of the Nazi tank tacticians, shown here atop the dashboard of his reconnaissance car, took over the Axis command and on Mar. 24 unleashed a surprise attack on El Agheila, forcing the light British units there to withdraw quickly. Still underrating Rommel's strength and strategic skill, the British were amazed when his armored divisions swept into Mersa Brega a few days later. The outflanked Benghazi division was forced to re treat. Between Derna and Mechili the British attempted to make a serious stand, but again the fast-moving Nazis outflanked them and in a daring, gangster-like night raid Nazi motorcyclists pulled two British generals out of the retreating column. By April 9 the British had retreated to Tobruk. Rommel swept around it to seize Bardia on April 12, cutting Tobruk off from Egypt by land. In less than a month all British gains, except Tobruk, had been lost.

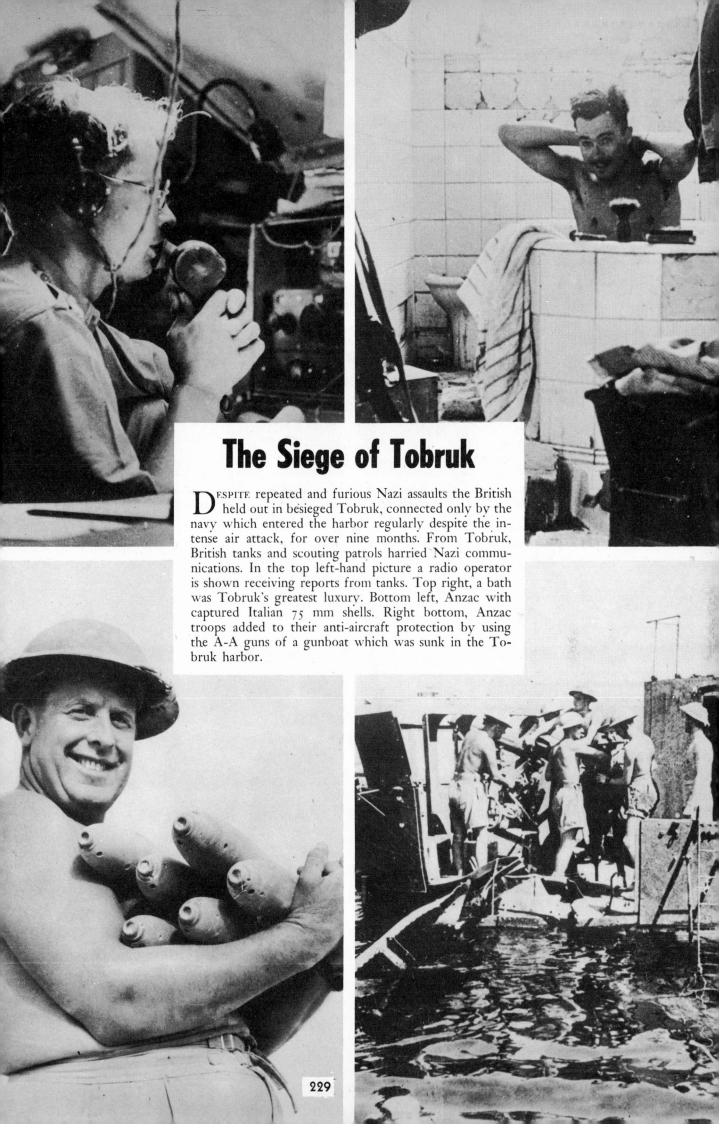

The Siege of Tobruk

DESPITE repeated and furious Nazi assaults the British held out in besieged Tobruk, connected only by the navy which entered the harbor regularly despite the intense air attack, for over nine months. From Tobruk, British tanks and scouting patrols harried Nazi communications. In the top left-hand picture a radio operator is shown receiving reports from tanks. Top right, a bath was Tobruk's greatest luxury. Bottom left, Anzac with captured Italian 75 mm shells. Right bottom, Anzac troops added to their anti-aircraft protection by using the A-A guns of a gunboat which was sunk in the Tobruk harbor.

THIS REMARKABLE PICTURE shows a New Zealand patrol guarding two members of a Nazi tank crew whom they have wounded. Note the apprehension of the patrol because of their lack of cover. During the summer months the intense heat put such a strain on the men and machines that fighting practically ceased. Exhausted, both sides limited themselves to patrol skirmishes. But on Nov. 18 the British opened up an intense drive on Rommel. By a series of swift thrusts and encircling maneuvers they got within ten miles of Tobruk on the third day and were joined by the Tobruk garrison which fought its way out to meet them. Rommel fought a series of delaying actions, escaping from every trap laid by the British, with his forces nearly intact.

ROMMEL RETREATED to El Aghelia and on Jan. 17 the British took Halfaya. Then on Jan. 22, Rommel began pounding the British, who were exhausted from their long drive, with heavy artillery. The above picture shows one of his range-finders at work. His mobile 88 mm. anti-tank guns shattered the British tank columns. To save time, he sat at a microphone shouting his orders in plain German. Though the British heard him, by the time they had put their counter-orders into code and the tank commanders had decoded them, Rommel's tanks had encircled them. The British were never given time by Rommel, who was as famous for his cruelty as his skill, to organize any defense. By Feb. 4 they had abandoned Derna and Rommel was again within striking distance of Egypt.

LARGE NUMBERS OF U. S. M-3 TANKS were used by the British but their effectiveness was limited by the Nazi 88 mm. gun. The British anti-tank gun had a shorter range. The British fell back constantly—but slowly, until they reached Bir Hacheim, held by the Free French. After a fierce two week battle Bir Hacheim and Knightsbridge fell, permitting Rommel to cut off Tobruk and trap there 25,000 men and large supply stores. The British command, thinking Rommel would require a week to reorganize his forces, was caught flatfooted when he immediately charged the fortress with every weapon he could muster. On June 21, after 48 hours of fighting, Tobruk fell. Moving eastward, Rommel managed, at Matruh, to draw British tank forces into ambush and move on Alexandria and Cairo.

TO AID THE BRITISH, whose position had now become desperate, U. S. bombers were rushed in to bomb Rommel's bases. Gen. Auchinleck replaced Gen. Ritchie as British commander. Finally, at El Alamein on July 3rd, the British, greatly reinforced by their Syrian armies and U. S. supplies, hurled the Nazis back. The exhaustion of Rommel's troops indicated a new turning point in the see-saw battle had been reached. In Commons Churchill faced stiff criticism for the conduct of the war but won a new vote of confidence by an overwhelming majority. Everywhere the people realized that the opening of a second front in Europe would cut Rommel's supplies to the point where he could not replace his losses and towards that front England bent all her efforts.

Roosevelt began U. S. rearmament on May 10, asking for a billion dollars. By Dec. ten billion had been appropriated.

AMERICA

TO HEAD UNITED STATES' DEFENSE PRODUCTION
Roosevelt originally picked W. S. Knudsen of General Motors, Edward J. Stettinius of U. S. Steel, and Harriet Elliot.

S INCE 1936 there had been a growing American minority that recognized the appeasement of the dictators must eventually end in either war or complete betrayal. Yet no one proposed, when Poland was invaded, that we go to war against Hitler. America's profound desire for peace found reassurance in the President's declaration of U.S. neutrality on Sept. 5 and his vigorous reinforcement of American defenses to prevent a "black-out of peace" here. But the United States, though neutral, made it clear she would do everything in her power "short of war" to aid the democracies. A special session of Congress, Sept. 25, 1940, lifted the arms-embargo provisions of the neutrality act which prohibited the sale of arms and loans to belligerents. Intended to keep us out of war, this arms embargo had actually aided the Axis, because it prevented China and Spain from pur

Beside President is Orville Wright, inventor of airplane.

SECRETARY OF STATE Cordell Hull made the first step toward hemisphere defense at Havana, July, 1941, when he got the South American nations to agree not to recognize any transfer of colonies in this hemisphere that might result from the war. Argentine Foreign Minister Melo (right) was at first reluctant but finally agreed. Nazi influence in South America was strong.

PREPARES

nasing arms here. Under the revised act the democracies vere allowed to buy arms on the "cash-and-carry" plan, or U.S. ships were barred from transporting munitions to elligerents. From the first President Roosevelt's defense measures fell into three categories: strengthening of our national defenses, the building of hemisphere solidarity and efense, and aid to the Allies. In Sept., 1939 President Roosevelt appointed a War Resources Board headed by dward J. Stettinius to survey our industrial defense needs. et it took the fall of the Lowlands to awaken America to s danger. On May 16 President Roosevelt initiated his rmament program with a request for a billion dollars. ut defense appropriations did not build tanks and planes nd on June 3 President Roosevelt asked W. S. Knudsen of General Motors to head U.S. defense production.

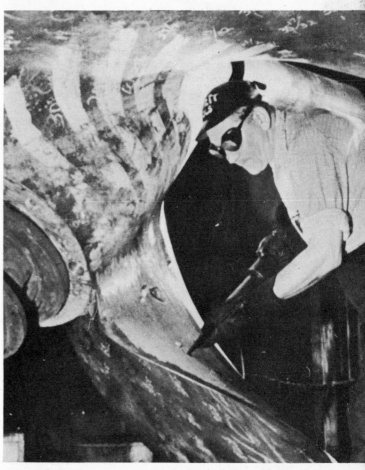

U.S. NAVAL CONSTRUCTION included 17 battleships, 60 cruisers and destroyers. Roosevelt had tried to build up the navy previously with some success. Until the fall of France, U.S. had always depended on Britain's fleet to patrol the Atlantic. But with the British fleet drawn elsewhere U.S. had to begin building a two-ocean navy at an initial cost of four billion dollars.

BRITISH SAILORS RAN UP THE UNION JACK on 50 over-age destroyers which were exchanged by President Roosevelt, Sept. 3, 1940, for 99-year leases on eight Atlantic bases from Newfoundland to the Caribbean. This strengthened American defenses and at the same time bolstered the British destroyer fleet which had suffered many losses since the start of the war.

ON OCT. 29 SECRETARY OF WAR STIMSON drew the first draft number in the first U. S. peacetime conscription of an army. The draft bill, conscripting men between 21 and 35, passed Congress on Sept. 14. The number Stimson drew was 158.

THESE MEN WERE AMONG THE FIRST inducted. Induction began all over U. S. on Oct. 25. The original draft bill limited the number of draftees to 900,000 in one year. Army camps sprang up everywhere, but by spring many men were still without weapons.

BY THE FALL OF 1940 the Office of Production Management had barely begun to swing U. S. industrial might into war production. Many plants were already producing arms for Britain and half their production was now diverted to U. S. needs. Defense plants began expanding. Machine-tool production, doubling 1939's production, reached $423,000,000 by the end of 1940 and doubled again in 1941.

TO ENGLAND the U. S. shipped large numbers of bombers such as these Lockheed-Hudsons. U. S. produced only 5,480 planes in 1940. But by Jan., 1941 production had reached 1,000 planes per month. U. S. got no tanks in 1940, but by Sept. 1941 production in the Chrysler plant alone had reached 10 per day. Yet by the end of 1941 U. S. was spending only a third of what Germany was.

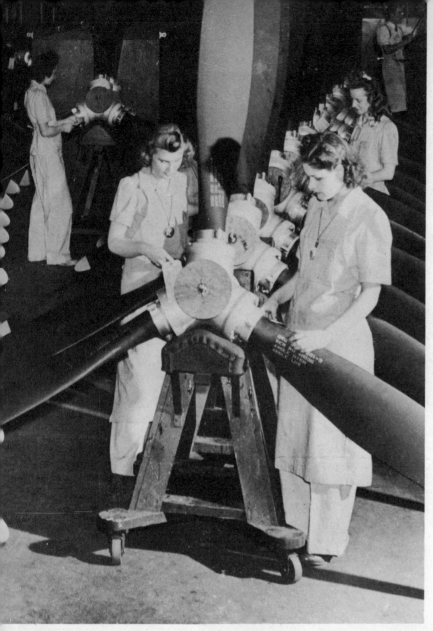

EMPHASIS WAS PUT ON AIRPLANE CONSTRUCTION because of the decisive role planes played in the war in Europe. The original plans called for 15,000 planes. By Sept. 1941 this had jumped to 44,000.

Although OPM had cleared $9,900,000,000 worth of defense contracts by Nov. 31, 1940, actual production got under way slowly. The titanic job of organizing and co-ordinating the nation's industrial machinery and resources fell largely on the shoulders of Edward R. Stettinius, head of the Industrial Materials Division; W. S. Knudsen, head of the Production Division; Sidney Hillman, head of the Labor Division, and Leon S. Henderson, head of the Division of Price Stabilization. Perhaps the biggest "bottleneck" holding up production was the shortage of machine tools which prevented the re-tooling of industrial plants for arms production. Machine-tool production reached $423,000,000 in 1940, doubling 1939 production, and was expected to top $823,000,000 in 1941. Yet it was not until Sept. 9, 1940, that OPM established preference ratings saying who should get these tools first, and not until Jan. 31, 1941, that OPM set up rigid priorities under Donald M. Nelson. Later to become head of the War Production Board, Nelson was to co-ordinate raw materials, priorities, and production. Defense boom towns began to appear all over America in the spring of 1941 as expansion of our industrial capacity rose and America's great auto plants were converted to arms production. Meanwhile, in December, Britain, liquidating industrial property owned by her nationals here, made it plain she could not carry the financial burden of the war alone much longer. In Jan. 1941 the Lease-Lend bill, authorizing the President to sell, lease, or lend U.S. weapons to any country whose defense the President deemed vital to the U.S., was introduced in Congress. Although vigorously opposed by isolationist groups and pro-Nazi organizations as a step which would lead us into the war, it was passed and signed by the President on Mar. 11. The bill provided for no specific repayment. Under it Britain was immediately allocated $1,080 million for the purchasing of much-needed supplies here.

OPM EXPERTS TURNED DOWN recommendations in 1940 that our steel capacity be increased 20%—from 84,000,000 tons yearly to 100,000,000 tons. By May 1941 shortages threatened and capacity was increased.

FUND-RAISING PARTIES, held throughout America by Bundles for Britain, raised millions of dollars for the relief of suffering in England.

N JULY 7, 1941, PICKED AMERICAN TROOPS TOOK er Iceland, advanced outpost of the Western hemisphere which had en occupied by the British after the fall of Denmark fourteen onths before. Previously U.S. had occupied Greenland as part of its licy of hemisphere defense. On July 1, in an exchange of letters th the U.S. Government, Iceland, which had suspended Danish au-

thority when Denmark was seized, had agreed to the occupation. U.S. promised to respect Iceland's integrity and independence, to adequately garrison the island, and to withdraw immediately upon war's conclusion. In mid-September a large field force of the U.S. Army was transferred to the island. This virtually ended the danger of Iceland becoming a Nazi stepping stone into this hemisphere.

ITISH FORCES WERE WITHDRAWN slowly to relieve ops at home, the Far East, Africa, leaving U.S. troops to hold the nd. U.S. forces included every branch of the services.

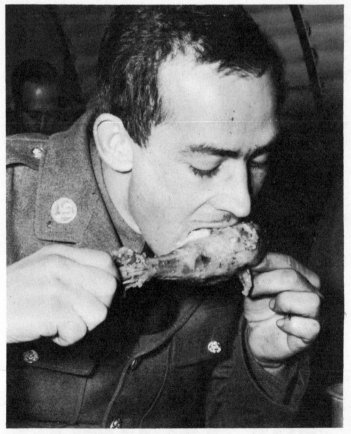

WELL-FED, WELL-CLAD U.S. TROOPS liked everything about their new post except its monotony. Soon U.S. soldiers were a part of island's life, were popular with Icelanders.

A Nazi sub lookout watches an English tanker go down. United States released 50 civilian tankers to Britain in May 1941.

THE BRIDGE OF SHIPS ACROSS THE ATLANTIC

THE coming of spring brought a renewal of the Battle of the Atlantic. In January only 205,475 tons of British shipping were lost, the lowest figure since March 1940, but in February losses amounted to 275,574 tons, in March 348,118 tons, and in April, 346,208 tons. A new high was reached in May when 380,035 tons were sunk by submarines and raiders. When the war began Britain had approximately 20,000,000 tons of shipping and during the first year of the war she was able to hold her own with new construction, seizures, and purchases. But against losses running at a rate

Though torpedoed off Nazi coast, H.M.S. Kelly did not sink. Towed across North Sea and repaired, she again put to sea.

of over 3,000,000 tons a year, her shipyards could produce only approximately 2,000,000 tons a year. Unless enemy sinkings abated and the United States supplied more ships, Britain was doomed to slow strangulation by the Nazi blockade. At the same time it became obvious that no matter how many arms, tanks, and planes the United States could produce, they were worth nothing if they could not be delivered to England. Except for big bombers which were being flown from Newfoundland to England, most U. S. arms seemed destined for the bottom of the Atlantic because

Britain had been forced to divert many of her naval vessels from convoy duty to the Mediterranean to meet the Axis thrust toward the Suez. The problem the United States faced was whether it would permit these sinkings to continue or use her own naval forces to protect them. Said the New York *Times*, March 13, "The Axis governments will be wrong if they think we intend to produce vast quantities of finely finished weapons for our allies, only to have these weapons sunk in the Atlantic Ocean. . . . by one means or another we shall see that they reach their destination."

Bombs from an American-built R. A. F. plane brought this Nazi sub to the surface. British officers are about to board it.

CONVOY BOUND FOR BRITAIN.

In a series of speeches in April Secretaries Stimson and Knox urged the use of the navy to assure England's continued resistance and called for repeal of the U. S. Neutrality Act. There was little possibility that U. S. shipbuilding, even when combined with Britain's, would meet the losses. Less than 700,00 tons of shipping was planned for construction during 1941. Meanwhile, on May 22, R.A.F. scouting planes warned the British Admiralty that the Nazi pocket battleships, *Bismarck* and *Prinz Eugen*, were preparing to put to sea in Bergen harbor. The Admiralty sent the cruisers *Norfolk* and *Suffolk* to watch for the Nazi ships between Iceland and Greenland.

Ships laden with war materials from the U. S. were convoyed by British flying boats and Royal Navy on their journey's last lap.

On the evening of May 23 the Nazi battleships were sighted speeding southwest through the snow and mist. The cruisers hung onto the trail while calling for support from heavier British ships. The next morning fighting was opened at long range by the *Prince of Wales* and *Hood*, newest and oldest of Britain's battleships, which had moved up during the night. A hit was scored on the *Bismarck*, but the *Prince of Wales* was damaged and the *Hood*, whose armor was badly placed although she was the largest battleship in the world, received an unlucky shot in her powder magazine which blew her up with all hands. This put the whole prestige of the

British navy at stake. The Admiralty rushed every available ship into the chase, including the home fleet headed by the *King George V*, the western Mediterranean fleet headed by the *Renown*, and the battleships *Rodney* and *Ramilles*, which left the ships they were convoying to join the search. About 350 miles south of Greenland the *Bismarck* and *Prinz Eugen* dropped from sight and it was 30 hours before an American-built Catalina plane sighted the *Bismarck* again. This was at 10:30 A.M., May 26, 500 miles off Land's End, too far away for the battleships to catch up. More planes were ordered up and their torpedoes damaged the *Bismarck's* steer-

ing gear and cut her speed. That night British destroyers caught and hit her with torpedoes fatally diminishing her speed. At 8:30 A.M., on May 27, the *Rodney* and *King George V*, closing in from two sides, opened fire on the trapped *Bismarck*. The *Bismarck* answered as long as her guns could fire. But by 9:30 her turrets had been shattered although she was still afloat. An hour later the cruiser *Dorsetshire* sent her to the bottom. The luckier *Prinz Eugen* escaped. Meanwhile, to relieve the strain on British naval forces, President Roosevelt inaugurated the north Atlantic "patrol" which gave ships en route to Britain protection as far as Iceland.

Heroes of the Sea

THE real heroes of the Battle of the Atlantic were the merchant seamen of America, England, Norway, and Holland. Despite the constant threat of U-boats and surface raiders, they took their ships across, many unarmed, especially in the early days of the war. Hundreds of them died in the attempt. Those who survived lived through terrible days on small boats and rafts, days of starvation, hunger and thirst, of madness, of being frozen by wintry storms and scorched by a blazing sun. Yet they came back to sail again. Their courage made the "bridge of ships" possible.

This unusual picture was made by a survivor of the tanker *Charles Pratt* when it was sunk off Freetown with a loss of two U. S. seamen.

A Nazi U-boat captain made this picture of the survivors of a ship just torpedoed Below, lone, starving survivor of another ship.

Harold Johnson

Walter Shotwell

Bill Caves

Frank Garcia

Harry Nerle

Marty Ganier

John Rainier

John Sovota

Charlie Moss

Texas Henderson

Earl Wolf

On May 6 Stalin became Premier of Soviet Russia.

Nazi Number 3, Hess: "I have come to save humanity."

TIME BOMB

THE MONTH OF MAY 1941

ALTHOUGH May, 1941 opened with the British invasion of Iraq and witnessed the air-borne invasion of Crete, the month was marked with significant indications that the war might shortly change its course. The first came on May 6 when Joseph Stalin, leader of the Communist party in Russia, became Premier. Under no delusions about Hitler's promises, the Soviets had been laboring furiously since the signing of the Nazi-Soviet Non-Aggression Pact to strengthen their defenses and to implement them by erecting around themselves a vast buffer territory. On April 13 the Soviets had further increased their defensive strength by concluding a non-aggression pact with Japan, leaving them free to concentrate on any threat from Germany. The assumption of the premiership by Stalin for the first time in that country's history was a sure sign that dangerous times were ahead for Russia. Nazi troops had already begun concentrating along the Polish border while Russia's defenses were not scheduled for completion until August. Determined to offer no provocation to the Nazis before Russia was fully prepared, Stalin acceded to the long-standing Nazi demand that Soviet recognition of Nazi-occupied countries be withdrawn and indicated that Russia might increase its trade with Germany. Nazi relations with Russia were both overshadowed and high lighted by the spectacular flight of Rudolf Hess, No. 3 Nazi and Hitler's closest friend, on May 10 from Augsburg, Germany, to Scotland, where he

Matsuoka moves within striking distance of the Philippines.

"We will not permit . . . Nazi shape of things to come."

arachuted to earth. He landed on the Duke of Hamilton's estate where he was captured by a farmer named Jack McClean armed with a pitchfork. Hess announced pontifically: "I have come to save humanity." In London there was a tendency to welcome him as a convert from Nazism, but this ended when Ernest Bevin, speaking for the government, denounced him as a murderer. Gradually the theory that his flight was evidence of the cracking up of the Hitler regime gave way to the more probable one that it was ordered by Hitler in a last attempt to win England to a "holy crusade" against the "Red Menace" of Soviet Russia. The Nazi High Command, which in 1939 had insisted on a non-aggression pact with Russia if it were to risk war in the west, had reversed itself in April, insisting Russia must be conquered before England could be successfully invaded. The Soviet policy of surprise expansion at German expense had kept vast armies of the Nazi troops immobilized in the east. High Nazi circles felt the English would be willing to accept a Hitler Europe and peace if the Nazis were to invade Russia. Hess's mission was to contact former appeasers and offer peace on this basis. He expected to be received as an envoy and allowed to return with England's answer. Instead the Churchill government threw him into jail and renewed its pledge to continue the war until Nazism had been smashed.

MEANWHILE, on May 6 American-educated Foreign Min-

ister Yosuke Matsuoka had successfully concluded negotiations with the Vichy Ambassador, Charles Arsène Henry, for the Japanese economic control of French Indo-China. There was no doubt, either in Washington, Tokyo, or London, that Japanese economic control would soon be followed by Japanese occupation, putting the Mikado's men within striking distance of Malaya, Burma, Thailand, the Dutch East Indies, and the Philippines. Simultaneously, Nazi penetration of Vichy-owned Syria had begun. A conference between Admiral Darlan and Hitler on May 11 indicated that Vichy was turning over her colonies to the Nazis for military use. A few weeks later British forces attacked Syria before the Nazis could become too strong there. Meanwhile, American attention to the Far East was momentarily diverted to near-by Vichy-held Dakar and its possible use as a base for Nazi U-boats by the sinking of the unarmed U.S. passenger ship *Robin Moor* off Brazil. Vigorously protesting, President Roosevelt declared on May 27: "We do not accept, and will not permit the Nazi shape of things to come . . . We shall give every possible assistance to Britain and to all who, with Britain, are resisting Hitlerism or its equivalent with force of arms."

Thus within the month of May the new course of the war had been indicated in Europe and Asia, and both United States and Britain had assured Russia of their support if Hitler should invade.

Hitler Invades Russia

A T dawn on June 22, 1941, the Nazis invaded the Soviet Union on an 1,800-mile frontier that extended from Finland to Rumania. An hour and a half later, while Hitler screamed over the Berlin radio that he could no longer put up with Anglo-Russian conspiracy, the Nazi Ambassador in Moscow informed Foreign Minister Molotov that Germany intended to go to war. The Nazi attack usually was preceded by demands with a time ultimatum. This time, however, the Nazis made no demands; months later Ambassador Litvinov revealed the Soviets had planned to unleash a violent attack on the Nazis the moment they presented demands to upset their invasion plans and seize the initiative. The bulk of the Nazi forces, estimated at 180 divisions including 20 armored divisions, was spread along the front from the Baltic to the Carpathians. Hitler rallied his satellite nations to a "crusade" to save "Christianity" from the "Red Menace." Although Finnish and Nazi troops attacked Russia on June 22, Finland did not formally enter the war until June 25. Hungary and Rumania entered the war on June 27. Italy sent several divisions and in France Laval began recruiting volunteers for the "crusade," which notably did not have the backing of the Pope. Most military experts gave Russia, which had not yet completed her mobilization, only a few weeks. Yet from the first day it was apparent that the Nazi blitzkrieg machine had run up against something in Russia never encountered in any other country.

FINLAND'S BARON VON MANNERHEIM, (right) shown here with Nazi General Stumpff, who headed Nazi air forces in Finland, directed a simultaneous attack by Nazi-Finnish troops against Soviet Russia at the same time Hitler invaded.

SHORTLY AFTER DAWN on June 22 swarms of Nazi Stukas descended on Russian airports, following the blitzkrieg pattern which had worked so well in the west, in an attempt to smash the Russian air force. The picture below shows some of the Red planes they trapped by their sudden attack. But despite the damage they did, the Nazis were far from destroying the Russian air force, which was estimated by Max Werner, military authority, to consist of 10,000 first-line planes. Though the Nazis immediately claimed to have wiped out the Red air force, they achieved only local superiority. Both the Nazis and the Reds fully realized the value of air power.

DVANCING NAZIS FOUND that the frontier guards, whom ey had expected to fall back in the face of a far superior foe, ught with a stubborn fury and retreated only at the very last inute. Even before Stalin called for a "scorched-earth" policy on ly 2, retreating Red troops were setting fire to everything as they left each town. This added greatly to the discomfiture of the Nazis, for while they advanced steadily they found every town in flames and its water system blown up. They suffered much from thirst. But even worse were the strong Russian counter-attacks, below, which let them pass and then attacked their flanks and communication lines.

DRIVING HARD, the main Nazi force struck north of the Pripet Marshes area, taking Brest-Litovsk within a few days, and moving northward to cut off the Baltic States. Another Nazi push went south of the Pripet toward the Ukraine. Without the initiative that accompanies a surprise attack, the Red forces were temporarily at a loss. The bulk of them had been awaiting the attack in the Ukraine and their transportation northward took time. Meanwhile, Nazi pincers moved on in an effort to encircle Minsk.

ON JULY 3 THE NAZIS entered Minsk, much of which had been destroyed by the retreating Reds. Near Bialystok the Minsk pincer army joined with one from Grodno, trapping 400,000 Red soldiers. The Nazis announced "resistance of the Soviet armies is broken." However, the trapped Red units continued fighting, and weeks later the Nazis admitted they were still fighting; many eventually fought their way out. Within two weeks the Nazis had advanced almost 200 miles. Yet they were still far from any vital objective.

250

HITLER'S COLUMNS EXPECTED to be welcomed as liberators of the Ukraine but instead the peasants, such as these who have destroyed their home and barn but saved their cow, organized guerrilla bands to harass them. The main Nazi thrust into the Ukraine by-passed Przemysl, moved on Lwow. In a large-scale battle engaging 4,000 tanks the Reds stopped this drive until June 30 when Hungarian reinforcements forced withdrawal from Lwow. Under Marshal Budenny the Reds slowly withdrew.

STATUES OF LENIN and Stalin were torn down by the Nazis. Schools, libraries and museums were ruthlessly destroyed. This picture was taken in the marketplace of a small Ukrainian city.

RUMANIAN DICTATOR Antonescu visited the front but he had little cause for rejoicing. The Red army was inflicting terrible losses on Rumanian troops. Red bombers fired the Rumanian oil fields.

WRECKAGE LEFT AFTER A BATTLE NEAR MINSK IN WHICH THOUSANDS OF ROARING TANKS, PLANES, AND MEN CLASHED

MONG THE MOST DESTRUCTIVE IN HISTORY, SUCH BATTLES WERE TITANIC INFERNOS SPREAD OVER AREAS MILES DEEP.

Roosevelt, Churchill, and aides attending church services during their historic meeting at sea, Aug. 1940.

THE ATLANTIC CHARTER

HITLER had hoped his "crusade" against the Soviets would bring, if not peace with England, at least complacency and no aid to Russia. But Churchill swiftly disillusioned him the very day Russia was invaded, declaring: "Any man or state who fights against Nazism will have our aid. . . . The Russian danger is our danger and the danger of the United States, just as the cause of any Russian fighting for his hearth and home is the cause of free men and free people in every quarter of the globe. . . ." Echoing Churchill's remarks, President Roosevelt paid tribute to the "magnificent" fight of the Red army and dispatched Harry Hopkins to Moscow to learn what the Russians needed most. On July 12 Britain and Russia signed a pact of mutual assistance. Similar pacts between Russia and the Polish and Czech governments-in-exile followed; Soviet Russia agreed not to recognize her move into Poland in 1939. On Aug. 2 the United States and the Soviets exchanged notes recognizing Nazism as their common enemy. Meanwhile, the R.A.F., in an effort to aid Russia, launched mass daylight raids on Germany and the occupied countries. England and United States were preparing to pool their resources to aid Russia while England faced the task of opening a second front in Europe. On Aug. 12 President Roosevelt and Churchill met secretly at sea aboard the *Prince of Wales* off the coast of Newfoundland to discuss these problems and set up the guiding principles for the peace which was to come when victory had been won. Both countries were fully represented by their military, naval, and supply chiefs, and for three days the discussions went on. The result of this conference, the Atlantic Charter, was announced on August 14. Its chief points pledged no territorial aggrandizement, no territorial changes that were not in accord with the wishes of the peoples concerned, the right of all people to choose their own form of government, free and equal accession to the raw materials and trade of the world by all nations, disarmament after the war. On Aug. 15 Churchill and Roosevelt sent a joint letter to Stalin, who had signified his acceptance of the Atlantic Charter, suggesting a conference in Moscow on increased aid to Russia. Stalin immediately invited delegations. The U.S. sent Harry Hopkins and W. Averell Harriman while Britain sent energetic Lord Beaverbrook.

"The Enemy Is Cruel and Implacable ..."

To both England and the U.S. the invasion of Russia brought a sharp sense of having been given more time to prepare, build up their armies, mobilize their industries. How much time, it was realized, depended almost entirely on one man—short, stocky, silent Joseph Stalin—on how well he had prepared Russia for war, how well he could lead its 190,000,000 people. Of Stalin and the Red army the average American or Englishman knew little that gave cause for hope. Probably no man had been more maligned. Few military experts gave the Red army longer than two weeks. The political collapse of the Soviet and revolution were universally predicted. However, twenty-odd years before Stalin had helped fight off one invasion of Russia. Ever since he had been preparing to fight off another. No country was better prepared for the onslaught. Stalin emerged as a great, determined war leader and world statesman, a man who had the confident backing of all his people, who could mobilize and inspire them to victory and win allies among nations. Warning of Russia's danger, he said on July 5, "The enemy is cruel and implacable. He is out to seize our lands . . . to restore the rule of landlords, to restore tsarism, to destroy national culture . . . the issue is whether the people of the Soviet Union shall remain free or fall into slavery." He called for a vigorous "scorched earth" policy and incessant guerrilla war: . . . "conditions must be made unbearable for the enemy . . . they must be hounded and annihilated at every step." Lastly, he made it clear that Russia was not fighting a revolutionary war, nor a war for territory, but a "national" war "in defense of our country." After his speech there was no doubt that Russia was solidly united behind Stalin's leadership and would follow him to the last.

At 63 Stalin faced the greatest task of his life: saving Russia.

To Defense Commissar Timoshenko went the job of saving Moscow.

Voroshilov, who mechanized the Red army, moved to Leningrad.

Famous cavalry expert Budenny was assigned to defend the rich Ukraine.

STALIN

Patiently easy-going yet determined, a theoretician and an intuitive politician, coldly analytical and frank, pipe-smoking Joseph Stalin has had the most remarkable career of all the world's leaders. His story is that of the Russian revolution. For years the most controversial figure in world politics, charged by his political enemies with every crime imaginable, Stalin won the respect and confidence of free peoples everywhere by the skillful way in which he organized and led Russia's fight against Nazism. His name will go down in history as the man who developed socialist Russia in twenty short years from a backward, illiterate, undeveloped agricultural country to one of the most highly educated, powerful, modern industrial countries of the world. Stalin's energetic political career began when he was expelled from a seminary in his native Georgia in southern Russia for studying Marx. He got himself a job reading scientific instruments in the Tiflis Observatory, spent his nights organizing oil workers, studying more Marx and Lenin. Unions and strikes were illegal under the Czar and it was there that Stalin, much harried by the police, first developed the determination, the patience, the political sense, organizing ability, and "long view" of events for which he is now famous. These elements in his character were forged in the unsuccessful 1905 revolution and the decade that followed when Stalin struck out the police terror, built the Communist party into a formidable, well-knit revolutionary organization. When Lenin died in 1924 the job of building socialism had only begun. Yet through Stalin's three Five-Year Plans, Russia was industrialized, her farms mechanized and collectivized, her living standards raised, her people educated. Those were grim, hard, struggling years for Russia, years of toil and sacrifice. There were blunders and mistakes. Stalin himself had to reprimand the overzealousness of the Communists in collectivizing the farms. There was sabotage and suffering. At times, it would seem today, only the determination of Stalin bridged the gap between chaos and socialism. But the plans did succeed, and when the war broke out Russia was well on the way to becoming one of the most powerful industrial nations of the world. The Five-Year Plans were the backbone of Russia's preparedness. Without them the Red army would have been powerless. As head of Russia's Communists, Stalin has been the bold, resolute leader of the "dictatorship of the proletariat." He has struck with full vigor at anything within Russia which threatened its life. Yet in 1936 Stalin voluntarily insisted that education and socialism had advanced far enough to relax the "dictatorship." Correspondents have noted his warmth, personal magnetism, that he laughs easily and often. He refuses credit for Russia's advances, gives it to "the people." When he is applauded by an audience, he applauds too—but he is applauding "the people." When H. G. Wells asked him what he was doing to change the world, he said: "Not so very much."

STALIN WAS BORN JOSEF DJUGUSHVILI on Dec. 21, 1879, in Gori, near Tiflis. His peasant father had become a cobbler and earned little. Fellow revolutionaries gave him the name "Stalin," meaning "steel" in Russian, during his underground days before the revolution.

STALIN'S MOTHER, Ekatrina Djugushvili, was determined he should not be a cobbler. When he was nine she sent him to the Gori ecclesiastical school to become a priest. Interviewed years later by H. R. Knickerbocker, she said Stalin had always been "a good boy."

THIS RARE PICTURE of Stalin (XX) was probably taken about 1894 when he was graduated to the Tiflis Theological Seminary. He began his political career at 15.

AT THE SEMINARY Stalin became acquainted with Marx's work, quarreled with the corrupt Russian priests, was expelled as a "radical" for organizing trade unions.

BY 1900 STALIN was the leader of the revolutionary movement in the Caucasus. He is shown here urging the oil workers to strike. His fame spread through Russia.

THE CZARIST POLICE hunted Stalin daily. This record was taken from their files after the revolution. He was arrested 8 times.

THIS IS THE SIBERIAN log cabin to which Stalin was exiled from 1913 to 1917. Exiled eight times, he escaped seven times.

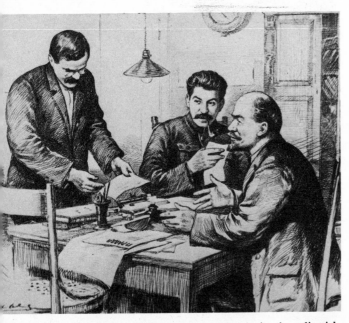

MOLOTOV, STALIN, AND LENIN are shown in the editorial offices of *Pravda*, of which Stalin was editor. Stalin corresponded with Lenin for years before he met him. In 1910, when Lenin formed the Communist party, Stalin joined it immediately.

STALIN WAS A LEADER OF THE RED ARMY, then ragged, starving, poorly armed. His superior ability as a strategician defeated the counter-revolutionary armies in three major battles—Leningrad, Smolensk, and Tsaritsyn.

257

STALIN, LENIN, the founder of the Soviet Union and father of the revolution, and M. I. Kalinin, now president of the Supreme Council of the U.S.S.R., posed for this picture in 1919 when Stalin was People's Commissar for Nationalities. The Czarist regime had attempted to Russianize the 160-odd nationalities within its borders, suppressed their languages, maintained its own rule by keeping the various national groups fighting one another, refused them school and economic development. To win full support of these national groups for the Soviet Stalin encouraged these national cultures and tongues, insisted on the fullest political equality for every nationality and race, and the economic and educational development of every region. This was his greatest contribution to Marxist theory.

LEON TROTSKY, who had not been a Bolshevik before the revolution, fought Lenin's "N.E.P." policy of 1921 which temporarily delayed collectivization. Lenin and Stalin argued socialism could not be built without the fullest support of the people, that they were not ready for socialism. Trotsky was voted down. On Lenin's motion in 1922 Stalin was elected general secretary of the party. With a handful of followers Trotsky continued to oppose Lenin and Stalin, who had become Lenin's right-hand man.

BUT STALIN, shown here crossing the Kremlin yard to a party conference, decisively defeated Trotsky in every debate and denounced him as traitorous. Trotsky was exiled in 1929. Years later, in 1937, Trotsky was found to be working with the Nazis for the overthrow of the Soviets. Trotsky's agents included eight Red army generals and numerous top Soviet officials. At a public trial they confessed their guilt and were executed. Trotsky was assassinated by one of his own followers in 1940.

STALIN'S CHIEF ADVISERS on foreign policy were Molotov and Maxim Litvinov. In the 1930's, certain war was coming, Stalin sent Litvinov to the League of Nations in the hope of making it a stronghold of collective security. Though Litvinov was the ablest diplomat at Geneva, he was unable to prevent the continual appeasement of the Fascist powers, wrecking the League.

MEANWHILE, WITH ORJONIKIDZE Stalin was pushing the development of heavy industry, particularly at Magnitogorsk, deep in the Urals, where they built one of the largest steel centers. By a series of Five-Year Plans which were fulfilled by the Soviet people with much suffering and sacrifice the Soviet Union was made practically independent of the world and more fully prepared for war.

N 1935 STALIN decided the U.S.S.R. had progressed ar enough in education and industry to permit the extension of democratic rights to all citizens. At his suggestion a new constitution was drafted to replace that of 1924 which, while permitting non-Communists to hold office, barred rich kulaks and others from voting. The new constitution, adopted in 1936, introduced universal, equal, and direct suffrage with secret ballots. Stalin warned the party it must reduce inefficiency, bureaucracy, and produce results if it was to maintain its leadership under the new system. Above: Stalin voting.

STALIN'S OFFICE in the Kremlin is well furnished but not magnificent. He lives in a small apartment elsewhere in the massive Kremlin, but also has a comfortable country house outside Moscow. His pay is very small. He has three children by two wives, both of whom died. He has taken pains to see that his children receive no special privileges because he is their father, once revamped Soviet education because he felt much of what his children were learning was unimportant. His second wife was given a religious burial. Unlike Mussolini and Hitler, he dislikes pomp and ceremony, can take criticism. He suffers from a heart murmur. His intimates: Voroshilov, Molotov, Kalinin with whom he has been working closely for forty years.

RUSSIA'S SCORCHED EARTH

IN his July 5 "scorched-earth" speech
Stalin called for the utter destruction
of everything in the Nazi path. The Russian people carried out the heart-breaking

struction with a thoroughness that dis-
ayed the Nazis. They had never before
countered "total defense." Railways,
idges, power plants, factories were
own up. Villages and cities were
veled. Water systems and granaries
ere destroyed. The fields themselves
ere set afire. Nothing was spared. The
itside world watched this awe-inspiring
ectacle with regret that it had not been
rried out in Europe, now the source of
any Nazi arms.

NAZI PIONEERS SPENT most of their time rebuilding bridges and
railway lines which the Russians had blown up in their retreat. By August
the "scorched-earth" policy had become a major weapon.

RED TROOPS DROVE their own supply train over this river bank when
the danger arose that the train would fall into the hands of the Nazis.
Peasants even knocked holes into buckets they had to leave.

WAITING FOR THE NAZIS to pass by while their village burns, these
peasants and thousands like them joined guerrilla bands to carry out
Stalin's order to "hound and annihilate" the Nazis.

NOTHING CAUSED THE NAZIS more discomfort than the blowing up of the water systems. During June, July, and August they advanced during an intense heat wave and suffered much from thirst.

NAZI SS TROOPS RUSH to save one of their trucks after Soviet guerrillas set fire to a near-by building in a surprise raid. The guerrillas took special delight in harassing the picked SS troops.

ALL THE NAZIS FOUND in the Baltic port of Talinin were wrecked docks, shattered factories, leveled warehouses. Somehow the railroad cars in the foreground escaped complete destruction.

NEARLY EVERY VILLAGE was set afire by the peasants as the Nazis approached. Later, when the rains began, and still later, when winter set in, the Nazis suffered acutely from lack of shelters.

EVEN THE GREAT DNIEPERSTROY dam, one of the greatest power projects in the world, was blown up by the Red army. Built by years of toil, it was a symbol of Russia's growing industry.

TRAPPED BY THE WATERS released when the dam blew up, the Nazis lost many men and much equipment. Trucks are shown here slogging through receding waters.

THIS DESTROYED REFINERY was only one of thousands of plants which were blown up after the machinery had been moved eastward. "No, this is not a joyful march," wrote one Nazi soldier to his family. "The weather is dreadful, the lack of food is hard to bear, and, what is worse, the Russians are attacking without pause. But our boys can stand it. . . . They only hope that help will soon come."

Well-trained and equipped members of the civil voluntary defense society led the organization of guerrilla warfare.

Russia's Unconquerable Guerrilla Fighters

THOUGH the Nazi war machine was able to plunge deep into Russia, it was never able to maintain anything like a stable rear. The cause of its troubles were several million guerrillas, who constantly raided their lines, captured high officers, blew up newly repaired bridges, attacked Nazi-held villages at night, kept the Red army informed of troop movements, ambushed tank columns. The Soviets had for years considered the people a part of the Red army and vice versa. Consequently the Red guerrillas were no untrained, pitchfork army, but organized, trained, and equipped under Red army leadership. A voluntary civilian defense group

known as Osoaviakhim formed the backbone of the guerrilla organization. It included men, women, grandparents and children. On the opposite page typical guerrillas a shown in action against the Nazis. They knew how to p out an incendiary bomb and how to stop a tank with bottle of gasoline. In the prewar years nearly every colle tive farm's Osoaviakhim received rifles, machine guns, an tank guns, mine throwers, grenades, and two-way radi They specialized in American-style Indian fighting, shar shooting, and hand-to-hand fighting. Their courageous fig immobilized almost 1,500,000 Nazi soldiers in the rear.

Guerrillas from a collective farm move off to the forests from which they harass Nazi supply lines. Note girls with rifles.

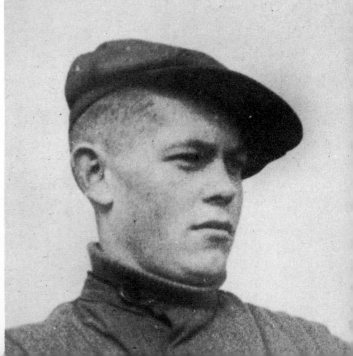

265

COSSACK GUERRILLA CAVALRYMEN, shown here receiving gas masks from a Red army man, inflicted heavy losses on Nazi bases in surprise raids. Their mobility made it virtually impossible for the Nazis to catch them. Nazi punitive forces sent out to destroy them were usually ambushed and annihilated in the forests.

TWO GUERRILLAS from the Leningrad area pictured outside their forest base. Guerrillas who were captured always tried to lead Nazi troops into prearranged traps at the risk of their lives.

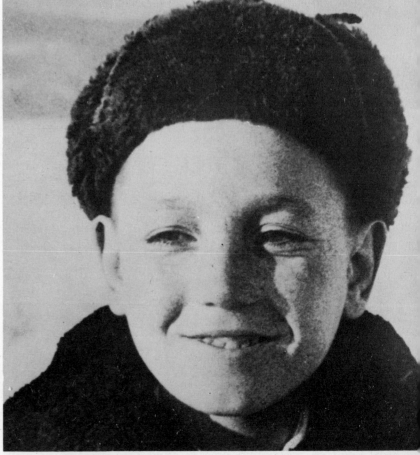

SIGNING THE GUERRILLA OATH: "I, a Red guerrilla, swear to my comrades in arms that I shall be brave, disciplined, and merciless to the enemy. To the end of my days I shall remain faithful to my country, my party, and my leader Stalin. If I break this sacred oath, may severe punishment be meted out to me at the hands of guerrillas."

VANYA ANDRIANOV, 14-year-old guerrilla, won the Order of the Red Army for slipping into a Nazi camp, learning the strength of the unit and guiding the guerrilla attack. Children acted as scouts, lookouts, and messengers, and were often tortured by Nazis who sought to find guerrilla hideouts.

A GUERRILLA SHOWS a white-robed Red army scout how his native Ukrainian village, occupied by the Nazis, can be attacked. The bitter cold and deep snows of the Russian winter forced the poorly equipped Nazis to stay close to villages. Therefore the partisans made special efforts to fire all buildings during their surprise raids. Whole areas, some of them containing several hundred square miles, were liberated by guerrillas, who successfully defended their "pockets" and waited for the advancing Red army.

A SCHOOLTEACHER, Muzalevskaya, of the Tula area, won the Soviet Badge of Honor for her bravery. Women guerrillas fought with their menfolk, nursed the wounded, acted as scouts.

A GUERRILLA LEADER decorates one of his men on the field. Whole families fought with unheard-of daring and heroism. For instance, the Balin family near Mozhaisk killed 74 Nazi soldiers, 5 officers, destroyed one tank, 21 trucks, 11 ammunition wagons, 14 horses, and captured 1,200 hand grenades.

Russian air strength was based on bombers, rather than fighters. These men are shown at the controls of a fast medium bomber.

Nazi Air Force Meets Its Equal in Russia

Lt. General Jacob Shmushkevich.

IN the Red air force Goering's Luftwaffe for the first time met a foe their equal in every way. The initial Nazi attack on Soviet airfields, prelude to every Nazi invasion, failed although it destroyed almost 500 planes, because the bulk of Red air strength had been concentrated at scattered bases far from the front around Leningrad, Moscow, and Kiev. The most air-minded people in Europe, the Russians had been the first to develop mass parachute jumping and the towing of gliders. At the outbreak of the war the Russians had about 10,000 front-line planes; they also possessed some thirty factories with an estimated production of 20,000 planes a year. In 1936 Russia had begun training 150,000 pilots; in 1941 she had eight men to replace each loss. While the most modern Red fighters were excellent, few had been built by July 1941. This constituted the Soviet's most serious air weakness, for her strength had long been concentrated in bombers, particularly heavy bombers. The Russian policy of constant attack, developed by Red Air Commander Lt. Gen. Jacob Shmushkevich, kept Nazi Stukas and Messerschmitts fighting dogfights when they were supposed to be blasting a path for Nazi tank columns and mechanized forces. During the first months Nazi and Russian plane losses rose to incredible figures. Both sides lost a plane every ten minutes.

Russian bombers taxiing into position before taking off to bomb Nazi tank columns. Each plane carries 4,400 pounds of bombs.

HIDDEN by a camouflage screen, this snub-nosed fighter plane is about to be pulled out onto the field for a take-off. This fighter is an improved model of the famous snub-nosed Chatos pursuit planes which the Russians gave to Loyalist Spain. In Spain they proved themselves to be superior to most of the Nazi and Italian planes flying for the Fascist forces and against which they were pitted.

THIS twin-motored Nazi bomber was brought down by Soviet fighters outside Leningrad. Losses of both Soviet and Nazi air fleets were fantastic in the early months of the war. In August the Russians admitted they had lost more than 500 planes, and estimated Nazi losses at 5,000. The United States and Britain agreed to give Russians 500 planes a month to help stem the German advance.

On Aug. 7 the "annihilated" Red air force bombed Berlin and Königsberg and other points deep in Germany. The men on these pages, known as "Stalin Falcons," were among those who participated in those raids, which continued as long as the Russian armies were able to hold the Nazis within bombing range of Germany. In the Ukraine the Soviets made much use of parachutists and in the first week of the war dropped them into Rumania. At Smolensk the strength of the Russian fighter force dealt heavy counter-blows to the Luftwaffe, making it possible for the Soviet armies to hold off the Nazi advance for over six weeks. Soviet women flyers ferried planes to front from factories in Urals.

A medium bomber prepares for a night flight.

Junior Lieutenant Sergeant M. I. Kolomeets.

Lieutenant N. I. Koltyshev.

Lieutenant A. M. Koviazin.

LIEUTENANT VERSHININ shot down two Nazi fighters accompanying bombers on his first day of combat—a Junkers 88 and a Messchmidt 109. His plane was adapted from a U. S. model.

FIGHTER PILOT KAMENSHCHIKOV stands behind a Nazi bomber he brought down. At the time this picture was taken he had already won the decoration "Hero of the Soviet Union."

FIGHTER PILOT LT. DMITRIYEV brought down five Nazi planes the first week of invasion. He is shown here in the cockpit of I-16, a second-line plane armed with two 20 mm. cannon.

LIEUTENANT IVAN AKSYARIN shot down five Nazi bombers in one afternoon. When out of ammunition Soviet airmen tried to clip tail or wings of Nazi planes with their own plane's propeller.

THIS DRAMATIC PICTURE was made a second after a Russian tank was hit by the Nazi anti-tank gun in the foreground during a Russian counter-attack near Leningrad. The main Nazi Baltic drive toward Leningrad had started from East Prussia and overwhelmed the Red defenders of Kaunas after a two-day battle and taken the Lithuanian capital Vilna. Riga was captured on July 1. On July 10 the Finns launched a new drive against Russian defenses along the Karelian peninsula but failed, and it was not until August 15 that a new drive took Sortavella at the northern end of Lake Ladoga. Aug. 18 Russia offered, through United States, peace terms to Finla which involved, according to Secretary Hull, "the making of ter torial concessions by Russia to Finland." Partly to show her go faith, partly because they were needed in the south, Russia withdr 15 divisions and allowed the Finns to take Viipuri and advance their old border on Aug. 30. But Finland, firmly in the Nazi gr refused to negotiate or to talk peace.

WHAT FRIGHTENED THESE NAZIS is not known, but from their terror-stricken faces, particularly that of the soldier on the right, it must have been awesome. This is one of the few pictures the Nazis ever released showing their troops looking harassed or frightened. Nazi soldiers and communiqués continually complained of the ferocity of the Russians. Instead of surrendering when surrounded, the Nazis grumbled, the Reds fought on until the last man was dead, exacting a heavy toll from Nazis who thought their job was done when they trapped Red units. They denounced as "deceitful and inhuman" the Red tactics of letting advance units pass hidden fortifications without firing on them and suddenly bombarding at close range the unsuspecting main body of troops while the advance unit was ambushed further ahead. Meanwhile, in the Ukraine the armies of Marshal Budenny yielded slowly. Though the Nazis had occupied great areas, they were as far away from their main objective, the destruction of the Red army, as they had been in June.

GERMAN TROOPS ENTERED KIEV on Sept. 20 after hammering on the city's defenses since July 23. Budenny's armies had permitted themselves to be outflanked while they carried out Stalin's order to "bleed the German armies white." Then, when they were virtually trapped, they retreated, blowing up the great Dnieper dam on August 25. On Sept. 19 they withdrew from Kiev, again making a daring escape. The Nazis found little haven in Kiev, for the Reds had mined virtually every building and left the power station intact so that the Nazis, turning on the power, would blow themselves to pieces. Discovering the Russian trick, the Nazis dug out 10,000 mines in three days. But five days later much of the city blew up in their faces when Red time-mines exploded.

Much harassed, the Nazis pushed on after Budenny's armies.

Nazi motorcyclist pushes through another burning village.

EANWHILE, AT SMOLENSK the battle still raged. Though azi spearheads moved far beyond Smolensk, Russian spearheads oved equally deep behind German lines. Cut off behind German lines, Red troops "disintegrated," fleeing into the woods from which they raided Nazi bases. After a titanic three-month battle the Reds retreated on Aug. 18, leaving Smolensk in ruins.

275

Russia's Mud

ABOVE: A NAZI FIELD KITCHEN stuck in the mud in August. Note that the horse on the left has fallen down. Soldier in foreground is advancing to hook chain onto a tank. The Nazis knew about Russia's autumn mud before they started but they expected campaign to be over no later than the end of July. But in November, Nazis were still struggling in the mud on many roads (below).

ALTHOUGH the Nazis were claiming mud was delaying their advance in July, Russia's torrential autumn rains did not begin until late August and they continued until late in September. The heaviest within memory of most Russians, they produced practically impassable roads such as that in which these Nazi tanks are stuck. While the mud also reduced Red mobility, it hurt the Nazis most. Russian artillery and planes were able to hammer to pieces bogged-down Nazi tank columns. Most of all, the mud gave Russians more time. The mud did not prevent the Reds from attacking and at Yelna they smashed the Nazi 28th, 106th, 161st Infantry, and the 7th and 14th Motorized Divisions.

THE NAZIS DUG IN at Smolensk to stabilize the front, but Timoshenko, dealing the Germans their first defeat, swept them back and trapped eight divisions. With the coming of colder weather the Nazis regained their mobility and the Russians again retreated. The first snows found the Nazis, having swept around Poltava, advancing on the important industrial city, Kharkov. Below, Nazi scouts are seen sweeping around abandoned Red motorized artillery. In the south the Nazis, while failing to take Odessa, cut off the Crimea. The people of Odessa put up a courageous battle, making and supplying their own weapons until Oct. 16, when they were overcome.

THIS RUSSIAN TANK DRIVER was killed as he escaped from his crippled medium tank in the Leningrad area. Nazi communiqués grumbled because Red tank crews did not surrender when their tank was put out of action, but fled to any near-by cover from which they continued to fight with grenades and automatic rifles. Such tactics, backed by fierce Russian determination to stop the Nazis, slowed the drive toward Leningrad. Continuous Russian counter-attacks, such as the one below, along the Luga river held the Nazis until another column, moving eastward, swept through Staraya Russa, cutting the Leningrad-Moscow railway and the Russians withdrew.

The Siege of Leningrad

WHEN Narva, Kingissep, and Novgorod fell on Aug. 21 the Nazi threat to Leningrad became a siege. Optimistic Nazi communiqués announced the imminent fall of the second largest Soviet city, a powerful industrial center, and the Baltic port from which the Red navy was raiding Nazi convoys to Finland and Sweden. But the day Novgorod fell Marshal Voroshilov called on Leningrad's millions to rally to the city's defense. "Let us create," read his dramatic proclamation, "new units of the people's army to prepare to defend the city with arms in hands. Let us rise as one in defense of our city, our hearths, our families, our honor, and our liberty." The response of the people was instantaneous in its character. New fortifications were built and old ones improved. Cannon, munitions, tanks poured from the shops of the city. Every able-bodied man and woman became a soldier in some way. ". . . a crime," fumed the frustrated Nazis, "putting even the defense of Warsaw deep in the shade." The factories and machine shops fashioned armoured trains carrying heavy naval guns which, moving on the many railroad lines around the city, were able to lay down heavy barrages on Nazi concentrations miles from the city.

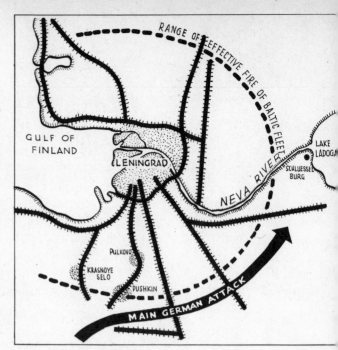

THE NAZIS MOVED SLOWLY EASTWARD to Schuesselbe on the tip of Lake Ladoga. They captured it on Sept. 9 after heav fighting. This completed the encirclement of Leningrad.

THE RED NAVY, BASED AT KRONSTADT, played a major part in defense of the city. Red warships were able to move through the Neva which permitted them to shell the Nazis at any point ten miles outside the city limits. This was one of the main reasons why Nazis moved on to Schuesselberg, which is out of range of the Red fleet's big guns. Communication with Moscow was kept up by radi and planes and by a road around Lake Ladoga and later across its ice covered surface. Nazi threats to annihilate the city only spurred o defenders, whose counterattacks, complained the Nazis, kept the from concentrating their forces. See map above.

THE WORKERS' BRIGADES DRILLED CONSTANTLY to defend the city house by house. A maze of strong fortifications were built through the streets. Nearly everyone in the city, regardless of his profession, participated; Shostakovich, famous Soviet composer, for example, served as an air-raid warden. Production in the factories increased in proportion to city's peril.

WELL-CONCEALED GUNS AND FORTIFICATIONS kept the Nazis outside the city, although early in October they managed to reach the suburbs. However, Red forces dislodged them within a few days. Hangö, the Soviet base on the tip of Finland, held out until Dec. 9, when Nazi-Finnish troops finally battered their way through its fortifications.

THOUSANDS OF NAZIS SURRENDERED to Red forces, whose incessant counterattacks took a heavy toll of the besiegers, and never permitted them to concentrate enough forces to strike a decisive blow. With the opening of the Soviet winter offensive many villages were recaptured from the invaders, but the siege of Leningrad was not broken until Feb. 13.

THE DEFENSE OF MOSCOW

On Oct. 7 the Nazis unleashed a mighty two-pronged offensive with almost two million men in a last desperate attempt to take Moscow before the bitter Russian winter set in. One prong smashed toward Kalinin from the Valdai Hills while the other, moving from the central front, took Orel on Oct. 8 and Bryansk on Oct. 12. Though his troops had conquered most of European Russia, the only major Soviet cities Hitler had been able to take were Kiev and Odessa—and only after a long and costly struggle. The ultimate goal of the Nazis—the destruction of the Soviet armies—was far from achievement. The Soviet armies were not only intact but their resistance grew stronger. Hitler needed the capture of Moscow to sustain his prestige, already badly mauled, and to spur morale at home and in the field. But the people of Russia were determined not to yield, if necessary, to carry on from the Urals.

In July the people of Moscow had gone into the fields outside the city to dig trenches and tank traps. More fortifications were built within the city. The people took the Nazi threat calmly. "Everyone," reported Life magazine, "had his job to do and did it."

OSCOW'S WORKER BRIGADES manned the inner defenses of city to relieve the maximum number of Red army troops for the nt-line fighting at Tula, Vyazma, and Bryansk. Thousands of men and children, historic treasures of the Soviets, and much chinery were evacuated to the east. Correspondents who had seen the panic of Paris were amazed at the calmness with which men and women shouldered guns, built fortifications, prepared for a long siege, and the house-to-house defense of the city if necessary. Below: The finishing touches are put on a tankette for winter warfare with the Nazis only 65 miles away. Munitions production spurted upward.

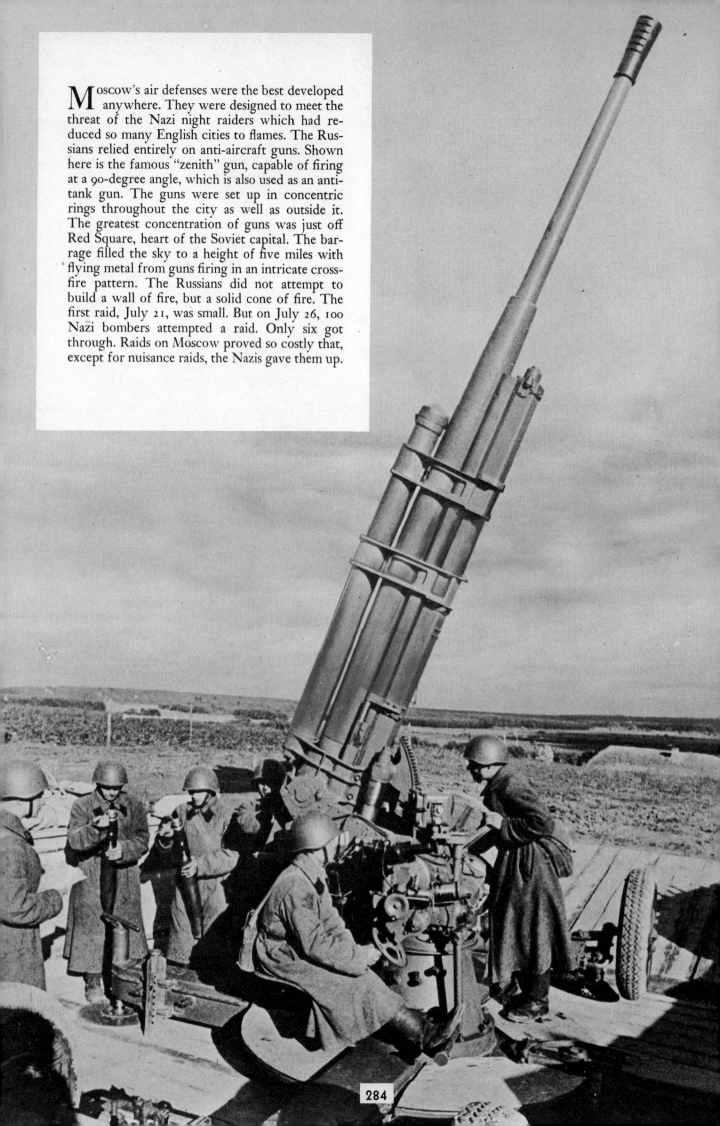

Moscow's air defenses were the best developed anywhere. They were designed to meet the threat of the Nazi night raiders which had reduced so many English cities to flames. The Russians relied entirely on anti-aircraft guns. Shown here is the famous "zenith" gun, capable of firing at a 90-degree angle, which is also used as an anti-tank gun. The guns were set up in concentric rings throughout the city as well as outside it. The greatest concentration of guns was just off Red Square, heart of the Soviet capital. The barrage filled the sky to a height of five miles with flying metal from guns firing in an intricate cross-fire pattern. The Russians did not attempt to build a wall of fire, but a solid cone of fire. The first raid, July 21, was small. But on July 26, 100 Nazi bombers attempted a raid. Only six got through. Raids on Moscow proved so costly that, except for nuisance raids, the Nazis gave them up.

OWERFUL ANTI-AIRCRAFT GUNS such as this took care of the area below the fire of e zenith guns. False rooftops were painted on Red Square and its famous red glass stars were ainted a dull color. The Kremlin was carefully camouflaged with false shadows and windows.

TRAINED FOR THEIR JOB for years, Moscow fire fighters worked efficiently and calmly. Every citizen participated in A.R.P.

L MOSCOW'S SCHOOLS, nurseries, and apartments had been uipped with air-raid shelters for years. These children are shown ing their suppers in the shelter of their nursery. At night thou- ds slept in the subways as the people of London had done a few nths before. Everyone between the age of sixteen and sixty gave e night or day a week to the air-raid precautionary system of his neighborhood and another to his factory. As a fire-precautionary measure the lofts and attics of all buildings were filled with several feet of sand. But Moscow's greatest danger came from the approach- ing Nazi armies, which pushed ever closer. By July most Moscow factories and vital equipment were being moved eastward. Moscow's citizens calmly prepared for any eventuality.

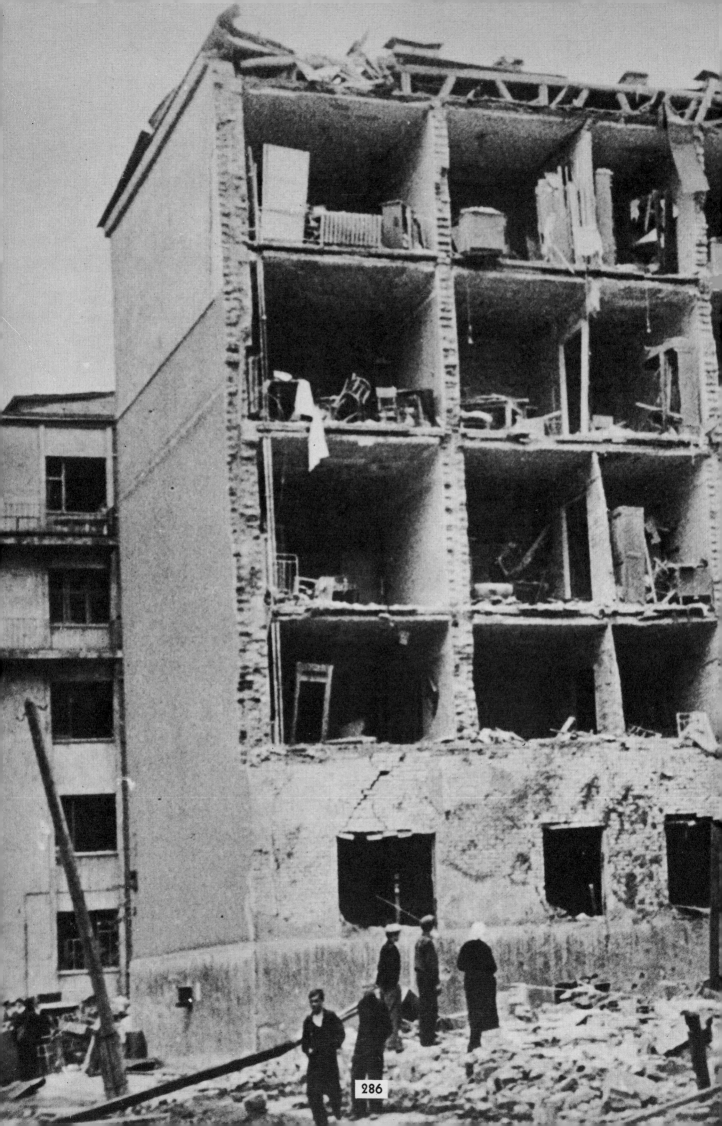

A Nazi bomb load knocked the entire wall off this Moscow apartment house. A section of the Kremlin was also damaged. However, compared to London, Moscow's damage was slight. Below is one of the Nazi bombers brought down by Moscow's intense anti-aircraft fire. One official of an English commission, sent to help organize civilian defense, explained to a U. S. reporter that teaching Moscow about air defense would be like "teaching the New York Yankees baseball."

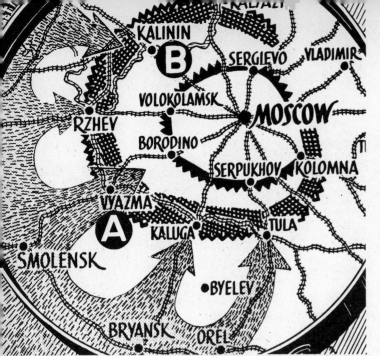

THIS CLOSE-UP of the Moscow area shows the main Nazi drives on Moscow. On Oct. 12 the Reds were driven from Vyazma and the Nazis smashed through to Borodino.

On Oct. 14 the Nazi armored units smashed into Kalinin and Mozhaisk, bringing the Nazis within sixty miles of the Soviet capital. That night the Moscow radio said: "Comrades, Moscow is in danger! The enemy is on the point of reaching the capital," and gave detailed instructions of where to get rifles, how to build barricades, and make hand grenades. As Moscow's semi-military civilian brigades marched off to the front, her newspapers, ever conscious of the time and materials that went into every gun, warned: "Lost arms, lost honor. Guard your arms better than your life. From every stone on the approaches of Moscow the enemy must be met with fire and steel." On Oct. 19, while titanic battles raged from Kalinin to Tula in a great semi circle about Moscow, Stalin declared a state of siege in Moscow, and government, foreign correspondents, and diplomats were moved eastward to Kubyishev. However, Stalin remained behind to direct personally the defense of the capital with Marshal Timoshenko. "No retreat" was the order of the day. Volunteers from Moscow tank factories went to the front line to repair damaged tanks on the battlefields. The prospect of facing another London or Leningrad filled the Nazis with rage and indignation.

NAZI MOTORIZED INFANTRY, who have just outflanked Red troops on the other side of the hill, await the command to pinch them off. Heavy Russian counter-attacks on Oct. 22 drove the Nazis back in the Kalinin area. But renewed Nazi charges carried them into Kalinin on Oct. 31 and through the outer defenses of Tula where the greatest Nazi tank forces were making a furious effort to break through. Tank battles raged over areas miles deep as steel monsters, spitting fire, hurled themselves on one another in the midst of screaming shell fire; men who lived through it described it later as an "inferno." Embattled Russia called for a second front as the ferocious struggle at Tula continued. But Britain was far from being ready to invade the Nazi-held continent.

REDS MET EVERY NAZI CHARGE with a furious counter-attack and on Nov. 3 a major counter-offensive began at Kalinin and opened at Tula a day later. It not only stopped the Nazis but drove them back, killing thousands. With the initiative now in their hands, the Reds announced the German drive on Moscow had been def- initely stopped. In Red Square, on Nov. 8, the anniversary of the Communist revolution, Stalin declared "Another few months, another half year, one year maybe, and Hitlerite Germany must burst under the weight of its own crimes. The German Fascist invaders are facing disaster."

RUSSIAN TANKS ROARED FORTH in a mighty offensive to smash the stalled Germans as the first snows fell. In Berlin, Nov. 8, Goebbels admitted the possibility of a Nazi defeat for the first time, saying "all the worries and distress which we must all bear in war would pale in the face of the inferno which would await us if we were to lose." With great frankness Stalin admitted 1,748,000 Russian casualties and asserted 4,500,000 Nazis had been killed, wounded, or captured. As he spoke the Red offensive destroyed over 400 tanks and two Nazi regiments at Maloyaroslavets and drove the Nazis back five miles near Tula. Meanwhile, the United States extended a billion dollars in lend-lease aid to Russia and took steps to begin larger ship- ments of supplies for the Red Army.

THE NAZI RETREAT in Russia began when the Red army began its great winter offensive on Dec. 7. The Nazis had not prepared for sub-zero weather, having confidently expected to be in Moscow no later than Sept. 15. Freezing, the Nazis stripped Russian villages of all clothing, begged Berlin for warm coats. Note the man wearing a nightgown for additional protection.

SOVIET COUNTER-OFFENSIVE

THE heavy snows and sub-zero weather of the Russian winter set in late in November as the Nazis finally battered their way to Klim, just fifty miles outside the Soviet capital. Winter found the Nazis ill-prepared. Their overcoats were not warm enough. They had few skis and fewer skiers. Their tanks and mechanized equipment were largely immobilized because their oil was too light. Their guns jammed. The extreme cold made breathing difficult and men needed to rest frequently. Few Nazi planes were equipped with skis, and the Luftwaffe virtually disappeared from the air. Nazi morale sagged as the legend of Nazi invincibility cracked on the defenses of Moscow and the men complained bitterly of their leaders' lack of foresight. Operations were necessarily restricted and the Nazis clung close to villages and towns which afforded them shelter. Against them the Russians, who had made intensive preparations for just this type of winter, sent well-equipped armies of ski troops and cavalry, tanks pulling infantry sleds, and motorized ski sleds to deliver heavy blows to the freezing Nazis.

IN CONTRAST to the Nazi sufferings, the Red army was well clothed and equipped for winter and pressed forward on all fronts. By Dec. 16 they had retaken Klim and Kalinin.

MONSTER CAMOUFLAGED Russian tanks charged through the snow in a series of small encircling movements which gradually bit off hundreds of square miles of Nazi-held territory. By Dec. 17 their drive had reached such proportions that Hitler, acting on "intuition," kicked out Gen. von Brauchitsch and took over command of the Russian campaign himself.

NAZI-HELD VILLAGES were recaptured by the hundreds. Their lack of preparation for severe winter weather forced the Nazis to stick to the villages and towns which the Reds pinched off one by one. On the defensive everywhere the Nazis began building defense fortifications along the old Russian border and along the Bug and Oder rivers in Poland.

ARMORED SKI SLEDS, driven by airplane propellers, enabled the Red troops to flank Nazi strong points and make sudden swift raids, such as the one shown in this picture. The Nazis had no ski sleds, had to flounder through bad roads, and could not operate at all in the open fields. The Russians also used large armored sleds which, filled with infantry, were towed by tanks especially designed to operate in deep snows. The picture below, one of the most remarkable ma[...] during the war, shows the charge of Russian cavalry across a sno[...] covered plain. The shock of seeing hundreds of yelling, saber-swin[...] ing Red cavalrymen charging down on them in a snowstorm so d[...] moralized isolated Nazi units and they often surrendered immediate[...] This picture was made under fire by Soviet cameramen.

THOUSANDS OF RUSSIAN RESERVE TROOPS pushed forward, driving the Nazis backward steadily, although in the Crimea a Nazi Gen. von Rundstedt was smashing back Russian defenders. Nearly every Soviet communiqué told of the recapture of "several hundred villages." Pictured below are two Soviet women ski parachutists who have just been decorated for their bravery under fire. Each has a tommy gun slung about her neck. Soviet parachutists continually dropped behind Nazi lines to wreck their communications; they usually came down in the dead of night because it afforded them more protection and increased the shock of their raids on the Nazis. The Red army also made extensive use of parachute nurses and doctors, dropping them into units that had been cut off temporarily.

The fleeing Nazis abandoned thousands of heavy guns, troop carriers, trucks, and tanks to escape the advancing Red Army.

THIS REMARKABLE ACTION PICTURE was made as the Russians advanced to the outskirts of Mozhaisk in mid-March. In the background can be seen the dim outline of the famous Mozhaisk cathedral. The man in the foreground has just charged up and is about to throw himself on the ground. Meanwhile, in the rear, Marshals Voroshilov and Budenny began training vast reserve armies to help meet the expected Nazi spring offensive, and Marshal Timoshenko, one of the greatest generals produced by the war thus f took over Budenny's perilous post in the Ukraine. In Moscow G Gregory Zhukov replaced Timoshenko as commander of the arm in that area. Northwest of Moscow large guerrilla forces holding s eral towns sallied forth to meet the Red Army.

To ease the strain on their overworked munitions plants, the Russians salvaged much of the equipment won from Nazis.

THE REUNION OF A GUERRILLA FIGHTER and his wife brings happy smiles to the faces of his fellow guerrillas. Scenes like this took place in thousands of villages which had been "liberated from the Nazi yoke." But often there was no happiness. Soldiers and guerrillas frequently found their loved ones had been murdered by the Nazis or had been driven westward to become slave laborers for the Nazi regime. Even prisoners of war were slaughtered. Orders to the German 60th Motor Infantry Regiment, No. 166-41, reads ". . . it is impermissible to tolerate a humane attitude toward war prisoners. Destruction of the enemy by fire or other weapons must continue until he is rendered completely harmless." Gen. Von Reichenau declared feeding war prisoners "unnecessary humanism," ordered it stopped.

FREEZING NAZIS gave themselves up by the thousands to the advancing Russians. By Jan. 2 Red troops had recaptured Staritsa and Maloyaroslavets. A heavy counter-attack from Leningrad pushed southwest.

THIS UNUSUAL PICTURE shows shivering Nazis waiting in a shallow trench for a Soviet charge. The man lying on the left has frozen to death.

THIS PICTURE WAS TAKEN as Red soldiers charged a Nazi position. By Feb. 8 the Russian armies had pierced the lines of the besiegers of Leningrad and five days later the siege of that city was lifted as the Nazis floundered in the snows of Vyazma and Zaikov. Slicing away at one Nazi position after another, the Reds had pushed their way to Dorogobuzh, fifty miles east of Smolensk, by Feb. 23. At Staraya Russa the entire Nazi 16th Army was encircled and smashed. Hitler now announced that the "Bolsheviks . . . will be annihilatingly defeated by us in the coming summer." Nazi morale at home sagged even more than it did in the field.

THIS NAZI WAS STEALING A SAMOVAR from the home in the background when a guerrilla sniper killed him and his fellow-looter. Nazi troops deliberately destroyed the homes and priceless manuscripts of Tolstoy, Tschaikovsky which had been preserved as cultural museums. Despite availability of firewood, Nazis burned books and manuscripts "to keep warm."

DEMORALIZED NAZIS are shown in the above picture surrendering to Red troops. Between Jan. 1 and Mar. 1 Hitler threw 38 Nazi divisions, totaling 500,000 men, to back up his faltering lines. On Mar. 19 he was forced to recall the generals his intuition had ousted in December. Two months later Goering was to tell of Nazi troubles in Russia: "There was not a front line. . . . There was only a dugout here, a dugout there, a lightly fortified village or a small wood. . . . The Russians were in our rear—in the north, in the center, in the south. Guerrillas blew up railways and ambushed our supplies. Our troops nearly froze. . . . Our engines could not run."

The Nazi Drive Into the Crimea

RED STRETCHER-BEARER KOROVIN brings in a wounded soldier and his gun during the Crimean fighting. The Russians, regardless of danger, always made every effort to save their weapons.

WHILE the determined Red army and heroic people Moscow and Leningrad were fighting for their liv in the north, equally furious battles were raging in t Lower Dnieper region of the Ukraine where Marshal B denny's armies stood their ground time and again until th were outflanked and then made miraculous escapes wi their forces still intact. Aside from the annihilation of B denny's troops, the immediate Nazi objectives in the sou were the great industrial Donets basin around Kharkov a the Caucasian oilfields. With the fall of Kiev after a 69-d siege on Sept. 20 the Nazis unleashed two new drives: o moved on Kharkov while the other, under Gen. von Run stedt, pushed across the Dnieper at Kherson to threaten t Crimea. But the Red army fought the Crimean drive to standstill in a ten-day battle on the narrow isthmus of Pei kop. Finally Rundstedt gave up the siege for the mome to send his tanks eastward, to the Sea of Azov, which th reached on Sept. 22, isolating the Crimea. After much ha fighting this Nazi column took Mariupol and on Oct. battered its way into Taganrog. As it pushed on to Rost Rundstedt finally was able to invade the Crimea. Rostov w taken on Nov. 22. Meanwhile, in the north the Nazi arm took Kharkov on Oct. 25 after weeks of bloody battlin The Russians mobilized every man, woman, and child the Crimea for total defense, just as Leningrad and Mosco had. The people of Sevastopol, Soviet Black Sea port, p pared to emulate those of Russia's two main cities. Bar cades were erected and the citizenry armed for a long sie

THE BLACK SEA FLEET of the Red navy was based at Sevastopol; its loss would seriously cripple control of the Black Sea and the Caucasian defenses. On Nov. 5 the Nazis reached its outer defenses as the Red army split to defend it and Kerch. Although Kerch fe on Nov. 17, Sevastopol stood up under the Nazi hammering with the aid of the Red navy's heavy guns and its civilian defenders.

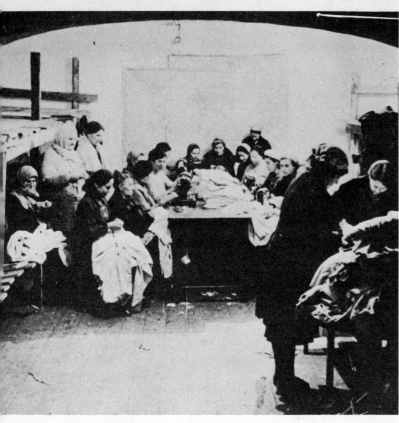

THE HEROIC PEOPLE OF SEVASTOPOL carried on their lives underground during the long siege of the city. Even munitions factories continued production underground.

POWERFUL UNITS of the Red fleet constantly shelled Nazi positions around Sevastopol and landed marines to threaten Nazi lines from the rear on Jan. 6.

THIS UNUSUAL PICTURE OF THE RETAKING of Rostov by the Red army was made on Nov. 29, seven days after the Nazis had occupied the town, as the Russians advanced from house to house. On Nov. 30 the Russians bypassed Taganrog and cut over to the Azov, trapping the Nazis until reinforcements came to their aid. On Dec. 30 the Red army recovered Kerch and seven days later Red navy marines landed at Yalta and Eupatoria, threatening the Nazi rear and lifting the siege of Sevastopol. But on Jan. 19 the Nazis began a sledge-hammer offensive which stopped the Red drive. By the end of May, 1942 the Nazis still held Taganrog, had reoccupied Kerch, and had unleashed an all-out drive to take Sevastopol in a supreme effort to cut off the Black Sea.

THE NAZIS SLAUGHTERED over 500 civilian men, women, and children from Kerch outside that Crimean city when they found they could not hold the city in Jan. 1942. A terrible revenge, it was among the most cold-blooded massacres of the European war. The close-up above shows a mother and her two babies. Note the three-month-old baby lying across her chest. What crime could this infant have committed? Below, the grief-and-horror-stricken people of the city come out to the bloody field to begin the horrible search for the bodies of their loved ones. The woman in the foreground has just found the body of her husband. The massacre enraged Russia. Molotov, reporting on the Kerch massacre and others, promised "punishment for all these incredible crimes."

ALL THE GRIEF AND THE HORROR of war are registered in this dramatic picture of a Russian mother and father who found their son among the slaughtered at Kerch.

YOUTHFUL COMMUNIST guerrillas listen to a Nazi pronounce the death sentence on them with the hope of teaching other guerrillas and recalcitrants a lesson.

BRAVELY—almost eagerly—they climb onto the crude trap that will send them to their death. Scores of partisans died this way. But guerrilla warfare went right on.

WAGONS FILLED WITH THE DEAD had to be pushed through the mud back to the city, where the victims of the Nazi ruthlessness were given a mass burial.

NAZIS LEFT their bodies hanging for days as an example to others. But the Nazis found their terror only deepened Russian hatred—intensified resistance.

LORD BEAVERBROOK AND W. AVERELL HARRIMAN, representing England and the United States, had arrived in Moscow in October 1941 to speed delivery of Anglo-American supplies. On July 12 Britain and Russia had signed a mutual-assistance pact, and on August 2 the United States and Russia exchanged notes which recognized Nazism as their common enemy. Credits were granted the Soviets in both U.S. and England and by early September the first shipments of supplies from the U.S. were arriving at Vladivostok. Other shipments went to Murmansk and Persian Gulf ports. All tanks built in England the week of Sept. 22 were earmarked for Red Army.

Mechanics assembled American trucks landed in Iran, then drove them through the Caucasus to the Red Army.

...E-COVERED CONVOYS braved Nazi raids and Arctic weather ...winter long on the Murmansk route as the stream of supplies ...w. England, keenly aware of the breathing spell and the promise ...ultimate victory in the magnificent fight of the Russians, gave up ...r rights on tanks and planes in order to fulfill Russia's needs

before Hitler's spring offensive. The U.S. extended $1,000,000,000 in lend-lease funds to Russia and promised her 500 tanks a month. But it was not until March that aid began to assume sizable proportions. Meanwhile, the Russians called vigorously for a western front, but neither England nor America was prepared for an invasion yet.

...ULL WING OF R.A.F. FIGHTERS flew to Russia to aid in her defense ...y in September. Assigned to the Murmansk front, R.A.F. pilots are shown ...ng to helmeted Captain Safanov of the Red Air Force. The R.A.F. vigor- ...y participated in the air defense of Murmansk harbor. Meanwhile, indirectly ...elieve Russia, the R.A.F. began heavy raids on Nazi industry from England. ...e bombs fell in Germany in June than the Nazis dropped in England in April.

ONE OF THE MOST DARING R.A.F. FLIERS in Russia, Sgt. Charles Haw, downed so many Nazi bombers that the Russians awarded him the Order of Lenin. As British and American planes replaced their losses, Russians flew Tomahawks, Airacobras, Spitfires, and Hurricanes, but liked their own Stormoviks best.

"SO SORRY..."

SINCE May, when Vichy France gave Japan economic control of French Indo-China, Japanese-U. S. relation had been under increasing strain as Japan moved toward greater power in the Pacific. With the invasion of Russia by Hitler, the Japanese announced their policy was "immutable." It was expected in many quarters that Japan as the eastern Axis partner would attack Vladivostok. But the eastern Red Banner armies had smashed Japanese troops two major "border clashes" in 1938 and 1939 and any doubt about the "immutable" Japanese policy were resolved June 23, when Vichy accepted Japanese demands for military bases and the right of transit for troops. The new Tokyo move menaced Burma, Malaya, and Singapore, well as China's Burma Road, the Philippines, and U. power in the Pacific. President Roosevelt, who for years had maintained a conciliatory policy toward Japan while like most Americans, sympathizing with the Chinese people heroic fight for freedom, made it clear that United State could no longer view Japan's expansion without alarm. July 25 Britain and the U. S. froze Japanese assets. England canceled her own, Burma's, and India's trade treaties with the Japanese. President Roosevelt ordered the calling up of the military forces of the Philippines under Gen. Douglas MacArthur. On Aug. 1 the President placed an embargo shipment of aviation gasoline and oil to Japan while the Dutch followed suit in a stern demonstration that the ABCD powers (America, Britain, China, Dutch), were united and meant business.

JAPANESE AMBASSADOR Kichisaburo Nomura, shown entering the White House, initiated talks with the United States at the end of August "to establish a new basis for U. S. relations with Japan," which was spending almost $7,000,000 a year in America on propaganda. Meanwhile, Tokyo began the economic penetration of strategic Thailand, already overrun with Jap 5th columnists.

THAILAND OFFERED the Japanese direct access to Burma and British Malaya. The fall of these points would greatly endanger the Philippines. To allay U. S. fears Tokyo released optimistic reports of their belief in peace with the United States and cancelled their intended protests against American shipments of oil to Soviet Russia through the Pacific port of Vladivostok.

BY SEPT. 21 SECRETARY HULL and Nomura found themsel deadlocked. The Japanese demanded U. S. aid to the brave Chin be stopped and their "new order" be recognized. This the U. S. fused to do. But as negotiations broke down Tokyo announce was sending Saburo Kurusu to Washington with a new formula continue negotiations for a peaceful settlement.

NOMURA MET KURUSU on his arrival by plane in Washington on Nov. 15. His dramatic flight brought new optimism to the U. S. Although Washington continued to believe there was little hope for peace. Premier Tojo had said on Oct. 26: "Japan must go and develop in ever-expanding progress—there is no retreat. . . . Nothing can stop us. . . . Wars can be fought with ease." Japanese troop transports flowed steadily southward. Meanwhile, Kurusu began his talks and on Nov. 27 saw President Roosevelt. But by Dec. 3 talks had reached an impasse. Yet the Japanese were not ready to give up negotiations, insisted that they continue, reiterated their desire for peace. They made a new appointment with Secretary Hull for December 7th.

AT 2:05 P.M. ON DEC. 7 Nomura and Kurusu arrived at the U. S. State Department to see Secretary Hull. Theirs was one of the most treacherous roles in history. Both men probably knew when this picture was made that Japanese planes were bombing Pearl Harbor, the Philippines, and other U. S. Pacific outposts. Note their bland expressions of serenity.

THE PERFIDIOUS JAPANESE AMBASSADORS LEFT Hull's office trying their best to look like martyrs. Just before they talked to Secretary Hull, word had arrived of the surprise attack on Pearl Harbor. But the report was unconfirmed and Hull restrained his angry denunciation of their government to a note they presented which attacked the United States.

AT 6:30 A.M. on Dec. 7 a Navy supply ship sighted a Japanese sub off the great U.S. Pacific naval base, Pearl Harbor, at Oahu, Hawaii. Within five minutes the sub had been sunk by a U.S. destroyer and plane. Yet no alert was sounded. At 7:02 A.M. Corp. Joseph Lockard, operating the base's aircraft detection system in voluntary practice, located a large fleet of planes 130 miles northeast of Oahu, but his superiors dismissed them as U.S. planes. Yet on Oct. 16 and Nov. 27 Washington had notified Gen. Walter C. Short and Admiral H. E. Kimmel, who commanded U.S. forces at Pearl Harbor, of the imminent danger of a Japanese surprise attack. Neither officer, however, put his forces on alert. At 7:45 a Japanese sub was sighted inside of submarine nets of Pearl Harbor. Ten minutes later large fleet of Japanese dive bombers dropped out of the skies from all sides, turning the ship-filled harbor and near-by Hickam Field into blazing infernos. Spies had given pilots the exact location of hangars, munitions, anti-aircraft guns, and each plane hurled its death load at a specific objective. U.S. soldiers, sailors, and fliers fought heroically amid flaming wreckage to beat off the attack, but the initial Japanese raiders hit so many of the harbor's defensive

eapons that they were able to do little. New waves of
iiders struck at 11:29, at 11:59, at 12:22, at 7:15 P.M.
nd at 9:10 P.M. By the end of the day the Japanese had
rippled the striking power of the U.S. Pacific Fleet and
ere free to proceed to the invasion of Malaya, the
hilippines, and the Dutch East Indies. The powerful
attleship *Arizona*, shown above with her flag still flying,
ad been sunk along with the *Utah* and the destroyers *Cassir,*
haw, Downes while the battleship *Oklahoma* had capsized
nder the Japanese blows. Also lost were tremendous num-
ers of planes and 2,897 valuable soldiers and sailors.

JAPANESE DIVE BOMBERS DESCENDED IN WAVES and from all directions to confuse anti-aircraft crews. This plane has just reached the bottom of its dive. Note flaps.

JAPANESE CONCENTRATED ON PEARL HARBOR and near-by Hickam Field where this picture was taken of Hangar No. 11, which was completely shattered by the bombers' attack.

THIS IS THE MOTOR OF A JAPANESE NAVAL BOMBER, one of the 41 downed by U.S. anti-aircraft. Many U.S. pilots tried to take off, but were downed on the runways.

THIS P-40 CURTISS FIGHTER HAD ITS WINGS CLIPPED by a bomb which also buckled its landing gear. A squadron of "Flying Fortresses" arrived from the U.S. in the midst of the Japanese attack. All but one, which was shot down, managed to land safely. Parts from smashed planes were salvaged by ground crews after attack.

Smoke from the stricken *Arizona* rolls back over the shattered hangars of Hickam Field.

THIS WING OFF A DOWNED JAPANESE BOMBER littered a Honolulu lawn. Civilians, thinking Japanese might attempt a landing, armed themselves and prepared to fight to the last man.

THIS ARMY TRUCK SUFFERED A DIRECT HIT just off Hickam Field's parade grounds from the first wave of Japanese planes. Note the burning tire in the foreground.

WAIKIKI RESIDENTS BEGAN CLEANING UP DEBRIS of their bombed-out homes after the attack. Following the same pattern of ruthlessness they had established in China, the Japanese had bombed civilian centers and schools. In Wahaiwa they machinegunned the streets. Over fifty civilians were killed, many more were wounded.

On Dec. 8 a grim President asked Congress to declare war on the Empire of Japan.

"Remember Pearl Harbor"

For months before the sneak attack on Pearl Harbor the people of the United States had been split over President Roosevelt's program of aiding the nations fighting the Axis powers. While the President had the solid backing of the majority of the people, he was under continuous attack by a sizable, organized minority called "America First." Its leadership, headed by Charles A. Lindbergh, Senators Wheeler, Clark, Walsh, and Nye, scoffed at the President's reiterated warning that America was in danger of attack and demanded a program of appeasement. At the news of the treacherous Japanese attack "America First" withered away to the pro-Nazis, the anti-Semites, and the Fascist Cough-linites who had been some of its most aggressive members. At noon on Dec. 8 President Roosevelt, grim, obviously angry yet calm, appeared before a joint session of Congress to ask for a declaration of war against Japan. "Yesterday," he said, "December 7, 1941—a date which will live in infamy—the United States of America was suddenly and deliberately attacked by naval and air forces of the Empire of Japan." Calling the attack "dastardly and unprovoked," he asked for a declaration of war against Japan. "Always will we remember the character of the onslaught against us. . . . We will gain the inevitable triumph." His whole speech took only ten minutes. Within half an hour the Senate had voted for war—82 to 0, and so had the Representatives—338 to 1, the lone dissenter being Jeannette Rankin. As on Dec. 11 the cry "Remember Pearl Harbor" swept America, and as the South American countries moved closer to the U.S. in hemispheric solidarity, the other two nations of the Axis, Germany and Italy, declared war on the United States. Screamed Reichschancellor Adolf Hitler to his heiling Reichstag, "I cannot be insulted by Roosevelt . . . because I consider Roosevelt to be insane. . . . We know, of course, that the eternal Jew is behind all this." Separate declarations of war on Germany and Italy were made by Congress on the next day. On Dec. 13 the Axis satellite nations, except Finland, declared war on the United States. They included Hungary, Rumania, Bulgaria, Manchukuo. Britain had declared war on Japan several hours before the United States. Their vast man power and industrial resources assured the ultimate victory of the anti-Fascist states, although it was certain that there would be defeats for some months to come, particularly in the Pacific. But in Russia the Nazi armies were being bled white and there was no doubt that a second front would be opened at the right time by Britain and the U.S.

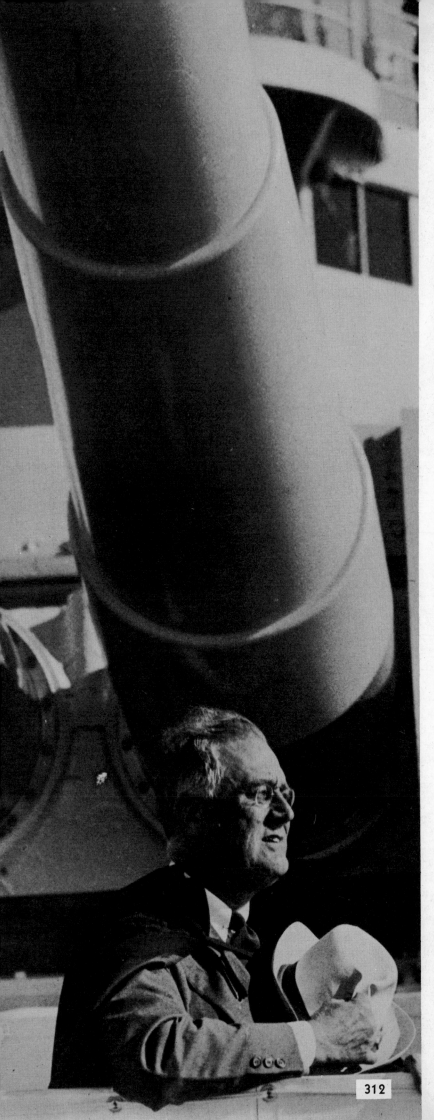

ROOSEVELT: WAR PRESIDENT

Franklin Delano Roosevelt is the seventh President to lead the United States in time of war. That it is the greatest war the world has known assures him of a place in history beside Washington and Lincoln. Yet even if he were not a war President his stature would hardly be less. He is the first President to be re-elected for a third term. He is the greatest social reformer the Western hemisphere has produced. He is a spectacular President in spectacular times. In 1922 his political career seemed at an end, for he was bedridden and paralyzed. Yet with the determination, confidence, courage few men possess he overcame his affliction. Wealthy, cultured, cosmopolitan, aristocratic, Franklin Roosevelt might well have become a stuffy corporation lawyer. Instead he became the champion of the underdog, the downtrodden, and the oppressed. In 1932 that included nearly everyone. The financial disaster of 1929 was still taking its toll. 15,000,000 were unemployed, banks were failing everywhere, faith in our economic system was shattered. Roosevelt's frank, intimate, confident speeches were in startling contrast to politicians' platitudes. By millions he was hailed as nothing short of a Messiah when he called for a "new deal" for the "forgotten man," bringing to America hope and a richer, fuller concept of what Democracy and Government might be. Few men have had greater ability to inspire great numbers of people. Called a "traitor to his class" by old and wealthy former friends, Roosevelt led the first years of the New Deal with crusading zeal, lessened his pressure for reforms when war overtook the world and threatened America. His reforms, once described as "communist-inspired," have, in less than a decade, been universally accepted as beneficial and necessary and have brought to America a greater appreciation of human life and happiness. A master politician, a dynamic and vigorous humanitarian, buoyant with a fine sense of his own place in history and with an indomitable confidence in himself, he has smashed tradition after tradition without hesitation whenever it seemed necessary for the welfare of the country. He has made few long-range mistakes, has foreseen and prepared for many of the disasters of the war. His "Good Neighbor" policy, bringing to the possessive Monroe Doctrine the same democratic concepts and friendly warmth his New Deal brought to the United States, was begun in 1936, years before most Americans awoke to the vulnerability of our country; its value, in terms of American lives saved, is infinite. His mistakes seem small in historical perspective. Physically and mentally, President Roosevelt has borne the burden of his office far better than past Presidents have, far better than most men could. He likes it.

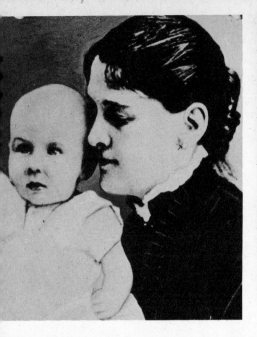

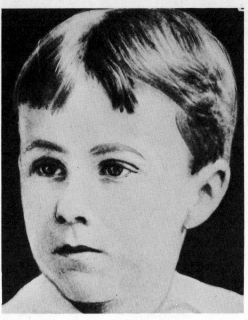

HIS PICTURE OF FRANKLIN and his mother was taken when he was about one year old. His father, James Roosevelt, was 53, and his mother, 27, when he was born at the old family estate, Hyde Park, N. Y., on Jan. 30, 1882. His oldest ancestor was Claus Martanszan van Rosenvelt, a Dutch merchant who had come to New Amsterdam in 1649. Theodore Roosevelt, later to become President, was a fifth cousin. The Roosevelts were wealthy, his great-grandfather having made a fortune in real estate around New York. They lived quietly in the family mansion at Hyde Park, but also maintained a home in New York City where they spent part of the year.

WHEN HE WAS FIVE, Franklin was precocious. He had few playmates, spent most of his time with his father and tutors. The family took him often to Europe. At eleven (right) he was an excellent horseman, owned a pony and a gun, studied bird life with his father. When he visited the White House, Grover Cleveland, who was a friend of his father's, said to him: "I'm making a strange wish for you, little man . . . I hope you'll never be President of the United States." He loved history, memorized most of Admiral Mahan's famous *History of Sea Power*. He liked outdoor life, particularly sailing. One of his few playmates was his cousin Eleanor.

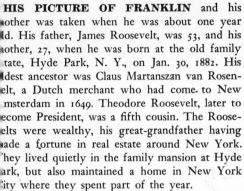

AT 14 HE ENTERED GROTON, an exclusive prep school. He rowed, played football; he is the white-sweatered boy in the center above. A brilliant student, he won the school's Latin prize, finished the six-year course in four with honors, and entered Harvard.

WHILE A HARVARD STUDENT, Franklin posed for this picture with his parents. At Harvard he was a crusading *Crimson* editor, socially popular, and finished his course in three years. Prankish, he swiped a pen from the Kaiser's yacht while vacationing.

HE MARRIED ELEANOR, niece of his fifth cousin President Theodore Roosevelt, in 1905 while a Columbia Law student. He had known her all his life. The President gave away the bride and "stole the show," much to the newlyweds' chagrin.

IN 1910 HE WAS ELECTED state senator after an automobile campaign throughout Dutchess County. It was the first Democratic victory there in 28 years. As Senator he fought against fire traps, child labor. In 1912 he led the N.Y. Wilson forces.

WILSON APPOINTED HIM Assistan Secretary of the U.S. Navy on Mar. 17, 191 Roosevelt was then only 31 years old. Nav power had been an obsession with him sin youth. He owned 9,000 books on sea powe tactics, navies, studied them constantly.

ROOSEVELT, SHOWN HERE WITH SECRETARY DANIELS and Admiral McGowan, had alarmed many stuffy admirals when he entered the Navy by declaring it was overrated, its battleships obsolete and undermanned. Slashing at red tape, he reorganized its yards, supply centers, stimulated construction of modern ships, increased its man power during the war from 78,000 to 500,000.

WHEN U.S. WENT INTO WORLD WAR I Roosevelt spoke fr quently in the Liberty Bond drives. He is shown here with ear movie stars: kneeling, Marie Dressler, Charles Chaplin, standir Douglas Fairbanks and Mary Pickford. Meanwhile, Secretary o Navy Josephus Daniels had practically turned the actual administ tion of the Navy over to him.

WITH JAMES M. COX as his Presidential teammate, Roosevelt ran for the Vice-Presidency in 1920. The two candidates (above) were decisively defeated by Harding and Coolidge. Roosevelt, disappointed but not discouraged by the failure of the U.S. to join the World Court and League of Nations, retired from political life to become vice-president of a banking firm.

MEANWHILE, THE ROOSEVELT FAMILY was growing. Shown here with their parents and grandmother, Sara Delano Roosevelt, are: Elliott, John, Franklin Jr., Anna, and James. It was at Campobello in 1921 that Roosevelt was stricken with infantile paralysis. He began his heroic fight to overcome the ailment by learning everything known about the disease.

AFTER THREE YEARS of constant exercise but little improvement Roosevelt went to Warm Springs, Ga., to bathe in its tepid waters. There were immediate benefits. He was able to return to political life, nominating Alfred Smith for President at the 1924 Democratic convention. The picture was made in 1926 when Roosevelt, his handicap overcome, went swimming in Miami.

IN 1928 ROOSEVELT became governor of New York in the same election in which Herbert Hoover defeated Smith for the Presidency. Re-elected in 1930, Roosevelt reformed utility laws, and when the depression hit America he advocated a public-works program to cut unemployment. In 1932 he defeated Smith to win the Democratic Presidential nomination. His theme: "The Forgotten Man."

James A. Farley

IN the fall of 1931 James A. Farley, no reformer but a political machine-builder of the first magnitude who had attached himself to Roosevelt during his governorship, made a national tour to urge Roosevelt's candidacy among Democratic party leaders. Farley's trip set in motion the machinery that was to bring to troubled America its great social reforms. In Roosevelt's concept of democracy the Government was responsible for the welfare of its people. To prevent an uncontrolled economy from running amuck, creating waste and suffering, the Roosevelt administration enacted banking reforms and established the Securities Exchange Commission, regulated agricultural production through the AAA, established TVA as a utility "yardstick," raised the national income and health standards by wages-and-hours legislation, provided for public works through WPA to absorb unemployment, enacted a social-security program to care for the aged and unemployable, and through the National Labor Relations Act brought the relations of labor and capital under Government supervision. Feared at first by conservatives, all these measures had become accepted as necessary and beneficial by 1940. Only over their execution was there any real controversy.

ROOSEVELT DEFEATED PRESIDENT HOOVER in Nov., 1932, winning a plurality of over seven million votes and carrying 42 states. The picture above shows President Hoover and President-elect Roosevelt leaving the White House for the inauguration, Mar. 4, 1933. The failure of the Hoover administration was largely attributed to its seeming unwillingness to take active steps to reduce unemployment and extend relief.

FOUR HOURS AFTER HIS INAUGURATION Roosevelt called a special cabinet meeting and decreed a "bank holiday." Banks had been failing at an increasing rate for over a year. The above picture shows a crowd around a closed bank. Over 15 million Americans were unemployed. Relief agencies were unable to cope with the situation. The national income had been cut in half.

ROOSEVELT'S FIRST STEP toward recovery was the N.R.A. (National Recovery Act). He appointed gruff Gen. Hugh Johnson above, with Secretary of Interior Harold Ickes, to administer the act. It regulated wages and hours and guaranteed collective bargaining by unions which resulted in wage increases stepping up the buying power of the nation. Other reforms: the AAA, Guffey Coal Act.

the famous "Nine Old Men": Brandeis, Van Devanter, Hughes, McReynolds, Sutherland, Roberts, Butler, Stone, Cardozo.

IN 1935-6 THE U.S. SUPREME COURT declared unconstitutional ost New Deal reforms, including the NRA, the AAA, and the .Y. Minimum Wages and Hours for Women and Children Law. oosevelt declared his reforms were being killed by a "horse-and-uggy" court. He proposed adding six new members to the Court, rovoking the most violent parliamentary battle of the New Deal's history. Meanwhile, in Mar. 1937 the Court reversed itself on two New Deal reforms previously condemned, and upheld the National Labor Relations Act. This new-found flexibility slackened Roosevelt's pressure for a new Court. Within the next few years most of the conservative justices of the Court had resigned and had been replaced by enthusiastic followers of the New Deal philosophy.

THE W.P.A. WAS BEGUN IN 1935 when private industry left million still unemployed. Most W.P.A. funds were spent on dams, ads, schools, athletic fields, and later defense work. To three million pression stricken people it meant a job that lifted their families from e doldrums of a meager relief, gave them a chance to maintain eir morale, self-respect.

IN 1936 ROOSEVELT DEFEATED Gov. Alfred M. Landon of Kansas, carrying every state but Maine and Vermont. Labor, which had made tremendous strides through the Wagner Labor Act, gave him strong support. Although relief and W.P.A. had already cost ten billion dollars, Landon's inability to offer a better program than mere economy resulted in his defeat.

The Toll of Ten Years

These pictures dramatically show the physical effect ten years' constant toil and nervous strain have had on President Roosevelt's face.

1932: After his nomination for President.

1936: Accepting his second nomination.

1942: Serving his third term—a war President.

HARRY HOPKINS, shown holding his daughter Diana, had become the President's personal emissary and adviser by 1940. A social reformer, Hopkins had headed WPA in its biggest days, later was Secretary of Commerce. He moved into the White House in May 1940, and at the Democratic convention served as the President's delegate. Roosevelt was nominated by acclamation for third term. Due to the war conservatives were split over the third term issue.

ROOSEVELT WON HIS RECORD-BREAKING THIRD TERM by majority of almost five million over Wendell Willkie, Republican liberal candidate. Demonstrating the unity of America on our anti-Nazi foreign policy and aid to Britain, Willkie refused to make it an issue although he waged vigorous campaign on domestic issues. Two years later Willkie put his party on record as being against postwar isolation.

VISITING ARGENTINE and Brazil in Dec. 1936 Roosevelt emphasized the sincerity behind his "Good Neighbor" policy toward South America. Conferences at Lima, Havana, Panama decreased Axis influence in South America and the South Americans joined U.S. in hemisphere defense.

AS THE DEFENSE PROGRAM BEGAN Roosevelt did not press for new social reforms in the interests of national unity. But he refused to give in to Congressmen who demanded anti-labor legislation. "We need not swap," he said, "the gain of better living for the gain of better defense. I propose to retain one and gain the other." By May 1942 defense industries had absorbed all but 2,600,000 of our unemployed.

VICE-PRESIDENT HENRY A. WALLACE, shown here riding with the President when he returned to Washington after being elected for a third term, has been one of the President's closest advisers since Wallace became Secretary of Agriculture in 1932. A scientific dirt farmer, Wallace's work in agriculture had been brilliant. As head of the War Economic Board, Vice-President Wallace became the Presidential spokesman on postwar plans and war aims, and especially interested in the problems of South America. President Roosevelt's suggestion in 1942, that Puerto Rico be given its freedom in 1944 or when the war ended, indicated that our plans for peace and freedom for small nations would be begun by cleaning up our own backyard.

Japan's Drive into the South Pacific

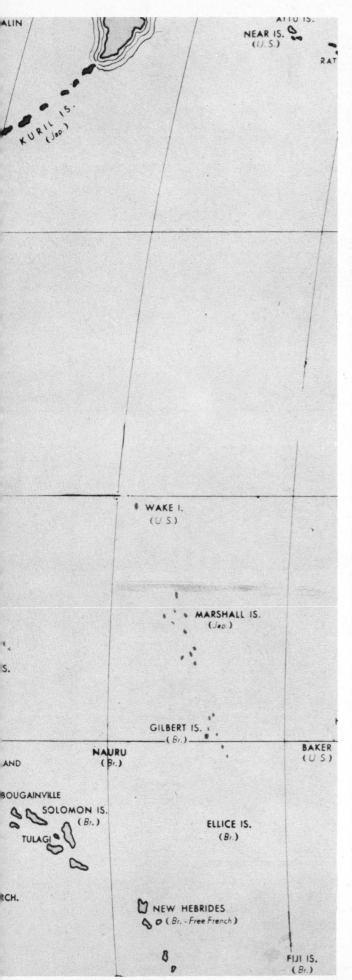

ALIN

ATTU IS.

NEAR IS.
(U.S.)

RAT

KURIL IS.
(Jap.)

WAKE I.
(U.S.)

MARSHALL IS.
(Jap.)

GILBERT IS.
(Br.)

NAURU
(Br.)

BAKER
(U.S.)

AND

BOUGAINVILLE

SOLOMON IS.
(Br.)

TULAGI

ELLICE IS.
(Br.)

RCH.

NEW HEBRIDES
(Br.-Free French)

FIJI IS.
(Br.)

THIS map shows the main battle area of the South Pacific during the first few months of the Japanese attempt to conquer all of Asia. Pearl Harbor and the United States are so distant that they cannot be shown in a map of this scale. With the United States Pacific Fleet temporarily crippled at Pearl Harbor it was not difficult for veteran Japanese troops, overwhelming in numbers to push rapidly into the South Pacific. The main Japanese strength was concentrated in French Indo-China, which had been turned over to them by the Vichy government in midsummer. On Dec. 7 these troops, under fat, gruff Gen. Yamashita, invaded Malaya while lighter forces moved into Thailand to begin the push that would ultimately cut off the Burma Road. The first objective of Yamashita's forces was Singapore, one of the world's largest naval bases, which dominated the hundreds of islands in the South Pacific, including the Dutch East Indies, Borneo, and the approaches to Australia. By gaining it they could advance from island to island until they had gained the entire archipelago, cut off Burma, threaten India, put Australia in desperate peril. Simultaneously with their invasion of Malaya, Japanese naval forces attacked U. S. outposts at Guam and Wake. Garrisoned by a small number of men and weakly fortified, Guam fell on Dec. 12. At Wake heroic U. S. Marines and construction workers held out against numerous Japanese assaults and the fire of heavy guns until Dec. 24. Meanwhile, Japanese troops which had been assaulting the British stronghold at Hongkong intensified their efforts and on Dec. 25 the bedraggled British forces there surrendered. With the exception of the Philippines where MacArthur's men were still holding out, this cleared the area of U. S. bases, permitted the Japanese navy to concentrate on the islands off Malaya and Australia. Sarawak was occupied without resistance on Jan. 1 and ten days later the Borneo port of Tarakan was captured. The Japanese made no attempt to conquer the inland areas of these islands, from which guerrilla bands continued to operate, but instead seized the main cities and ports, used them as jumping-off points for their next objective. The outnumbered U. S.-Dutch naval and air forces, seriously weakened by the sinking of the British battleships, *Repulse* and *Prince of Wales*, by Japanese aircraft Dec. 9 off Malaya, were never able to gather enough strength to do more than harass the Japanese with light raids. On January 23rd Japanese forces landed in the Solomon Islands and in Papua, which brought them to Australia's front door. Meanwhile Japanese forces had been gathering in Sarawak and Borneo for an invasion of Java. In a furious five day battle U. S. and Dutch naval vessels and aircraft smashed the invasion fleet as it steamed through the Makassar Strait between Borneo and Celebes. But they had been unable to prevent the Japanese from landing earlier in Sumatra and on Feb. 17, the day after Singapore fell, the Japanese seized the richest oil fields at Palembang. Desperate attempts were made by the United Nations' forces to hold Java as a base from which operations might be conducted against the Japanese, but heroism was not enough and on February 28 the Japanese occupied the northern coast of Java.

This map, drawn June 22, 1941, shows Japanese held areas in dark grey, United Nations territory in light grey.

TOKYO HAD BEGUN CONCENTRATING TROOPS in Indo-China in June. By December 200,000 Japanese troops were ready to embark for Malaya or stationed along the Thailand border. On Dec. 7, simultaneously with the bombing of Pearl Harbor, they struck, landing at the mouth of the Kelantan River in Malaya on Dec. 8. 25 Japanese transports landed many men along Thailand's Malayan border on Dec. 9. The next day they took Kota Bharu and split into two columns, moving south toward Singapore along the east and west Malayan coast. Other Japanese pushed northward across the Kra Isthmus into Burma, taking Victoria Point on Dec. 15

MEANWHILE, JAPANESE BOMBERS were hammering Singapore. Fires raged through the grass-roofed native quarter despite the work of the hastily organized, ill-equipped civilian firemen. Moreover, the early failure of the British commander, Brooke-Popham, to take the Japanese threat seriously and his reluctance to mobilize the native population laid the foundations for the fall of the city. On Dec. 26 Brooke-Popham was replaced by Gen. Pownel but by now the Japanese were within 200 miles. Adept at jungl warfare, naked, grease-covered Japanese slithered through underbrus to trap British units bogged down with useless artillery.

AN AUSTRALIAN ANTI-TANK CREW stops two Japanese tanks. The outnumbered Anzacs could stop the Japanese on the roads but could not check their jungle infiltration.

A CLOSE-UP OF THE TANKS HIT. On the ground lies the body of a Japanese. But by Jan. 26 the Japanese had taken Batu Pahat, western anchor of Malaya's defense line.

MEANWHILE, Japanese troops were advancing rapidly toward Rangoon, port of entry for most of China's military supplies. With no planes Japanese held control of the air, bombarded Rangoon unmercifully. In the picture above a terror-stricken native tells his story to Burma governor, Sir Reginald Borman-Smith. The Japanese, whose total strength amounted to only four divisions, advanced rapidly against a few poorly trained Burmese battalions and an Indian division. Veteran Chinese troops, which had placed themselves under British command, offered to defend Rangoon, but their offer was rejected and the Chinese were kept in the north, largely because Burmese ministers did not want them. On Mar. 8 the Japanese took Rangoon and moved north to complete their conquest.

A Japanese bomb has just killed this grief-stricken Singapore mother's child, whose body lies on the right.

By Jan. 28 the Japanese in Malay had passed Sangarang and neared Kulai, only 18 miles from British Singapore. By Jan. 31 the British were forced to evacuate the city proper on the Malayan mainland and retreat to Singapore Island, where the naval base was located. The British had never counted on an assault from the mainland, and once it began Singapore's ability to command the sea approaches to the Dutch East Indies, Australia, and India diminished. After the sinking of the *Repulse* and *Prince of Wales* on

Dec. 10 the British could not prevent the Japanese seizure of Sarawak and North Borneo by landing forces on Dec. 1 These were followed by landings at Tarakan, Minahass and the Celebes Islands on Jan. 11. Hard-fighting Dutch an U. S. air and naval forces, however, managed to break up 100-ship invasion fleet bound for Java in the Macass Strait in a battle that raged from Jan. 23 to Jan. 28. The sank two Japanese warships and eleven transports and dan aged 18 others, including nine warships. Meanwhile, only

Bomb fragments have hit the other woman in the leg. This is one of the most remarkable pictures of the war.

lf mile of water separated the British on Singapore Island om the gathering forces of Gen. Yamashita on the main- nd. On the 14-by-16 mile island were packed 750,000 ngry, thirsty people of virtually every race and nationality the world. On Feb. 8 the Japanese captured the stoutly fended Singapore airport to end what little air protection e base had. Repeated attempts to land on the island were rown back until Feb. 13 when the Japanese captured the

Singapore reservoir, shutting off the meager water supplies of the defenders. Three powerful drives by 100,000 men crossed to the island, and on Feb. 15 Gen. Percival, com- mander of the base, found it impossible to continue resist- ance and surrendered. Fighting continued in the Dutch East Indies, in Burma, and in Bataan, where MacArthur's men had resolutely held and thrown back powerful Japanese offen- sives.

Gen. Chiang Kai-Shek sent his veteran troops into Burma to help China's new Allies protect her life-line.

CHINA FIGHTS ON

SINCE 1939, when the Japanese put full steam behind their "undeclared" war against China, the Chinese people, under the courageous, stubborn leadership of Gen. Chiang Kai-shek and his wife, had waged an epic battle in defense of their country and its freedom. Always retreating to draw the invaders deeper into their vast country, giving battle only when the Japanese least preferred it, they had killed and wounded 1,644,000 Japanese in four years. They had lost most of their great cities and industries, their entire coast and 900,000 inland square miles. They carried out a "scorched-earth" policy which left little for the invaders. Behind Japanese lines they organized guerrilla resistance. They literally clawed the Burma Road out of the Burmese mountains with their fingernails, although at first 200 of every 250 workers died of malaria. Deep in the interior they set up co-operative industrials to produce arms, munitions, clothing. Always with an eye on the day when they would advance, they tore up Japanese railroad lines and frugally buried the rails for their use later. After four years of intensive warfare the Japanese were as far from conquering China as the day they had begun. Their ruthless bombing of China's teeming cities, killing thousands, neither broke her people's heart nor her determination to fight on. Instead they won for China world-wide sympathy and aid. Throughout these years the Soviet Union shipped vast quantities of war materials to China while United States extended her $170,000,000 in loans for war equipment. At Changsha in October 1941 Chinese troops inflicted a disastrous defeat on the Japanese who lost 30,000 men and much material. When the Japanese launched their attack on Pearl Harbor and moved into Malaya and Burma, Chiang Kai-shek sent his battle-trained troops into Burma to defend the vital hard-earned road, China's most important route for supplies from Britain and the United States.

The Burma Road, built by hand by
thousands of Chinese in two years, despite malaria, danger, and air raids,
wound 726 miles from Kunming to
Lashio in Burma

THIS PICTURE, FAMOUS FOR ITS STATUESQUE quality, shows some of the 700 persons killed when a Japanese bomb hit their jammed air raid shelter. Most of them suffocated. Despite years of horrors like this the Chinese carried on and Japan found herself incapable of decisive victory. After five years of warfare against the poorly equipped Chinese the Mikado's men were still as far from victory as ever. After the fall of France Britain's position was so desperate that she was forced to accede to the Japanese demands that she close the Burma Road. The British closed the road from Aug. 9 to Oct. 9, 1940 and in the interim the Japanese tried to get Chiang Kai-shek to make peace with them. But Chiang, backed with new promises of aid from U.S., refused to become a Japanese puppet, turned down their peace offers. When U.S. and Britain became her allies, China moved speedily to help them.

ON JAN. 2 CHINESE TROOPS MOVED INTO BURMA to aid in its defense. Their offer to defend Rangoon was rejected by the British in deference to Burmese prejudice, and they were kept immobilized in northern Burma. The Japanese drive reached Marteban on Feb. 11 and, crossing the Sittang, captured burning, looted Rangoon on Mar. 8. The British retreated northward.

TOUGH, WIRY U.S. GEN. JOSEPH STILWELL, who had spent years in China, was given command of the Chinese troops in the Toungoo area after Rangoon's fall. Outnumbered, the Chinese were rapidly forced back. By Mar. 31 the Japanese had taken Toungoo and were forcing British troops up the Chindwin Valley toward India. As in Malaya the British were poorly equipped for jungle fighting.

THIS REMARKABLE PICTURE shows the Japanese conquerors riding through a Burma village as they consolidated their gains. Meanwhile Gen. Stilwell was cut off from his troops and, carrying his own tommy gun, led his party through 110 miles of dense jungle to India. As the Japanese moved up the Burma Road, the plight of China became more desperate than at any time in five years.

Two A.V.G. "armorers" load a Tomahawk's guns. The Japanese Zeros carried little armor, disintegrated when hit.

THE brightest spot in the disastrous Malayan and Burma campaign was the spectacular work of the "Flying Tigers," American volunteers serving in China's air force under U.S. Gen. Claire L. Chennault. In ninety days they destroyed 457 Japanese planes while losing only 15, although they were always outnumbered and flew obsolete P-40 Tomahawks. Chennault, who had been retired from the U.S. Army as a captain because of deafness, became head of Chiang Kai-shek's 100 plane air force in 1937. Though he lost most of his planes during the next four years, he became the best expert on Japanese air tactics outside of Japan. But he was an air chief without an air force, and it was not until Dec. 1940 that he obtained 100 obsolete Tomahawks from the U.S. through lend-lease. Without pilots or facilities for training them, he obtained permission to recruit volunteer pilots and mechanics from the U.S. Army, Navy, Marines. By Nov. 1941 he had two full squadrons of eighteen planes each and part of a third, trained in Chennault's own fighter tactics for teams of two planes. Chennault had worked out his tactics years before while serving in the U.S. Army but

A "Flying Tiger" awaits his squadron leader's signal to take off.

Chennault taught "Tigers" combat team flying.

Directed by a skeleton American ground force, nimble Chinese mechanics serviced the A.V.G.'s overworked Tomahawks.

ttle attention had been paid to them. Based on the fact that wo planes have a greater firepower than one, they took ombat flying out of the individualistic realm in which it ad been developed and made it a problem in highly co-rdinated teamwork. Yet "Tigers" retained the color and avor of the Lafayette Squadron of World War I. When ne Japanese struck at Pearl Harbor, Malaya, and Burma the 'Flying Tiger Sharks," as they were called by the Chinese, ioved into Burma. With the help of two British squadrons hey wrenched control of the air in south Burma from the Japanese. As the Japanese land forces advanced the "Flying Tigers" took the offensive, smashing Japanese airports with demolition bombs carried in their laps. Patching up bullet-riddled planes, moving from one makeshift airport to another to keep the Japanese from learning where they were based, outflying and outshooting numerically and qualitatively superior Japanese planes, the "Flying Tigers" became the most colorful air force in operation anywhere. With Burma lost they returned to China to carry on the fight as members of the U.S. Air Force.

Jack" Newkirk died, but not before downing 28.

Chinese mechanics improvised spare parts for shot-up planes from tin cans.

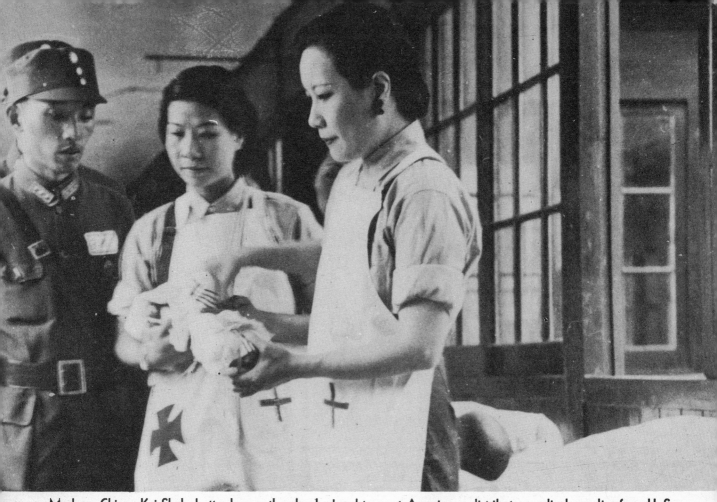

Madame Chiang Kai-Shek, better known than her husband to most Americans, distributes medical supplies from U. S.

IN CHINA MADAME CHIANG KAI-SHEK, busy distributing the last medical supplies to come up the Burma Road, and the Generalissimo prepared to carry on, although China's plight was more desperate than at any time during the preceding five years. From America President Roosevelt promised "ways will be found to deliver airplanes and munitions." In December, when the Japanese attacked Burma, China sent 150,000 workmen to hack out a new Burma Road across the perilous Himalayan Mountains to Sadiya, India. Meanwhile, at Changsha, Chuhsien, and Nanchang the Japanese opened powerful drives to knock China out of the war.

THE CHIANG KAI-SHEKS HAD VISITED INDIA in March to help settle the problem of Indian home rule. They sympathized with Pandit Jawaharlal Nehru, leader of the Indian nationalists, shown speaking here. Through Sir Stafford Cripps, Britain offered Dominion status to India and the right of individual Indian states to secede from India after the war. In return Britain asked for control of India's defenses during the war. The talks failed, and on April 28 Cripps revealed that the problem of Indian secession after the war had deadlocked negotiations. With the Japanese on India's borders, with Nehru determined to resist invasion, with Gandhi determined not to resist, India's defense became vital to China, for its loss would practically end the last possibilities of supplying China. Meanwhile, in the U.S. Chinese boys (below) were learning to fly with U.S. forces. In them and in the U.S. China put its hope.

The Defense of the Philippines

THIS REMARKABLE PICTURE, SHOWING JAPANESE LAND-ING barges approaching Luzon on Dec. 9, was developed from film found on the body of a dead Japanese on the beach.

COURAGEOUS, WELL-TRAINED FILIPINO TROOPS smashed the first Japanese attempts to land, but by mid-December the Japanese had effected landings at three points in northern Luzon.

THE blow which devastated Pearl Harbor did not have the same effect in the Philippines where Gen. Douglas MacArthur, former U.S. Chief of Staff, had been preparing the islands' defenses since 1935. And it was on the Philippines that the brunt of the Japanese drive fell. Regardless of the Japanese advances in Malaya, the Philippines offered a jumping-off point for attacks on Japanese communications and simultaneously immobilized Japanese naval and army forces badly needed elsewhere. The Japanese attack on Dec. 7 attempted to knock out Manila's great naval base, Cavite, and near-by Nichols Field. The next day Japanese transports appeared off Vigan and northern Luzon to attempt landings. But these were driven off by hard-fighting Filipino troops, and not until Dec. 9 were superior Japanese forces, at a frightful cost, able to seize beach heads. MacArthur's forces totaled less than 100,000 men, of whom only 10,000 were regular U.S. troops. Their lack of planes and tanks made it doubtful if they could hold out for long. Nichols Field and other Philippine air bases were under almost continuous attack as more Japanese troops landed in the north and at Lingayan. Meanwhile, other Japanese forces had landed in Malaya and were besieging the British sea base at Hong Kong from its defenseless land approaches. In Malaya the British fell back rapidly. Japanese propaganda that they were waging a war against the "white oppressors" of the yellow race had a powerful effect in Malaya and Burma, and contributed much to the British inability to stem the tide. But this propaganda made no headway in the Philippines, where the people, who had been armed and promised complete independence in 1946, fought furiously against the invaders. But they were unable to prevent a Japanese landing at Legaspi, south of Manila, on Dec. 11, and the invaders now began a drive for Manila from north and south.

FIRST AMERICAN HERO of the war was Capt. Colin Ke who, on Dec. 11, dived his flaming, bomb-laden Flying Fortr into a Japanese battleship, sinking it immediately.

CIVILIAN MANILA WAS BOMBED FREQUENTLY as the Japanese attempted to set fire to its grass roofs. Meanwhile, the British suffered a severe blow when Japanese dive bombers sank two of her greatest battleships, the *Prince of Wales* and *Repulse* off the Malayan coast on Dec. 10 with great loss of life. On Dec. 11 the heroic U.S. forces at Guam were finally forced to surrender. On Dec. 14 Japanese forces drove into Burma across the Kru Isthmus from Thailand, where fifth columnists had surrendered on Dec. 7. By Dec. 15 the British had abandoned Victoria Point on the Malayan peninsula. Below: Eyeing the approach of Japanese bombers apprehensively, a Filipino family flees Manila and heads into the countryside. Thousands of other Filipinos died before they could escape.

THIS FILIPINO FOUND HIS WIFE and three children had been killed by a Japanese air raid on San Pablo, near Manila, Christmas Day, while he served as a member of a first-aid squad. Japanese ruthlessness spurred the determination of the Filipino people to fig on, and in the jungles of Luzon their guerrilla bands exacted a heav toll from the invaders whom they ambushed frequently.

AN AMERICAN SOLDIER AS HE IS ABOUT TO HEAVE a "Molotov Cocktail," a bottle of flaming gasoline, into the path of an onrushing Japanese tank—a trick learned in Spain.

THE THOUSANDS OF JAPANESE TAKEN PRISONERS MacArthur's men became a difficult problem as the siege went for there was barely enough food for Filipino and U.S. troops.

PRIVATE AVON SHERMAN AND LT. H. H. ROBERTS grab doughnut en route to the front. Sherman, a tireless fighter, won the Distinguished Service Cross, the Silver Star, and the Purple Heart, and accounted for more than his share of Japanese. But on Dec. 24 reinforcements for the Japanese poured from 100 transports off the Lingayen Gulf.

THOUSANDS OF THE MIKADO'S MEN DIED as their officers ordered them to advance at any cost. MacArthur had calculated that the Japanese would not attempt to take the Philippines if it meant losing 60,000 crack troops, but as they kept throwing reserves into the firing line, it was clear they were ready to pay the price. Slowly the American and Filipino troops were forced backward.

ON JAN. 1, 1942, MACARTHUR SET FIRE TO CAVITE, shown burning here, and abandoned Manila's defense. Manila, though an "open city," had been ruthlessly bombed. Japanese reinforcements had forced MacArthur to shorten his lines. Most of Cavite's supplies were moved to Corregidor and the rest burned to render the naval base unusable. A few days before, on Dec. 25, the defenders of Hong

RETREATING SLOWLY TOWARD BATAAN, MacArthur's men let Japanese tanks pass such outposts as this and then pinched them off. Accurate U.S. artillery fire smashed the invaders back on re- peated occasions, and on Jan. 21 Gen. MacArthur unleashed a sur- prise counteroffensive which threw the stunned Japanese back all along the front and inflicted heavy losses on them.

Kong, who had exhausted their water, food and medical supplies, surrendered to overwhelming Japanese forces. The British had never thoroughly prepared Hong Kong's land defenses.

U.S. BOMBERS, numbering only 36 originally, fought hard but suffered heavy losses. On Dec. 25 Gen. Lewis Brereton moved those left to Java where new losses forced him to India.

MACARTHUR'S TROOPS APPLIED THE "SCORCHED-earth" policy of Russia and China to slow the Japanese advance. They are shown here preparing to dynamite an already damaged bridge. The native population aided the retreating U.S.-Filipino forces, supplying them with information about Japanese strength, concentration, and artillery emplacements, but by Feb. 1 the Filipino and American forces had been driven halfway down the Bataan peninsula, and in Malaya the Japanese were approaching Singapore.

GEN. MACARTHUR CONFERRED FREQUENTLY WITH
Manuel Quezon, president of the Philippines, at his headquarters on
Corregidor. Quezon had brought MacArthur to the islands in 1935 to
build their defenses when he realized that if the islands were to assume their independence in 1946 they must be prepared to defend
themselves. MacArthur had been U.S. Chief of Staff.

WOUNDED FILIPINO SOLDIERS are shown
here being transferred to one of the field hospitals in
Bataan, after having their wounds dressed by stretcher
bearers. Lack of medical supplies was one of the greatest shortages from which the heroic defenders of the
peninsula suffered. Food was also scarce.

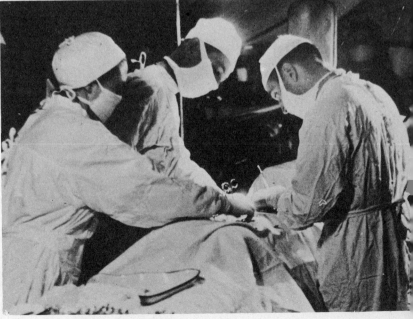

DOCTORS PERFORMED OPERATIONS ON THE SERIOUSLY WOUNDED
in steaming hot field hospitals not far behind the front lines. Meanwhile, as the
Bataan soldiers fought off attempted Japanese landings, President Roosevelt in Washington announced that United States had expeditionary forces in every corner of
the globe. Simultaneously, as commander in chief, he ordered Gen. MacArthur to
leave Bataan secretly for Australia.

Gen. Wainwright and Gen. MacArthur have a quiet talk before MacArthur leaves for his command in Australia.

BY HIS skillful resistance to the Japanese in the Philippines Gen. MacArthur captured the imagination of free people everywhere. Earlier, in Dec. 1941, President Roosevelt and Prime Minister Churchill had foreseen the possibility of the loss of Malaya, Singapore, the Dutch East Indies, and the Philippines, and had begun shipment of vast quantities of men and matériel to Australia. By early March Australia had become a great military base and Gen. MacArthur was ordered by the President to assume command of the A.E.F. there. MacArthur turned command of Bataan over to Lt. Gen. John Wainwright. Leaving Bataan secretly in three small P-T torpedo boats commanded by Lt. John Bulkley, who had already made himself and his boats famous by tor-pedoing a Japanese cruiser and several transports, MacArthur set out for Australia. The general's party included his wife and three-year-old son and President Quezon. After a dangerous and jolting three-day ride, during which time they were in constant danger of being sighted by the Japanese, the boats put in at a secret rendezvous island where their passengers were picked up by Flying Fortresses and flown to Australia. Arriving on Mar. 17 MacArthur was almost immediately appointed commander of all United Forces in the Southwest Pacific. Meanwhile, the Japanese had taken almost all of the Dutch East Indies and were preparing to launch an invasion of the vast and vulnerable Australian continent by sea and air.

GEN. WAINWRIGHT, SHOWN HERE WITH HIS STAFF
OFFICERS as he mapped out the last-ditch fight to hold Bataan
and Corregidor, carried on in the same courageous and skillful manner as MacArthur. The forces now besieging Bataan were overwhelming, totaling seven full divisions with full control of the air.

On Mar. 10 Gen. Tomoyuki Yamashita, conqueror of the on
mighty British Singapore base, arrived to take command of the Ja
anese drive; Tokyo was irked by the brave fight of Bataan's d
fenders, for it upset their war time table and immobilized over 120,0
troops. Bataan's soldiers suffered much from shortages of all types.

HEROIC CORREGIDOR

FOR WEEKS the position of Bataan's defenders had been
desperate and without prospect of relief. Japanese air and
naval forces successfully blocked every attempt to send them
much-needed medical supplies, food, munitions. The fact
that some 45,000 Filipino and American troops were able to
stop 200,000 Japanese troops enraged Tokyo's High Command. Once Yamashita took control the tempo of the attacks
and bombardment doubled. The physical exhaustion of outnumbered, hungry men fighting without rest, day and night,
caused the collapse of Bataan's defense on April 9. Yet almost
10,000 troops managed to escape when the Japanese broke
through to the island fortress Corregidor, where for 28 days
they were under a bombardment that never ceased. In their
last hours they lit cigarettes with $100 bills to prevent
thousands of dollars taken from Manila banks from falling
into Japanese hands. By their heroic stand they wrote a new
page in the history of bravery. On the extreme right of page
343 is the last message heard from Corregidor, tapped out
on a radio key by Private Irving Strobing, a 22-year-old
Jewish boy from Brooklyn, N.Y. Our greatest writers could
not describe in more moving and realistic terms the story of
brave men under fire, how they feel and what they think
about as they go down before superior arms.

Corregidor, a tiny island fortress, supplied Bataan.

BATTERY MARSHALL

"... THEY are not near yet. We are waiting for God only knows what. How about a chocolate soda? ... Not many. Not near yet. Lots of heavy fighting going on. We've only got about one hour, twenty minutes before ... We may have to give up at noon. We don't know yet. They are throwing men and shells at us and we may not be able to stand it. They have been shelling us faster than you can count ... We've got about fifty-five minutes and I feel sick at my stomach. I am really low down. They are around smashing rifles. They bring in the wounded every minute. We will be waiting for you guys to help. This is the only thing I guess that can be done ... General Wainwright is a right guy and we are willing to go on for him, but shells were dropping all night, faster than hell. Too much for guys to take. Enemy cross-shelling and bombing. They have got us all around and from the skies. ... From here it looks like firing ceased on both sides. Men here all feeling bad, because of terrific nervous strain of the siege. Corregidor used to be a nice place but it's haunted now. Withstood a terrific pounding.

"... Just made broadcast to Manila to arrange meeting for surrender. Talk made by General Beebe. I can't say much. Can't think at all. I can hardly think. Say, I have 60 pesos you can have for this week end.

"... The jig is up. Everyone is bawling like a baby. They are piling dead and wounded in our tunnel. Arm's weak from pounding key, long hours, no rest, short rations, tired ...

"I know now how a mouse feels. Caught in a trap waiting for guys to come along and finish it up. Got a treat. Can pineapple. Opening it with Signal Corps knife ... My name is Irving Strobing. Get this to my mother, Mrs. Minnie Strobing, 605 Barbey Street, Brooklyn, N. Y. They are to get along O.K. Get in touch with them as soon as possible. Message. My love to Pa, Joe, Sue, Mac, Garry, Joy, and Paul. Also to all family and friends. God bless 'em all. Hope they be there when I come home. Tell Joe, wherever he is, to give 'em hell for us. My love to you all. God bless you and keep you. Love. Sign my name and tell my mother how you heard from me ..."

LAZING AWAY FURIOUSLY AT THE CONTINUOUS ATTACKING JAPANESE these guns of Fort Hughes and those of Corregidor and Fort Drum smashed one back after the other. But on Mar. 24 Yamashita began a frenzied artillery and air bombardment of Bataan. Badly battered, Bataan's defenders hung on until April 7 when 200,000 Japanese troops finally overwhelmed its 36,853 defenders. Only 9,000 escaped to Corregidor, where they miraculously held out for 28 days, until May 5.

Corregidor's exhausted defenders finally come out of their smoke-filled tunnel.

Roosevelt made Donald Nelson chief of the War Production Board. Nelson swiftly converted our industrial plants for war production

The Battle of Production

ALTHOUGH the United States had been rearming since May, 1940, the attack on Pearl Harbor found the nation's industrial capacity far from being fully mobilized for war production, its expanding army far from being fully equipped. Before the United States could put enough forces in the field to wrest the initiative from the Axis powers, the Battle of Production had to be won. Under the Office of Production Management industrial conversion had gone slowly despite Mr. Knudsen's diligent labor. Though it had made great strides in some fields, particularly aircraft, OPM officials had failed to expand the nation's steel and aluminum capacity and to develop synthetic rubber plants, concentrated war orders in big plants while neglecting to utilize small plants, and failed to overcome the reluctance of many industries to expand. Though labor was asked to make sacrifices, its spokesmen's demands for immediate and all-out conversion received scant attention. After Pearl Harbor it was clearly evident that OPM had outlived its usefulness and that to win the war a new organization was needed to mobilize fully the national resources, man power, and economy. To win the Battle of Production President Roosevelt created the War Production Board, put vigorous, far-sighted, hard-working Donald M. Nelson in charge on

Jan. 18, 1942. The President's Victory quotas seemed impos-sible; they called for: 60,000 planes, 45,000 tanks, 20,000 aircraft guns, 8,000,000 tons of shipping in 1942, and more than double those figures for 1943. But America went to work. Philip Murray and William Green, leaders of the American Federation of Labor and Congress of Industrial Organizations, announced labor would sacrifice its right to strike voluntarily, whole-heartedly supported Nelson's plan for joint labor-management boards to increase production in each plant. Industry labored night and day to expand needed facilities, developed new technological methods to speed production, surpassed all previous achievements in mass production. By June the War Production Board had won the Battle of Production, according to President Roose-velt, who declared our factories were producing 4,000 planes a month, 1,500 tanks, 50,000 heavy machine guns, 2,000 ar-tillery pieces exclusive of tank guns and anti-aircraft. The cost from June 1940 to June 1942: $228,811,233,542—nearly half again as much as the U.S. spent from the day it was founded until June 30, 1940. Pictured on the page opposite are a few of the men who played an important part in win-ning the Battle of Production and in mobilizing America's full strength for the offensive.

W. S. KNUDSEN headed OPM, became Nelson's production chief when OPM was replaced by War Production Board.

PAUL V. McNUTT'S job was to find the man power. He criticized discrimination against women and Negroes in industry.

W. H. DAVIS headed the War Labor Board set up to arbitrate labor disputes without strikes.

TREASURY Secretary Morgenthau directed the sale of War Bonds to pay for the war effort and check inflation.

ACTIVE Vice-President Wallace headed the War Economic Board, supervised all war agencies, called war a "People's Revolution."

BERNARD BARUCH, who headed War Industries Board in 1918, was the unofficial adviser of all Washington.

WILLIAM BATT, $1-a-year man and famous industrialist, was Nelson's materials chief, doubled as chief WPB trouble-shooter.

FIGHTING Leon Henderson battled politicians vigorously to hold prices down, and to prevent inflation. His title: Price Administrator.

SIDNEY HILLMAN, ILGWU leader, represented labor in OPM until poor health forced him out.

By May, 1942, P-38 interceptors, the fastest U. S. fighters, were rolling out of Lockheed plants every few minutes.

Thirteen months after it was begun Ford's gigantic Willow Run plant was aiming at producing a giant bomber an hour.

PLANES

In the same years that U.S. commercial aviation covered this continent and spanned the Atlantic and Pacific, military aviation was largely neglected. Only small amounts were spent on research and military production. On May 16, 1940, when President Roosevelt announced his defense program, the combined U.S. Army and Navy air fleets totaled only 5,047 planes. Of these, approximately 500 were fit for battle.

Orders from Britain and her allies, though comparatively insignificant today, were sufficient to educate most U.S. aircraft plants in the construction of military planes. Before the problem of mass production could be solved, however, the types of planes, the percentages of trainers, bombers, and fighters, of developing better planes and motors, of priorities, of expanding plant capacity had to be decided. Planes were hardly off the production lines when they were obsolete. Changes in specifications throttled production. Emphasis was shifted from fighters to long-range bombers to medium bombers. To an anxious public it seemed that new types of planes were being built every day, but none of them were being built in quantity.

U.S. plants had delivered to Britain and Canada only some 1,900 planes in 1940. For a while it looked as though the masters of mass production, the American engineers and workmen, had met their first defeat. When the President, in Jan. 1942, called for 50,000 planes for that year and 125,000 planes for 1943, they seemed impossible goals.

But American ingenuity and workmanship gradually ironed out production kinks. Spectacular records were achieved. The counterboring of holes in engines, for instance, which took 3½ hours in 1939, was taking only 36 seconds in 1942. Sub-assemblies were developed for whole sections of planes.

By May, 1942 some 13,000 combat planes had been delivered and total production had exceeded 3,500 planes a month. The goal of 50,000 planes for 1942 was assured, and a head start had been achieved on the 1943 goal of 125,000 planes—one every eight and a half minutes.

Note place for cannon and machine guns between twin motors.

Production of Vultee trainers for Army and Navy had begun to assume real proportions before Pearl Harbor was attacked.

PRODUCTION OF "FLYING FORTRESSES" had assumed large proportions before Pearl Harbor and they were in service in every part of the world. Heavily armed and armoured, they were among the most intricate assembling jobs ever attempted. Sub-assemblies built wings, tails, dashboards, noses, etc., which converged with the main assembly lines at the proper place and time.

Twin-engined PBY Navy patrol planes were being mass produced by Feb., 1942, to cover our coasts and protect ship convoys

IRCRAFT WORKERS put up their own slogans to inspire greater oduction efforts. Front line fliers returned to tell them how much eir work counted. By Jan., 1941, 115,000 planes were on order and each plant was producing one standardized type of plane. On June 8, 1942, President Roosevelt asked for another $11,043,000,000 for the air forces of the Army.

ass-production of glass-nosed, speedy, three-wheeled B-26 medium bombers was achieved at the Glenn Martin plants in 1941.

TANKS

PRODUCTION OF THOUSANDS OF SCOUT CARS moved rapidly once auto and truck manufacturers had retooled their plants. Roller helps lift truck out of deep ditches.

WHEN the United States began its rearmament program in May, 1940, the Army had only 446 tanks, none strictly modern and not more than 50 fit for any kind of battle. The great automobile factories of Detroit were already producing in small quantities some of the trucks, staff cars, "jeeps," reconnaissance cars, half-track troop carriers. The industry leaders were reluctant to convert their factories to war production; in fact, not until Feb. 2 did the last pleasure car roll off the assembly lines. Then the dies which had produced $4,000,000,000 worth of autos a year were junked and the conveyor belts torn down to make way for new belts and new dies which would produce the 45,000 tanks needed for 1942. By May, 1942, approximately 100 tanks were being produced each day and production was steadily rising.

MASS PRODUCTION OF MEDIUM TANKS, known as the M-3 or "General Grant," was begun in a few factories late in 1941. Over 6,000 tanks of various types were produced between 1940 and 1942. Production of monster 60-ton tanks was not begun until 1942. The hulls of United States tanks were made of cast steel and then welded, giving the crew greater protection than crews of Axis tanks. The first model M-4 tanks carried their heaviest gun, a 75 mm. cannon on the right, a 37 mm. anti-tank gun on the turret, and a 50 caliber machine gun. Later models carried the heavy cannon in the center to permit wider firing range. By the end of May production of M-4 had reached 3,000 a month and they were in active service in Egypt, the Far East and the battlefields of Russia.

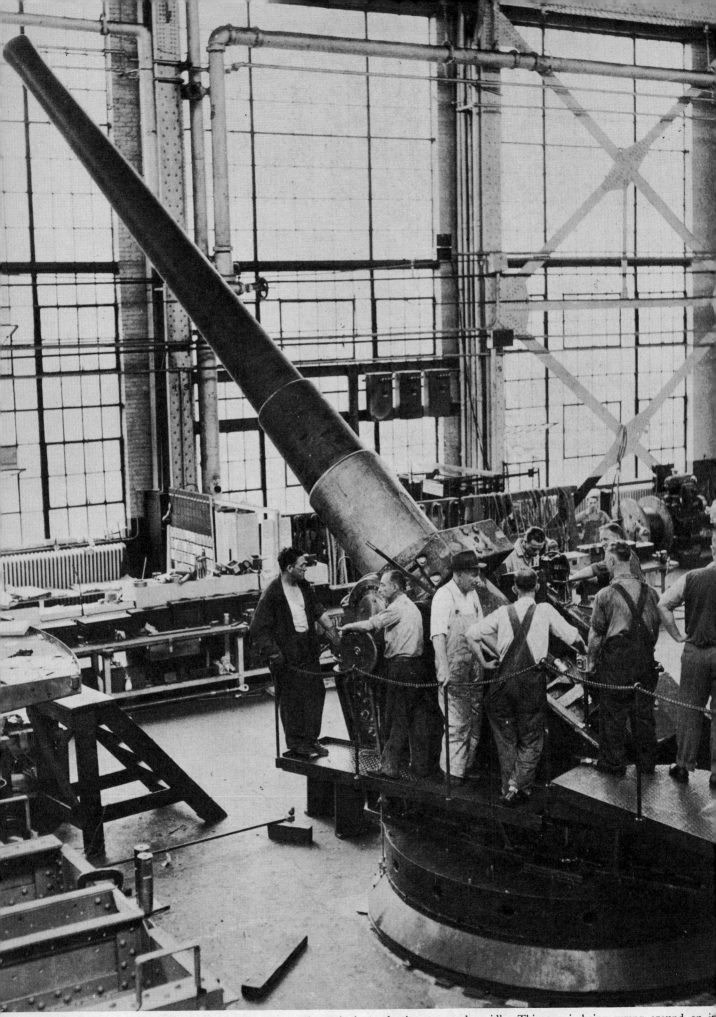

PRODUCTION OF HUGE RAILROAD GUNS took much time because none had been built since 1918 and such guns require delicate balance. The first one was completed in Jan., 1941, after that pro- duction mounted rapidly. This gun is being swung around on it swivel base inside the plant by inspectors who are checking its bal ance and recoil mechanism.

GUNS

HEN the rearmament program of the United States began in May, 1940, the Army had only 448 anti-aircraft guns of all sizes, enough artillery to equip the army of [1]0,000 men then in existence. There were almost no modern [art]illery pieces. Artillery ammunition amounted to only a [fo]ur-day supply in any big battle—and later tests revealed [th]at about a third of it would no longer explode. Our muni[tio]ns capacity was so small that an explosion at Bayonne, [N.] J. in the summer of 1940 virtually wiped out a third of [th]e nation's munitions production facilities. Progress was [slo]w. In May, 1941, soldiers were still drilling with logs [lab]eled "105 mm. howitzer." By May, 1942, however, over [20]0 artillery and anti-tank guns exclusive of anti-aircraft [an]d guns to be mounted on tanks, had been produced. Pro[du]ction of machine guns, including anti-aircraft, aircraft [an]d infantry amounted to over 50,000. Working night and [da]y by May, 1942, were 100 new ammunition factories.

Production of naval guns kept ahead of our naval construction.

INSPECTOR EXAMINES a trench mortar. Production of [the]se simple, powerful guns was easy; not so easy was production of [the] complex anti-aircraft and anti-tank guns a month.

THIS 105 MM. HOWITZER CARRIAGE was made in one plant, the gun itself in another. Only by making different parts in various factories was it possible to make over 800 of them monthly.

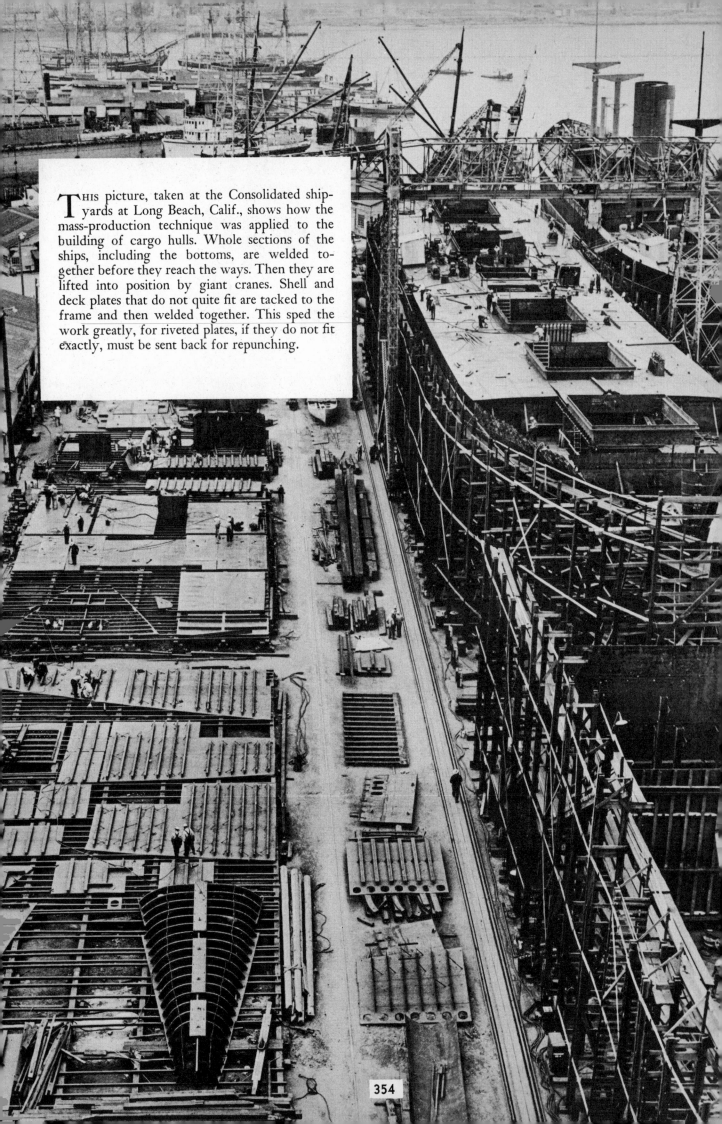

THIS picture, taken at the Consolidated ship-yards at Long Beach, Calif., shows how the mass-production technique was applied to the building of cargo hulls. Whole sections of the ships, including the bottoms, are welded together before they reach the ways. Then they are lifted into position by giant cranes. Shell and deck plates that do not quite fit are tacked to the frame and then welded together. This sped the work greatly, for riveted plates, if they do not fit exactly, must be sent back for repunching.

Merchant Shipping

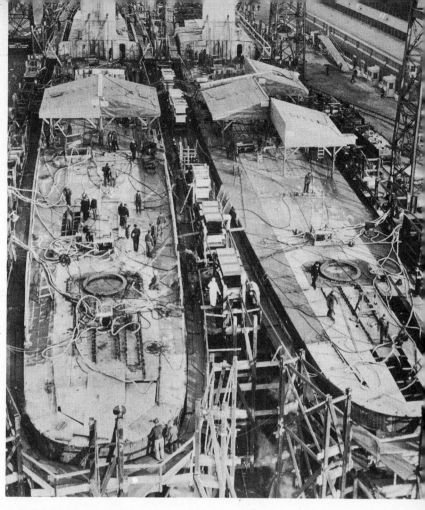

FACED with the problem of supplying our own fighting forces abroad as well as our Allies, President Roosevelt, in his January production speech, set a goal of 8,000,000 tons of shipping for 1942 and 15,000,000 tons for 1943. Between Jan. 1 and May 22, 1942, 138 ships were delivered, a remarkable number compared to what had been done a year before. But Nazi U-boat packs sank 191 ships in the same period, and by mid-June the total sunk numbered 269. It was clear that shipping was the weakest and greatest danger spot in the entire U.S. production picture. Battles on far-off fronts were being lost because there were no ships to bring them supplies that were waiting on U.S. docks. A score of critics, including Walter Lippmann, blamed the situation on the lack of foresight and co-ordination of Admiral Emory S. Land, War Shipping Administrator. By the end of June it was recognized that only through the mass production methods of Henry J. Kaiser, the builder of the Grand Coulee dam, would the 8,000,000-ton quota for 1942 be met. By mid-May Kaiser's yards were launching 10,000-ton Liberty boats 43 days after the keel had been laid and fitting them in another 26 days.

1,500 LIBERTY SHIPS, such as the two above, were the backbone of the new fleet. By April keels for 142 had been laid and 82 had been launched. By July three a day were coming off the ways and Admiral Vickery was promising 20,000,000 tons of shipping instead of 15,000,000 for 1943. Below: the first of the easily assembled, flat-bottomed Sea Otters. One of the chief advantages of the Sea Otter was that it could be powered with available gasoline motors.

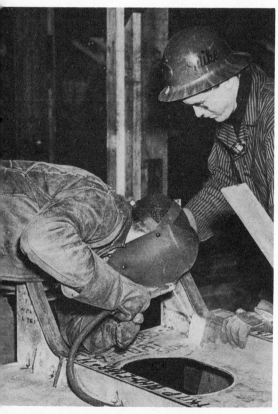

WELDING LIGHTENED THE WEIGHT of the ship by several tons and increased the boat's speed. Ironically, Germans first discovered its advantages.

THE AIRCRAFT CARRIER *HORNET*, the United States' seventh large carrier, was launched in December, 1940, but was not one of the twelve new carriers provided for in the two-ocean navy. When the carriers became the backbone of the fleet in the spring of 1942, the Navy began to train 30,000 pilots for their planes.

OVER A MILLION WORKERS, such as these Philadelphia Navy Yard employees, won "E" pins, awarded by the Navy Department in recognition of excellent work, efficiency, and increased production. Early in 1941 only six private shipyards were working on navy contracts; by June 1942 225 were at work.

CONSTRUCTION OF SPEEDY PC-BOATS, SUB-CHASERS, was stepped up to help ease the strain on merchant shipping. A thousand were under construction by Nov., 1940, and in June, 1942, 1,000 more were authorized. Note that a new bottom is being lowered onto the ways immediately after a launching.

TWELVE OF THE 166 NEW DESTROYERS had been built by Dec., 1941. After Pearl Harbor production records were shattered. Whole sections, including 40-ton bows and sterns, were fabricated ashore, then lifted onto ways by cranes. Time to build a destroyer was cut from 28 months to eight months.

NAVAL CONSTRUCTION

EXPANSION of the U.S. Navy began on May 17, 1938, when Congress authorized a 20% increase. Two years later a second expansion bill authorized an increase of 11%. But the fall of France and the danger that the British fleet, which had long guarded the Atlantic, might fall, brought immediate authorization, on July 19, 1940, of a two-ocean navy, increasing the navy 70% by the construction of 245 combatant ships. This would give the United States the greatest navy in the world. It provided for 17 new battleships, 12 new carriers, 48 new cruisers, 166 destroyers, 81 submarines. Production was begun in Sept. 1940, and during the coming year Congress added another three billion to the 26 billion already appropriated. Mass-production methods were introduced. By early 1942 six of the seventeen battleships had been launched. After Pearl Harbor production soared. Ships slid down ways in over 200 shipyards. In June Congress added $8,500,000,000 to the 20 billion odd dollars already appropriated to double the two-ocean navy. But simultaneously it provided for a new kind of navy. Plans for five monster 60,000-ton battleships which were ready for construction were scrapped. The era of the battleship had ended in the battles at Midway and Coral Sea. Though the battleships still under construction would be finished, the others were to be converted immediately to carriers. And the House Naval Committee revealed about 35 cruisers and merchant ships were also being converted. This would give the United States some eighty carriers and a navy larger than the combined navies of the world.

THE 1,500 TON *PETO,* long-range sub, hits the water in a sideways launching. U.S. had 104 subs when two-ocean navy was started. By Sept., 28 of the 83 new ones had been launched. Most new U-boats were of the long-range type, capable of cruising thousands of miles.

BY FEBRUARY, 1942 SIX OF THE SEVENTEEN NEW BATTLESHIPS had been launched. Shown above is the trim 35,000 *Indiana* just before launching. Nearing completion were four more. However, after the battle off Midway plans for 60,000-ton battleships were shelved. Many battleships on the ways were converted to carriers. Thus ended the 20-year-old argument over battleships *vs.* planes.

A MILLION AND ONE

B Y MARCH, 1942 over five million men and women were involved in war production; by the end of the year, another ten million would be needed. Most of them made the million-and-one things armies and navies need besides planes, tanks, guns, warships, such as surgical instruments, blankets, flashlights, needles, canteens, goggles, screw drivers, shoelaces, insulation for wiring, shovels, toothbrushes, lantern wicks. To make this huge multitude of things the battle of production was fought just as hard, if not as spectacularly, as it was in the basic war industries. Subcontracts on all kinds of equipment went to all kinds of plants, from tiny cellar machine shops to prison shops. Old prejudices against women and Negroes were shattered by the nation's need, and these new sources of man power assured America that the hands needed to meet our production goals would be available..

ALTOONA'S SPRAWLING RAILROAD SHOPS turned out these new wheels, ready to be fitted to 10,000 new freight cars.

FARM PRODUCTION for 1941 was 13% higher than the average of 1935-9, because U.S. was already beginning to feed the world.

UNIFORMS FOR AN ARMY OF 5,000,000 soldiers and for every climate kept the garment industry working 24 hours a day.

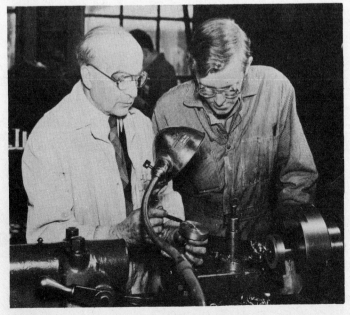

PURDUE UNIVERSITY'S MACHINE SHOP, like that of many other schools and colleges, was converted to war production.

MONTHLY PRODUCTION OF 50-CALIBER MACHINE guns, being tested above, went from 700 in 1941 to 1,500 in 1942.

IN ORDER TO SERVICE PLANES, more motors were needed than planes, but motor production easily kept ahead of schedule.

MILLIONS OF GAS MASKS WERE MADE to equip the Army, Navy, and Marines. Production for civilians began in 1942.

MOST OF THE SOLE LEATHER produced in the U.S. was required to make the millions of pairs of shoes needed for soldiers.

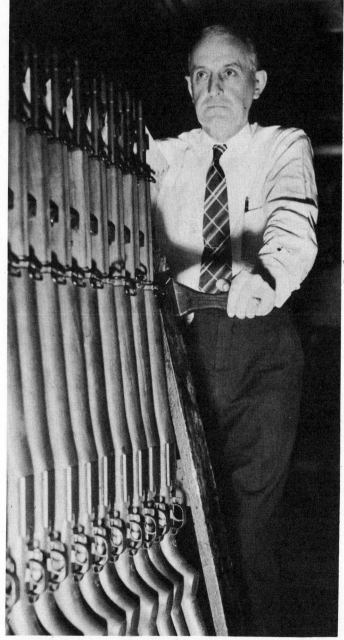

MUNITIONS PLANTS, BUILT IN 1941, sent the munitions production rate soaring in 1942. These are 155 mm. shells.

PRODUCTION OF GARAND RIFLES, one of the fastest, most accurate rapid-fire guns in the world, reached 1,000 a day.

IMMEDIATELY AFTER THE OUTBREAK OF THE WAR air interceptor commands were set up along both our Pacific and Atlantic coasts to head off possible air attacks on U.S. The shelling of the Pacific coast by a Japanese sub and of Aruba by a Nazi sub awoke most Americans to the fact that our coasts might become active w theaters. This picture shows a Pacific patrol receiving instructio before taking off. Note silhouettes of Japanese planes and submari hanging on the walls of the interceptor command's control room.

THE HOME FRONT

CALIFORNIA'S 113,000 JAPANESE were rounded up, taken to closely guarded work camps far inland to prevent fifth columnists and spies among them from aiding Japan.

TO GUARD NEW YORK AND OTHER COAST CITIES, interceptor comman worked from control centers such as this, modeled after England's. An air-raid alarm New York day after Pearl Harbor, though false, demonstrated U.S. unprepared brought thousands of civilians to defense headquarters to volunteer services.

Anti-aircraft guns emplacements dotted both coasts, ringed major cities, vital harbors and industrial plants.

U. S. Army patrols were set up to guard oil reserves, bridges, war factories, docks, and vital roads throughout the nation.

Drivers Corps

Messengers

Auxiliary Police

In Akron, O., raid drills included lunch in shelters.

This shelter served Stamford, Conn., plane builders.

Abandoned N. J. mines were reopened as shelters.

Able J. M. Landis became head of Civilian Defense Jan. 9.

THE HOME FRONT

THE millions of Americans outside the military services responded to the attack on Pearl Harbor by swamping the offices of Civilian Defense to volunteer as air raid wardens, plane spotters, first aid workers, firemen, anything to help defend America and win the war. Months before, Washington, learning a lesson from France where the populace had not been mobilized and from England and Russia, where the public had been mobilized, had set up Civilian Defense Services under the joint direction of Mayor F. H. LaGuardia and Mrs. Eleanor Roosevelt. In the pre-Pearl Harbor period Civilian Defense grew gradually amidst a welter of red tape, disorganization, and confusion as to what constituted Civilian Defense. In the view of Mrs. Roosevelt and Mayor LaGuardia, Civilian Defense included not only air raid wardens, but a national health and physical fitness program. When Civilian Defense offices bogged down under the rush of volunteers that followed Pearl Harbor, the economy bloc in Congress let loose with an attack on Civilian Defense' fitness program as "New Deal boondoggling." A Congressional free-for-all ended with LaGuardia and Mrs. Roosevelt being replaced by able J. M. Landis who reorganized Civilian Defense.

Rescue Squads

Air Raid Wardens

Auxiliary Firemen

AN AIR RAID WARDEN IN NEW YORK CITY turns off a stop-and-go signal during a test black-out. One of the most popular branches of civilian defense, air raid wardens gave up 24 hours monthly to patrol their neighborhoods.

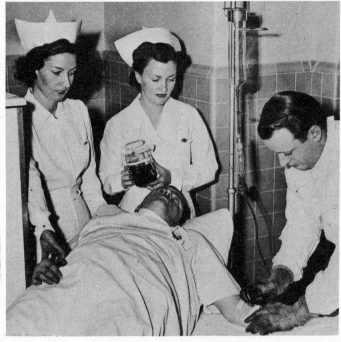

THOUSANDS BECAME BLOOD DONORS to give the Red Cross its goal of 1,000,000 pints of blood for transfusions at war hospitals. Use of blood plasma banks was developed by Russian scientists, was first used during Spanish civil war.

THROUGH THE RED CROSS American women gathered and mended clothes, made bandages, packed medical supplies for use abroad. These Honolulu women are sorting clothes originally intended for Britain to find wearables for Pearl Harbor victims.

TEXAS-BORN MRS. OVETA CULP HOBBY was selected to head the WAAC (Women's Army Auxiliary Corps). The WAACS were the first corps of women to serve with the U. S. Army. Their job was to relieve men from office and supply work.

Thousands of volunteer firemen and air-raid wardens learned how to extinguish incendiary bombs and render first aid.

WOMEN'S AMBULANCE AND DEFENSE CORPS on the West coast trained intensively. A San Bernardino unit is shown drilling with gas masks while smoke pots add realism to their work. In many sections of America, particularly the Southwest, guerrilla units we organized to meet the threat of invasion. Thousands of Americ women served in the American Women's Voluntary Service.

N MAY 3 the nation began sugar rationing to prevent later short-
es. Eight ounces per week was allotted to each individual. Above:
application for a ration book.

SS OF THE DUTCH EAST INDIES cut off U.S. rubber sup-
es. Above is one of the first synthetic tires produced in America.
re rationing went into effect in January, 1942. Gasoline rationing
the East coast began May 15.

BLACK-OUTS, common in Europe since 1938, began in America's
major cities on the Pacific within a few days after Pearl Harbor. By
May most East coast cities, including Washington, had undergone
test black-outs. The above picture was made in New York just before
the city was blacked out, while the picture below shows the same
scene during the black-out. The tall center building is the RCA
Building at Radio City; the white blob in both pictures is the moon.
To protect east coast ships which found they were being silhouetted
for the benefit of Nazi subs by an offshore glare most eastern coastal
cities were dimmed out for the duration.

INCREASE PRODUCTION of aluminum, much needed in air-
aft construction, 11,835,000 lbs. of old aluminum pots, pans, hair
rlers were collected in a national drive.

This striking picture was made of the top commanders of the army early in Mar., 1942, after the reorganization of the army.

The Reorganization of the U.S. Army

BY THE end of 1941 United States' military power had reached a stage where its rapid development was in danger of being strangled by over a century's accumulation of finely spun red tape and bureaucracy. On March 2, 1942, an executive order effected a sweeping reorganization of U.S. military administration, slashing away mountains of red tape. Numerous cumbersome and conflicting bureaus were dissolved into three supreme sections: Air Force, Ground Force, and Supply. Ever since 1939, when the President jumped young, brilliant, non-West-Pointer George Catlett Marshall over the heads of 20 major and 14 brigadier generals to the post of Chief of Staff, such a move had been rumored. Indeed, months before the President's order General Marshall had effected much of the reorganization.

The new streamlined high command, pictured above, included: Lt. Gen. H. H. Arnold, chief of the autonomous Air Force, who is showing his colleagues something on the map; Gen. Marshall, Chief of Staff, Gen. Lesley McNair, chief of the Ground Force, including all infantry, cavalry, and armored divisions; standing, right, Major Gen. Brehon B.

Somervell, chief of supply; left, Maj. Gen. J. T. McNarney, who is in charge of War Department reorganization.

On these generals falls the burden of directing United States' effort in global war. They are the brains of the Army. Yet each of them has many years of practical soldiering. Marshall planned and organized the Meuse-Argonne offensive in World War I. Arnold, a pupil of the late Gen. Bill Mitchell, directed the training of the air corps in 1917, foresaw the coming of air power, planned for and organized the world's largest air force for the U.S. McNair has been an infantry officer since 1904, fought with Pershing in Mexico, Funston in Vera Cruz, won fame in France with the first A.E.F. Somervell is one of the great organizing geniuses of the Army, solved Mississippi River Commission problems for Hoover, WPA problems for Franklin Roosevelt. McNair, an organizer like Somervell, has revamped the War Department's outmoded procedures, streamlined its necessary red tape. It is the high command's job to decide strategy, where U.S. forces shall be sent, how many, how to keep them supplied, pick commanders. It is a formidable task.

Yet by May there were hundreds of thousands of U.S. troops serving in every part of the globe, and the High Command was still building an army which would total 4,500,000 by the end of 1942. U.S. striking power, which was virtually non-existent two years before, was well on the way to be overwhelming. Over 1,800,000 of American troops had had over a year's training. The battles of Production and Preparation had been won and opening phase of offensive actions against the Axis had begun.

An anti-aircraft unit conditions its gun during 7,000-mile trip.

A.E.F. Troopships reach Australia

Gen. MacArthur assumed command of all United Nations' forces.

THE smoke had hardly cleared from Pearl Harbor when the U.S. High Command shipped to Australia a U.S. air unit. It arrived there at the end of December while Roosevelt and Churchill were planning the grand strategy of the war in Washington. Looking at just as black a picture as they could paint, the President and Prime Minister foresaw the loss of Malaya, Burma, the Philippines, and the Dutch East Indies before adequate reinforcements could arrive. They decided Australia's defenses must be made secure at once. Strategically located but hard to reach, Australia offered facilities for large troop concentrations and adequate harbors. Best of all, it offered a jumping-off point for a large scale offensive against the Japanese. As rapidly as convoys could be made up, well-trained American troops were shipped out on the long, hot 7,000-mile route to Australia. Mobile coastal guns, tanks, fighter planes were shipped with them in vast quantities. The arrival of the first large convoys was not announced until Mar. 14. Three days later it was revealed that Gen. MacArthur had flown from embattled Bataan to take charge of American forces. Later MacArthur was given command of all United Nations forces in the Southern Pacific.

THROUGHOUT APRIL, MAY AND JUNE U. S. troops from every corps continued to pour into Australia. Not a man was lost enroute but the crammed troopships were very uncomfortable traveling through the tropic waters with all portholes sealed. Life preservers were worn at all times. The sea-wise kept landlubbers watching for mythical buoys marking the Equator.

TRAVELING WITH THE TROOPS were several hundred Army nurses, full hospital units and large supplies of medicines. But few of the men suffered from anything but the intense heat.

THE A.E.F. INCLUDED many mobile anti-aircraft guns, such as the one being unloaded in the above picture. They were greatly needed for the defense of Australia's vast, vulnerable coast.

EQUIPPED WITH NEW GLOBULAR HELMETS, which offered more protection than the old style helmet, the American troops were shifted to Australia's most vulnerable points as soon as they landed. Meanwhile, on Mar. 17, Gen. MacArthur assumed command of all the United Nations' forces in the Southwestern Pacific. Japanese planes were already reconnoitering northern Australia.

BETWEEN AIR RAIDS by Japanese planes American boys played cards with battle-trained Anzacs who had fought in Greece, Crete and Libya and who had been brought home to help defend their own country. On April 25 more U. S. troops landed in New Caledonia, a Free French island colony, 800 miles east of Australia. By the end of March the Japanese had taken most of the East Indies.

U. S. ANTI-AIRCRAFT UNITS TRAINED constantly to bring their teamwork to perfection. Meanwhile, U. S. Army engineers scraped and leveled hidden airfields (below) for our air force. Bombers could be flown in but the much-needed fighters and interceptors had to be shipped in. On Feb. 20 the Japanese succeeded in taking Timor, a Portuguese island off northern Australia and an excellent base for air raids on Darwin, Australia's chief port in the north. In the Darwin area Anzacs and Americans rushed fortifications to prevent the Japanese from seizing a foothold. Meanwhile, February 27 the Navy and U. S. air force had smashed a great Japanese invasion fleet bound for Java in the Makassar strait inflicting serious losses and much damage to troopships and naval vessels.

S. P-40 FIGHTER PLANES, more than a match for the Japanese Zeros, were stationed along the northern and eastern coasts and around the principal cities to intercept bombing raids. In mid-May U. S. land-based bombers joined naval aircraft in a smashing defeat of the Japanese fleet in the Coral sea. Flying Fortresses began heavy raids on Japanese bases in the Dutch East Indies in May.

Though the Japanese raided Darwin (below) and their baby subs had penetrated the Sydney harbor, their main forces were concentrated in a major effort to knock out hard-pressed China. With the U. S. and Britain rushing the opening of a second European front, Australia had become, momentarily perhaps, a secondary front. American supplies and troops, however, continued to arrive in Australia.

First contingent of A.E.F. to Ireland reached there on Jan. 25, began handing out American cigarettes to British sailors.

ON TO BERLIN!

On JANUARY 25, 1942, less than two months after Nazi Germany had declared war on us, the first contingent of American Expeditionary Forces to Europe arrived safely in northern Ireland. A second contingent arrived a few weeks later, and on May 17 the Army announced that a new convoy to troopships had arrived. Thus, for the second time within the memory of most Americans, United States troops had arrived in Europe to fight Germany. The troops, numbering many thousands and including tank units, had made the crossing without the loss of a single man. Months before U.S. technicians had been busy building bases for them since January a great U.S. naval base had been in operation at London-derry, Ireland. New and larger contingents of U.S. troops arrived during the summer and on June 25 Major General Dwight Eisenhower arrived to take command of the U.S. invasion forces. As the summer wore on, new Japanese successes in the Far East and Rommel's success in Africa made the opening of a second front in Europe the only real hope of winning the war.

U. S. Marines arrived on May 17 wearing the newly designed combat helmet

First man ashore was Pvt. Milburn Kenke of Hutchinson, Minn.

To every man in every A.E.F. went this Presidential letter.

GEN. MARSHALL, U.S. CHIEF OF STAFF, reviewed A.E.F. orces at their bases in March when he flew to London to confer with he British High Command on the opening of a second front. Return- ng to America, he told the graduating class of West Point that American troops "are landing in England and they will land in France." This was the first official announcement that a second front would soon be opened. Meanwhile, the work of shipping to England munitions and supplies as well as more troops went forward steadily under the direction of U.S. Gen. Brehon V. Somervell. More daring Commando raids simultaneously increased Nazi nervousness and brought Gen. Rudolf Gerd von Rundstedt, Hitler's greatest strate- gist, to France to command the Nazi defenses of the coast.

373

OILING UP THEIR SUB-MACHINE GUNS, the A.E.F. began intensive training. The arrival in May of tank and heavy artillery units brought the number of troops to "many thousands." From Washington it was announced that British and American experts had long been at work standardizing the equipment, guns, and munitions of the two nations so that they could be interchanged at will.

MEANWHILE BRITISH GEN. H. E. FRANKLYN began planning with U.S. Gen. Russell Hartle for the transportation of the A.E.F. to invasion bases along the Channel coast. There were by this time close to four and a half million men under arms in Britain. Officers of the British and U.S. high commands shuttled back and forth across the Atlantic to complete invasion plans.

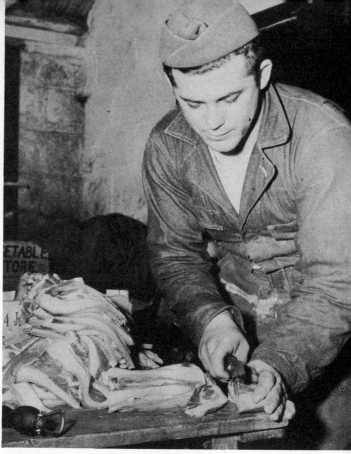

U.S. TROOPS brought their own food supplies to save dwindling British reserves and ate better than the average Britisher. Anglo-American food supplies had been pooled in Jan. 1942.

THICK SLICES OF IRISH BACON became a favorite of the A.E.F. But independent southern Ireland, one of the last neutral states in the war, was on the verge of starvation.

TOUGHENED BY OVER A YEAR'S TRAINING in the U.S., the A.E.F. set about its preparations for invasion in a businesslike way. Meanwhile, word of their arrival spread like wildfire throughout conquered Europe, brought underground anti-Nazi activity to new heights. Commandos were joined in a raid on St. Nazaire by Frenchmen who had hidden their guns.

MAJOR GENERAL DWIGHT D. EISENHOWER, picked by the U.S. High Command to head A.E.F. operations in Europe, arrived June 23. Texas-born, a West Pointer, "Ike" Eisenhower served in World War I as a lt. colonel, was MacArthur's right-hand man in the Philippines in 1935, headed the vital Operations Division of the General Staff, was America's best armored force expert.

NEW A.E.F. CONVOYS arrived in a steady stream with more men, supplies. This picture was taken while one of the convoys neared Ireland and anti-aircraft crews increased their watch.

Training maneuvers were carried out in the realistic atmosphere of bombed-out villages by troops using "live" ammunition.

RAINING UNDER EVERY POSSIBLE CONDITION they ...ight meet in the "big show," American troops were whipped into ...ape to take part in the coming invasion of the continent, then ...ipped southward to the English Channel coast to participate in ...ock invasions. Gen. Eisenhower's appointment was followed by ...at of Gen. Spaatz as head of the U.S. Air Forces in Europe, and American crews began participating in the mass raids of the British on Germany. Even without the A.E.F., Britain had approximately two and a half million well-trained, well-armed men ready for the invasion and another two million in her efficient Home Guard. By the end of July the lack of shipping was the toughest major problem delaying the invasion.

New, hard-hitting Russian bombers led the Red assault. In May 1,366 Nazi planes were destroyed.

The Russian Spring Offensive

Since Dec. 6 the Russians had been driving forward.

As the spring of 1942 began to melt the deep snows on the Russian steppes, world attention focused on the sprawling, uneven 2,000-mile Soviet front and awaited the much advertised and heralded Nazi spring offensive. Until now the Russians had done an incredibly magnificent job. They had not only checked the "invincible" Nazi war machine but they had hurled it back with staggering losses in men, planes, and tanks. Yet the Russians' own losses were immense and the question of whether the Red army would be able to withstand new and greater blows was fraught with significance for the whole world. As Gen. MacArthur put it, "On the worthy banners of the Red army rest the hopes of civilization." But Timoshenko was already supplying the Red army's answer to the promised deathblow. Determined not to let the initiative slip from his hands, Timoshenko stepped up the Russian assault in March. All along the vast central front he alternated one powerful thrust here with another somewhere else to keep the Nazi preparations in a constant process of reorganization.

USSIAN INFANTRYMEN MOVED into devastated Yukhnov, o miles from Moscow, early in March. Note that heat from burng buildings has apparently melted the snow. Meanwhile, Timoenko began placing the fresh armies Voroshilov and Budenny had en training all winter between Kharkov and Taganrog. From the great industrial bases in the Urals came new tanks which were supplemented by shipments from England and the United States. On April 6 Timoshenko began a thrust toward Kharkov which in 12 days destroyed some 40,000 Nazis and deepened the wedge the Russians had driven between Kharkov and Stalino.

TO KHARKOV, HEART OF THE INDUSTRIAL Donetz in, and communications center for the whole Ukraine, the Nazis hed reserves they had been gathering for an assault on Rostov and Caucasian oil fields. To increase the Nazi organizational problems, noshenko simultaneously drove giant pincers north and south of Smolensk. In Moscow on May 1 Premier Stalin, calling for a great offensive, gave an order that brought cheer to a world that had been thinking of victory in two years; "The entire Red army is to see to it that the year 1942 shall become the year of the final defeat of the German Fascist troops and the liberation of Soviet soil. . . ."

INCREASING QUANTITIES OF AMERICAN SUPPLIES were arriving at Murmansk, despite furious Nazi air assaults on the convoys off Petsamo. The above picture shows an American truck moving towards the front. Both Britain and the U. S., grateful for the time Russian resistance had given them, rushed all the equipment they could spare to enable the Russians to withstand the Nazi spring and summer offensive. Although they possessed great in dustrial plants in the Urals and had "leap-frogged" thousands of fac tories eastward beyond the reach of the Nazis, one of the most fan tastic feats of the war, the Soviet industrial losses had been enormou and aid was greatly needed. Agitation for a second front in Europ increased daily.

RUSSIAN AIR OFFICERS cooperating with the R.A.F. wing operating at Murmansk are shown here watching the R.A.F. in action. By May enough U. S. Tomahawks—called "Tomagauks" by the Russians—had arrived to equip full squadrons. Meanwhile, in mid-April, the Red army smashed Nazi attempts to seize the initiative.

IN THE U. S. RED GENERAL BARAYEU and Col. Bere inspected new planes seeking to obtain one adapted to flying con tions in Russia. Red Air force pilots liked the Airacobra best becau of its maneuverability, but found its famous tricycle landing g "too tender" for the make-shift air fields from which it flew.

IMOSHENKO UNLEASHED A POWERFUL OFFENSIVE n the Kharkov area on May 13, two days after the Nazi drive for ne Caucasus got under way in the Crimea. Low-flying, heavily ar- noured Stormavik planes, carrying a heavy cannon as well as two nachine guns, smashed Nazi counter-attacks with tanks. The above picture shows Stormaviks after smashing a Nazi tank column near Kharkov. Four of the tanks may be seen burning in the road. Timoshenko's own tank armies hurled themselves at Kharkov in a movement which threatened to flank the entire Nazi offensive in the Crimea and hold up the long heralded German drive.

HIS UNUSUAL PICTURE SHOWS Red Troops silencing a 'azi machine-gun nest with a light artillery gun at close-range in ne Crimea where a fierce struggle was being waged for the town f Kerch. Although putting up a furious resistance to every Nazi dvance in an effort to make them pay dearly for every yard won, the Red troops were pushed back into Kerch. Lack of bases forced the Red air force to yield superiority in the air to the concentrated Nazi Luftwaffe. To divert the pressure on Kerch the Red Navy landed marines in the rear of the Nazi drive, and counter-attacks were launched from Sevastopol.

HAND-PICKED, BATTLE-TRAINED RUSSIAN TROOPS, riding atop giant 50-ton "Voroshilovs" plunged toward Kharkov. In a desperate attempt to save their greatest Ukrainian base and prevent their Crimean drive from being outflanked the Nazis threw in reserve tanks and troops. In the Izyum-Barvenkova sector south of Kharkov, fighting reached the fury of Verdun. Heavy Red guns, shown below smashed Nazi fortifications and tank charges. Red Stormoviks and dive bombers swept down on Nazi air bases to wipe out most of the enemy's planes. Within three days Timoshenko's forces had hammered their way through the outer defenses of Kharkov.

PIERCING KHARKOV'S OUTER DEFENSES, the onrushing Red soldiers fought their way from house to house in the suburbs. Typical of the ferocious fighting is the story of one Nazi stronghold, a two-story stone house which could not be brought under artillery fire. Finally Russian infantry, under cover of a machine-gun barrage, advanced to throw themselves through the cellar windows. For a day and a half bloody fighting raged between the Nazis, who held the two floors, and the Russians in the cellar, with furious battles on the stairways. Finally the Reds managed to storm the stairway and clear out the Nazis. Meanwhile, as Timoshenko's main forces by-passed Kharkov and swept far beyond the city to establish a bridgehead on a river which the Nazis regarded as their last line of defense, the Nazis dropped numerous squads of 120 parachutists who were annihilated by Russian sniper units, containing some of the world's best sharpshooters. Tens of thousands of Russian engineers followed the Red advance to build fortifications and repair damage. Desperate psychological Nazi attacks led by brass bands were mowed down and only very heavy reinforcements saved the Nazis from a complete rout. The Kharkov battle did not inflict a decisive defeat on the Nazis but it did defeat their plans for a heavy spring offensive in the eastern Ukraine. The diversion of Nazi troops delayed the southern Nazi attack until mid-summer.

SOVIET TROOPS CAPTURED THOUSANDS of encircled Nazi troops; some of them are shown surrendering above. Most of the captured were young reservists, indicating deterioration of Nazi fighting strength. On May 20 Marshal von Bock attempted a counter-drive which failed to dislodge the Russians. After 19 days of fighting, Nazi losses totaled 90,000 dead, over 200,000 captured or wounded. Russian casualties totaled 75,000, indicating the projected Nazi drive on Rostov had been brilliantly checked but at great cost. Meanwhile Russian tank-borne infantry, shown below, were throwing back the besiegers of Sevastopol, last Russian stronghold in the Crimea.

HEROIC SEVASTOPOL

Although *the upper stories of Maxim Gorki Fort are in our hands and the battle line has moved some 1,400 yards forward, Soviet soldiers deep underground in the lower stories continue to resist. We have sent negotiators to explain to them that further resistance is useless, but they won't come out . . .*" complained the exasperated Nazi radio reporter. So it went at every pillbox and fort. This was Sevastopol. It had taken the Nazis 130 days to fight their way 300 miles from the Rumanian border to the Soviet base's outer defenses; it took them another 245 days to go the remaining 35 miles that meant conquest of the city. In Nov., 1941 one Nazi attempt to take the city failed, cost the Nazis 0,000 men. In December they tried again, lost 35,000 more. Their third attempt began on June 4 under Col. Gen. Fritz von Mannstein with 250,000 men who threw themselves upon Sevastopol's defenses in continuous assaults. The defending Red army and navy men and 80,000 civilians fought back furiously. Nazi bombers dropped tons of explosives, Nazi artillery fired at point-blank range. But Sevastopol's exhausted defenders only hung on. The Nazi dead covered the hills, lay rotting and stinking in the sun. After twenty-three days Mannstein claimed the city. The fighting went on for two days more. On July 3 the Red navy evacuated most of the troops, the remainder moved to Khersones Peninsula, where they continued killing Nazis until the last Russian had fallen. This third attempt cost the Nazis: 60,000 dead, 0,000 wounded, 300 planes, and 250 tanks. But they gained the main base of the Red navy, which was now forced to operate from its secret Caucasus bases.

IN SEVASTOPOL'S LAST DAYS Red navy marines, landing in rubber boats from submarines, attacked the Nazi rear. By heroic efforts they managed to divert the Nazi assault long enough for most of the city's children and women to be evacuated.

COUNTERATTACKING UNTIL EXHAUSTED, Red navy marines and civilians forced the Nazis to recapture many points a dozen times. The battleground: the British cemetery, where lay Tennyson's Six Hundred and 100,000 others who died in the 329-day siege of Sevastopol in 1854. Despite the enormous Nazi air superiority the Red navy moved about the harbor with ease, its big guns hammering the Nazis until the last minute. Of the "August city's" famed, beautiful buildings nothing was left but rubble.

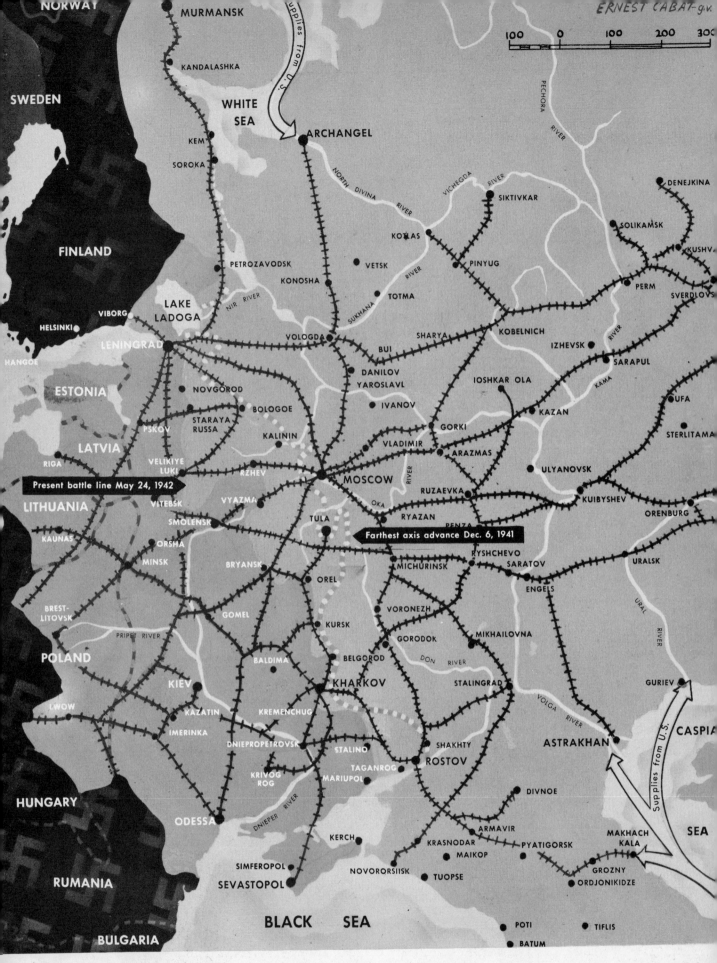

THIS MAP SHOWS the approximate lines of the Soviet-Nazi front after a year of fighting. The broken line shows the furthest point of Nazi advance during the year and indicates the amount of land recaptured by the Red Army offensive which began Dec. 6 at the gates of Moscow. The Germans made their greatest advance during July, August, and September. Their progress after October was little a was secured at terrible cost. The Nazi attempt to seize Moscow a Leningrad was, from a military viewpoint, not worth the effo virtually all Hitler's own generals opposed his Napoleonic dream entering Moscow.

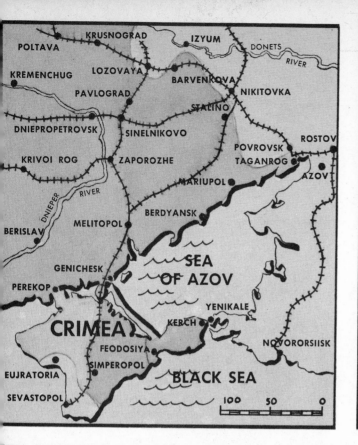

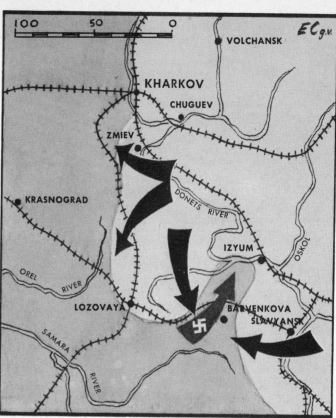

THIS CLOSE-UP shows the Crimea and lower Donets area where the Nazis massed their strongest forces for a spring and summer offensive which they planned to drive through the Caucasus and eventually effect a connection with the Japanese in Persia and India. The Nazi offensive began with the recapture of all Crimea, including Sevastopol.

TIMOSHENKO WRECKED THE NAZI PLANS, however, with a large-scale offensive in the Kharkov-Izyum area which forced the Nazis to reorganize their troops, rush them northward. This held off the main Nazi drive from spring to mid-summer, reduced the amount of good weather left before winter should set in again.

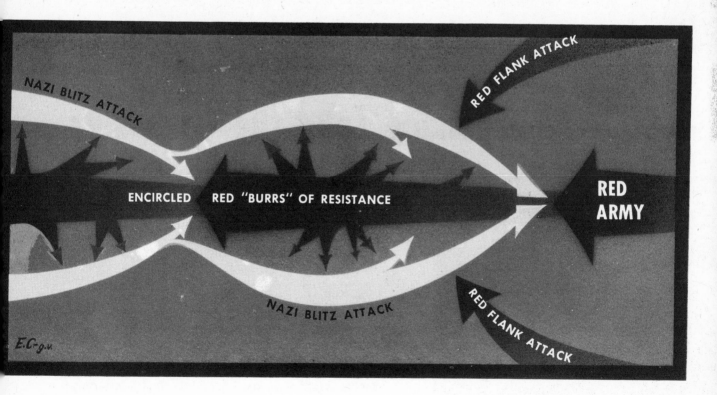

THIS CHART SHOWS the famous Red Army tactic which smashed the Nazi blitzkreig tactics that had been so successful in Poland and France. The Red Army mechanized units met the Nazi panzer divisions head on. But when the Nazis split and flanked them they did not fall back. Instead they drove steadily towards the Nazi rear while simultaneously bringing up forces to flank the Nazi pincers from their flanks. The encircled Russian "burrs" attempted to cut the Nazi tanks off from the infantry which followed them, leaving the Nazi tanks go

with the knowledge that units behind them would smash the isolated tanks. The encircled Russians also struck out at the thin Nazi flanks at various points. If they could break out easily, they did. If not they proceeded towards the base from which the Nazis had shoved off. This tactic put the Nazi communication and supply lines to their advance units out of commission and by late September the Nazis were forced to abandon their racing prong attack, keep their units closely together. Red troops, faced with annihilation, "disintegrated" in small bands.

This unusual picture was made during a Commando raid on the Nazi base at Vaasgo island on Dec. 27, 1941.

The Commandos Take the Offensive

DURING the summer of 1941 when Britain was threatened with momentary invasion, Sir Roger Keyes, World War I hero of Zeebrugge, began to organize small bands of volunteers for "hazardous assignments." Christened "Commandos" by Churchill, who took the name from the Dutch "Commandos" who raided British lines during the Boer war, their first assignment was to slip across the Channel, learn the progress of Nazi invasion preparations, sabotage, and return. The Commandos included burly East End longshoremen, truck drivers, aristocrats, novelists, and play-boys. Volunteers were closely scrutinized before being accepted. Those accepted, the cream of British soldiery, were given intensive "toughening-up" training, which included much hand-to-hand fighting, naval operations, guerrilla tactics. On Nov. 16, 1941, Lord Louis Mountbatten, famous British naval commander, was put in charge of their operations. On Mar. 4, 1941, the Commandos staged their first big raid on the Lofoten islands off Norway. By the summer of 1942 Commando raids on the coast of France had become so numerous and daring that they became a major part of the effort to relieve pressure on Russia and heralded the coming full-scale invasion of the continent.

Lord Louis Mountbatten was made Commando chief.

HE VAAGSÖ OIL FACTORY WAS SET AFIRE by the Commandos whose surprise attack caught the Nazis napping. The British anded under cover of a smoke screen while British warships and rcraft bombarded Nazi defenses. The kneeling Commandos below e watching for snipers. Above, Commandos are shown rounding o some of the Norwegian Quislingites on the Lofoten islands during the first big raid staged by the Commandos. Besides destroying oil stores, they captured 225 Nazis, sank all ships and destroyed a glycerine plant. Most of the local inhabitants welcomed them and some went back to England to join the Free Norwegian armed forces. The reckless daring and Indian tactics of the Commandos captured the imagination of the British and American public.

MOST OF THE VAAGSÖ NAZI GARRISON WAS CAPTURED.
They are shown above being escorted to barges to be taken back to England. Altogether the Commandos captured 225 Nazi soldiers and Quislingites in the Vaagsö raids. Below a wounded officer is shown being assisted back to the barges. Because the shock of the Commando attack was so complete, the Nazis raced around in confusion, fired on their own men, and caused few casualties among the Commandos. Discipline and timing were the two basic rules of the Commandos, for in a raid every man's life depended on the exact and immediate obedience to any order. Each man had a specific job to do at a specific time. Men who did not reach the barges at the appointed time had to be left behind, lest the entire force be captured.

This picture, the first to show Commandos on French soil, shows raiders boarding their barges at Boulogne.

LTHOUGH many more raids were known to have been carried out on the shores of Norway, France, and Holland by July, 1942, less than a dozen had been announced en fewer lent themselves to photographic coverage, for majority of the raids were carried out in total darkness. the raid on St. Nazaire no pictures exist, yet of all the ds few were more daring or significant. Landing silently the beaches at several points on the night of March 28, ups of Commandos wormed their way into the heart of town and Nazi U-boat base. The few sentries the confit Nazis had posted fell quietly—strangled, knifed, or ckjacked. Then suddenly the Commandos were disered by a Nazi who opened fire. Dazed Nazis stumbled m their bunks hardly able to comprehend what had haped. The British seemed to be everywhere with tommy s and hand grenades. Panic-stricken Nazis fired at every-g, including shadows and their own men, which revealed r positions to the British. Meanwhile, Commandos fired racks, supplies, and munition stores, and scores of French-, thinking an invasion had begun, pulled hidden guns and pons from secret hiding places and poured into the

streets to attack the Nazis from the rear. After doing considerable damage and seizing numerous prisoners, the Commandos effected a successful withdrawal under very difficult conditions. Two days later Berlin, with a bad case of the jitters, ordered an immediate shake-up of the French coastal defenses. No less daring than the St. Nazaire raid was the attempt of Commandos under Lt. Col. Geoffrey Keyes, son of Admiral Keyes, the founder of the raiders, to kidnap or kill Nazi Field Marshal Erwin Rommel in his Libyan headquarters. Slipping 250 miles into the Nazi rear, Keyes's small force reached the town where Rommel was planning his new drive on Egypt. With two other men Keyes eluded the Nazi guards in the darkness and made his way to the house where Rommel had his quarters. He rapped on the door and it was opened by a sentry who, sensing something was wrong, raised his gun. The sentry had to be shot, and the noise aroused the officers upstairs. Keyes shot his way upstairs but found his path to Rommel's room barred by two sentries, who managed to fatally wound him. He died as his comrades carried him out in an attempt to escape, which also failed.

THESE NAZIS WERE CAPTURED by Commandos on Feb. 27 when, moving in a coordinated attack with paratroops and navy forces, they raided an important Nazi radio-location station north of Le Havre.

NOT ALL COMMANDOS GOT AWAY on every raid This one was killed at St. Nazaire, France. Note Nazi who are searching for saboteurs left behind.

TWO OF THE COMMANDO LANDING BARGES are shown here returning from the successful raid on the radio-location station. The panels the men are holding are used to signal waiting British warships. Commandos wore rubber-soled shoes, blackened their faces to make them less discernible. Each man was trained in the use of a dagger and the first men ashore were assigned the bloody task of silently knifing any sentries. Often Commandos were ashore twenty minutes before they were detected and by then they generally ha control of the situation. Each Commando was taught how to sta and kill game so that, if left behind, he could hide in the woods ar live off the land until he could either find refuge with patriots escape to England. An underground railroad system regularly r turned R.A.F. fliers who were downed in certain sections of Hollan Belgium, and France to England.

A brave Norwegian boy shows his patriotism by leaning against an Oslo wall on which has been painted: "Long Live Haakon VII."

UNDERGROUND EUROPE

Some of the pictures on these pages are among the rarest taken during World War II. For they show the secret underground Europe that plagued the Nazis at every hour. Taken by trusted anti-Nazis, they were smuggled out at the risk of death to the bearer and any person recognized in the pictures. Even in America it would not be safe to publish these pictures without first blacking out recognizable features of the faces. Every effort has been made to certify their authenticity. As pictures they are often technically bad. They were taken by amateurs at the risk of their lives. Often the camera was concealed in a false book, basket, or underneath clothing. Yet it is precisely their poor technical quality, their incorrect exposures and blurred figures which give these pictures an authentic mood the best photographers could never capture.

HITLER's Nazi troops had hardly conquered a country when its suffering, distracted people forgot their grief and terror to begin harassing their conquerors. At first it was only a sign . . . betrayed Norwegians silently clipped paper clips together . . . a Polish worker locked his massive fingers . . . a French girl twisted two hairpins together . . . the Dutch used stamps of the old regime . . .

. . . signs like these swept Europe. They meant only one thing: unite against the Nazis. In every country, including Germany, the churches and particularly the Roman Catholic Church, became the center of the anti-Nazi underground movement. It was the only instrument through which legal opposition to the Nazis could be expressed. Through it masses of people could be contacted, directed, organized. Communists, nationalists, and Catholics formed the backbone of anti-Nazism in underground Europe. From homemade mimeograph machines and hidden presses poured thousands of anti-Nazi leaflets to be passed secretly from hand to hand. As the strength of the people grew, they gnawed at their Nazi conquerors in a million ways. Gradually open revolt, swift assaults on police stations to gain arms, the silent thrust of a long hatpin into a Nazi heart, and bombings spread. By the end of 1941 the underground movement was everywhere on the offensive, concentrating on obtaining arms. Desperate, the Nazis turned to massacre, but their terrorism held no fear for patriots. All over Europe silent people waited only for the opening of a second front as a signal to strike against the Nazis with all their might.

NORWEGIANS TURNED BREADLINES, such as this one in Oslo, into demonstrations against the Nazis at every opportunity. Strong bands of guerrillas continually harassed the Nazis in the northern areas while in the south small bands of saboteurs cut power lines, started fires, blew up bridges almost nightly. Street fighting between patriotic Norse and Quislingites was frequent. Many made daring escapes to England in fishing boats to join Norwegian forces there. Leading the struggle against Nazism was Bishop Eivand Berggray, head of the Norwegian church, who, with his fellow-bishops, defied Quisling's efforts to take over the church and was finally thrown into a concentration camp for openly agitating against the Nazi rule. Norwegians made up a "death list" of traitors.

THIS PICTURE, one of the best to come out of conquered Europe, shows how the Norwegians treated the Nazis. Everyone, except two small boys, has turned his back on the parading Nazi garrison at Drobak, outside Oslo. This was an invariable rule in every country. Nazis were shunned like poison to make them feel the hatred of the people for them. Restaurants emptied if they came in. Quisling was hated more than the Nazis. When he became puppet premier in Feb. 1942, Norwegian patriots cut the wires feeding the floodlights under which he was reviewing his followers. Norway's rocky, mountainous passes made it easy for guerrillas to cut Nazi supply and communication lines by blowing up bridges and tunnels and causing landslides. When Quisling took over the schools all the teachers resigned.

A French sailor, either a hostage or trapped while engaged in underground activity, awaits the shots of the Nazi firing squad.

FRANCE

FRANCE began to seethe with anti-Nazi activity when it became clear that the senile Pétain was in favor of collaboration with the Nazis. Thousands of Frenchmen listened to BBC religiously although it meant prison, perhaps death, if they were caught. Underground papers sprang up everywhere, despite the formidable tasks of securing paper and ink for them, to help organize resistance, combat the Nazi propaganda of Vichy. De Gaullists and Communists, the two main French underground groups, worked together, the Communists having their main strength in the industrial regions around Paris, the De Gaullists in unoccupied France.

A French worker meets the same fate. Nazi commander of Paris, Gen. Stulpnagel, killed 100 Frenchmen for every Nazi killed.

THE TWO MOST HATED MEN IN FRANCE, Marcel Deat and Pierre Laval, are shown above as they waited to inspect the Fascist brigade they had organized with Jacques Doriot to fight in Russia. A second later a 27-year-old patriot, Paul Collette, pretending he was a volunteer, stepped forth and sent a revolver shot into both of them.

THIS REMARKABLE ACTION PICTURE shows the wounded Deat being carried off by volunteers. Young Collette's aim was not good; both lived. Biggest problem of the underground was to find arms. To get them they ambushed Nazi patrols. Brave Frenchwomen, whose husbands and sweethearts were in Nazi prison camps, carried on much of the dangerous work in occupied France.

NAZIS ERECTED THIS GIGANTIC "V" on the Eiffel Tower in an effort to steal the symbol after BBC launched its "V" for Victory campaign. Within a fortnight after the BBC campaign began V's were being scratched everywhere. The Nazis claimed their "V's" symbolized the Nazi victory, but the German word for victory is *sieg*. Pétain and Laval turned French production over to the Nazis, but strikes were common and the slowdown strike almost continuous. Machinery was sabotaged, run without grease. Workers wasted precious oil. Tools were frequently lost and never could be found until the entire shop had been turned upside down. Waste was carefully but casually dropped into elevator shafts and then fired with a cigarette butt at the first opportunity.

TWO FRENCH UNDERGROUND WORKERS are shown in the above picture leaving a château which contained their headquarters. The picture below shows their sleeping quarters in the cellar. From the German underground, French learned how to rig up a board and a leaking bucket of water so that it would dump leaflets when the water ran out of the pail, giving the man time to escape. Leaflets were dumped from rooftops only when the streets were full of people because otherwise the Nazis would have time to clean them up an because in crowds it was easy for people to get leaflets without bein detected. By 1942 the R.A.F. was regularly dropping munitions an guns to the French underground, which diverted Nazi attention b setting forest fires.

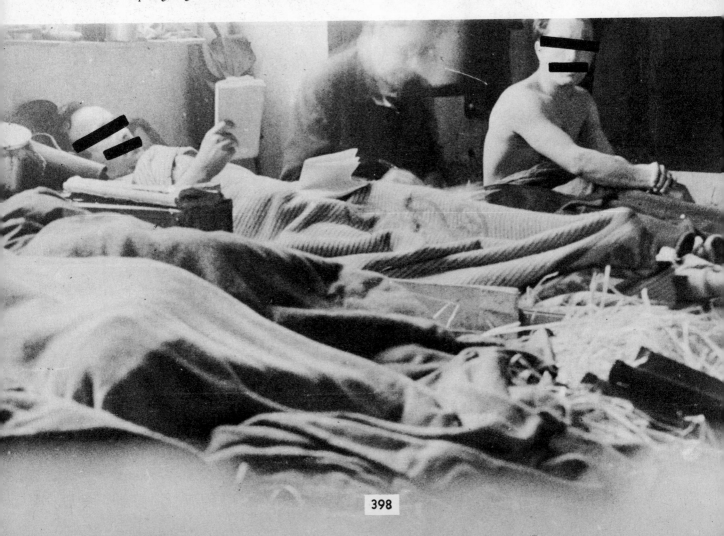

A Nazi notice that 24 Poles have been caught and sentenced for forming a secret military organization to attack the Nazis.

Poland

UNDERGROUND activity was hard to organize in Poland. Villages were far apart. There was much illiteracy, many old antagonisms. But by the end of 1939 illegal papers were being published in nearly every Polish city, groups were being organized for sabotage and guerrilla warfare.

By 1942, 400,000 Poles had been killed for sabotage and resistance. After Hitler invaded Russia underground activity mounted. Red airplanes dropped parachutists and supplies. Territory around Lublin and Zanosc became guerrilla strongholds and all Nazi punitive expeditions failed. Often they raided concentration camps, freed the prisoners. In one such raid Erich Guttart, the Nazi Gestapo master of Poland, was killed. Oil wells and fields were fired. Peasants harvested only enough grain for themselves. Constant raids on Nazi bases and airports permitted them very little rest.

apturing a lone Jew, some brave Nazis amuse themselves by pulling out his beard hair by hair. The dignity and courage with which the Jew looks straight into the eyes of his chief tormentor makes this one of the great pictures of World War II.

THE LOWLANDS

Tout le long de la rue Royale, de part et d'autre du petit square au cœur duquel à l'ombre de la Colonne l'Inconnu de 1918 dort dans sa glorieuse éternité, les sociétés patriotiques et les enfants des écoles font la haie.

Au milieu d'un peuple empoigné par l'émotion s'avancent les troupes victorieuses, qui d'Europe et d'Afrique. Dans le ciel nos ailes triomphantes tracent leurs V chargés de souvenir.

Et sur la tombe, encadré par ceux qui des deux côtés de la mer inviolée ont mené la lutte jusqu'à la victoire, le Roi-Prisonnier, dépose dans un silence de cathédrale, l'hommage de la Belgique à ceux qui, pour qu'elle vive, ont donné leur vie.

Ce Onze Novembre de l'an de la seconde libération, qu'il sera grand, qu'il sera beau.

Plus beau si c'est possible que le premier de tous les Onze Novembre, lorsqu'on entendit se répercuter l'écho du « Cessez-le-Feu » après cinquante-deux mois de campagne.

Le 11 novembre 1941, pour la deuxième fois depuis que la présence allemande souille à nouveau le sol de la Patrie, nous irons, en silence, en ordre pour ne par leur donner prétexte aux représailles criminelles qu'ils appellent « collaboration », incliner notre pensée devant la dalle de Bruxelles, devant l'humble monument de nos villages, ou plus intimement souvent devant la tombe d'hier ou d'il y a vingt-cinq ans.

Onze Novembre de guerre.

Onze Novembre d'occupation.

Jour de recueillement, de prière pour les croyants, de piété patriotique pour tous.

Nous penserons à nos morts pour penser à la Patrie vivante. Nous penserons à leur sacrifice pour ne pas perdre l'humble et persévérant courage de la résistance quotidienne. La Belgique qui a été, avec la maman, la compagne, les enfants abandonnés, leur pensée dernière doit, aujourd'hui être notre pensée unique.

Tous nos soucis, toutes nos espérances c'est de leur point de vue qu'il faut les examiner.

...ont le droit d'exiger que nous n'abandonnions pas une ligne des raisons pour lesquelles ils acceptèrent la mort.

Onze Novembre de guerre.

Onze Novembre des souvenirs.

Onze Novembre aussi des espérances confiantes.

Car il suffit de se reporter à douze mois en arrière pour apprécier le chemin parcouru.

Qu'elle apparaissait enthousiaste mais peu consistante notre certitude de l'an passé !

D'alliés il ne restait que, l'Angleterre, durement blessée.

Le Reich intact, écrasait de ses Panzer victorieux tout l'Occident, à la veille de voir par la force de choses s'offrir à lui des concours nouveaux. La Russie mystérieuse ravitaillait nos tortionnaires.

Un an a passé.

L'Europe écrasée est une suite ininterrompue de champs de bataille intérieurs. Dans le ciel les ailes à croix gammée fuient devant les avions anglo-américains. Le survol de nos provinces ne se fait plus de l'Est à l'Ouest mais de l'Ouest à l'Est. Et chaque nuit les bombes alliées portent la destruction au cœur du Reich. La Russie occupe, use, épuise les forces humaines et matérielles de l'orgueilleuse Wehrmacht. Les alliés forts du concours américain ne peuvent plus douter du résultat final.

En Belgique les traitres, hier plastronnant, en sont réduits à réclamer la protection policière de la Gestapo. L'opinion est unanime dans la résistance.

A ceux qui sont morts.

A ceux qui chaque jour font pour notre Patrie le sacrifice de leur vie.

A ceux qui mènent l'obscur, le tenace, l'héroïque combat de la résistance...

LA LIBRE BELGIQUE, leading underground paper, listed its editor as Peter Pan, its address as that of the Nazi field commander.

RESISTANCE to the Nazi "New Order" in Holland and Belgium centered about the Catholic Church. The Nazis had counted on easily winning the support of the people of these countries. But they had not reckoned with Cardinal van Roey of Belgium and the Archbishop of Utrecht, J. de Jong. All Nazi threats failed to move their firm anti-Nazi stand. Cardinal van Roey forbade his priests to give communion to any pro-Nazis or to sanction masses for any who died. When the Nazis tried to take over Brussels schools, the Cardinal preferred to shut them down. He foiled attempts to divide the people by setting the Flemish against the French-speaking Walloons. His priests repeatedly warned their congregations not to join the new Nazi organizations. The Cardinal's anti-Nazi Pastoral Letter resulted in threats of violence. The Cardinal's answer was the blunt statement that the first nine months of Nazi occupation had proved worse than the three years' occupation of the last war. In Holland Archbishop de Jong and four other bishops issued a secret pastoral letter forbidding Catholics to join Nazi organizations on pain of being refused the sacrament. Dutch Catholics, Protestants and Communists linked forces, and neither heavy fines nor threats of violence could silence them.

BOTH THE DUTCH AND BELGIANS demonstrated their anti-Nazism by burying R.A.F. fliers shot down over their countries with much ceremony, keeping their graves covered with fresh flowers. This is such a grave in Belgium. The placard says these six R.A.F. fliers were killed on a reconnaissance flight "for our liberation." Dutch patriots killed many Nazis, threw them into canals. Anyone who joined a Nazi organization was shunned. Sometimes pro-Nazis were captured and their heads were shaved. To show their sympathy with Jews the Dutch wore the Star of David. Hundreds were executed for wrecking anti-invasion fortifications in June 1942. Officers and soldiers of the former Dutch army headed this phase of the underground movements activities.

JUGOSLAVIA

THE fiercest anti-Nazi resistance came from the rugged mountains of Yugoslavia, where the most legendary figure of World War II, Gen. Draja Mihailovitch, and 150,000 followers held forth. Mihailovitch had retreated to the Serbian mountains when Yugoslavia was overrun in April 1941. There his Yugoslav regulars were joined by bands of Chetniks, skilled Serbian guerrillas, several thousand Greeks, and a handful of Australians, who had been cut off by the collapse in Greece. Women and children came too. Mihailovitch spent the summer of 1941 organizing his forces, equipping them with light artillery and machine guns by swift raids on Nazi supply trains. A mobile radio transmitter provided occasional contact with the outside world. Both the Russians and British parachuted supplies to him. Raids on Nazi prison camps added to his soldiers. By the fall he was ready to take the offensive. Catching Italian, Rumanian, and Bulgarian punitive forces in narrow mountain passes he dealt them terrible blows, expanded his "island of freedom." His guerrilla bands, hidden by peasants, slipped deep into the Nazi rear to raid headquarters, blow up bridges and stores. The Nazis, who left their Allies to mop up the Balkans, were forced to send their own crack troops after Mihailovitch's bands. At the end of June 1942 27 Nazi, Italian, Hungarian, Bulgarian, and Rumanian divisions were engaged in chasing Mihailovitch's men through the mountains. But they were meeting with only small success, many reverses, and the hour was drawing near when a second front would force them to withdraw and leave Mihailovitch free to strike more boldly than ever before.

CHETNIK SCOUT watches for the appearance of Nazi troops. Chetniks, including Mihailovitch , sometimes slipped into village taverns, mingled with Nazis, listened to their plans for smashing guerrillas.

THIS IS THE FIRST PICTURE of Gen. Mihailovitch to come out of his Serbian stronghold. A World War I hero, he was jailed by pro-Nazi politicians for urging close co-operation between army and people's organizations. He shared his men's hardships, fraternized with them, led them courageously.

No3. **die Fahne der** 10Pfg
Revolution
15. MÄRZ. ORGAN DER KPD SUDWEST 8. Jahrg

19. MÄRZ
Demonstration des Todes

This 1940 leaflet called for a "demonstration of death" during a blackout.

Food is a weapon. This leaflet asks: "Is a herring and potatoes enough?"

ES KOMMT DER TAG....

Another Communist leaflet warns the Nazis: "The day is coming. . . ."

GERMANY

THE day Hitler become dictator the secret anti-Nazi underground movement in Germany came into existence. Despite years of Gestapo terror it survived every attempt to root it out. Its leaders and members have been murdered, tortured and left to rot in concentration camps by the thousand. Others were forced to flee for their lives. Yet the work never ceased. However, after Hitler's bloodless conquest of the Saar the strength of the underground slowly ebbed. Each new Nazi victory demoralized and decreased resistance to the Nazis except among the best organized and disciplined groups. Strongest of these were the Communists and Catholics who worked together in an anti-Nazi front. Ever since Hitler assumed power the church has been the only legal means of expressing opposition to Nazism. The great Catholic leaders, Cardinal von Faulhaber of Munich and Bishop von Galen of Muenster, by challenging Hitler's Neo-paganism at the risk of their lives, became living symbols of anti-Nazism and were wildly cheered whenever they appear in public. The Church has become the meeting place and nerve center of the entire underground. On June 22, 1941, as the Nazi armies plunged into Russia, the Communists made a desperate attempt to lead a revolt. Within an hour after Hitler announced the invasion they had mobilized their units and by early morning, with brazen recklessness, they began open agitation in numerous cities for revolt, speaking at factory gates, street corners, markets, in the Nazi army camps. They had counted on the fear of a two-front war to swing the masses of people behind them. But shortly after noon, with the Gestapo taking a heavy toll, it was clear to the Communist that they could not rally mass support and they went underground as quickly as they had emerged. The German people, growing fat with the loot of Europe and easy victories, had come to look upon war as national past-time and, while they were uneasy, they were not yet ready to raise their hands against der Fuehrer. Yet within a few months this confidence had been dissolved by the failure of the Nazi armies to take Moscow or annihilate the Red Army. Morale and economic production sagged. Underground activity spread rapidly. The large groups of Czechs, Poles, Belgian and Dutch brought in to labor in the Nazi industrial plants became hotbeds of resistance. Deliberately they wasted materials, lost tools, did sloppy work. By Dec., 1941, the underground had at least two secret mobile radio stations in operation and the slogan *Down with the war* was replaced with more vigorous one: *Sharpen your knives. Down with Hitler.*

TRAVEL FOLDERS WERE a favorite medium for the underground before the war. Surreptitiously stuffed into station racks, they contained anti-Nazi essays. This one was written by Heinrich Mann, noted German labor leader, brother of novelist Thomas Mann.

Inside, an anti-Nazi leaflet.

EXCENTRIC SHAMPOO
Das Beste für die Haarpflege
Loyd PARFUMERIE

WOMEN BUYING POWDERED shampoo sometimes found anti-Nazi booklets inside the envelope. Almost every envelope type of package was used. Penalty for possession: death.

100 timbres — stamps — Briefmarken

STAMP AND SEED PACKAGES were bulky enough to contain long booklets attacking basic Nazi theories, and giving instructions for making leaflets.

Jeder Groschen für unsere Presse— Ein Schlag in diese Lügenpresse!

"EVERY PENNY FOR OUR PRESS IS A KICK IN THIS LIAR'S FACE," says this leaflet. The difficulties of organizing the publication and distribution of such a leaflet are enormous. Most underground meetings take place in theatres, restaurants, churches and underground units seldom consist of more than three so that a Gestapo spy cannot trap more than a few members. Until Europe was conquered much of the underground literature distributed in Germany was printed in France and Czechoslovakia, smuggled into Germany by daring anti-Nazis. Prospects of a second front in Europe results in a great upsurge of anti-Nazi activity in Germany. To meet the growing threat of revolt Himmler increased the SS corps to 750,000.

Wellington bomber crew maps its route to Germany. "Devastation" bomb in foreground is one of largest types.

The R.A.F. Smashes Nazi War Machine

WITH the Luftwaffe tied up in Russia giant R.A.F. night bombers struck heavier and heavier blows at Nazi Germany in an attempt to force Goering to withdraw planes from the Russian front and to smash the Nazi industrial might. The night raids of the winter were followed by daring, low-level daylight raids on Nazi harbors, plants, and rail junctions in the occupied countries. Late in March the R.A.F., which had grown steadily stronger, began the devastation of the Nazi war-production machinery at

THIS UNUSUAL PICTURE, taken when the R.A.F. and Commandos raided Nazi-held Vaasgo island off Norway, shows bombs exploding on runways of Herdla airport. On May 3 R.A.F. bombers severely damaged Nazi battleships Gneisenau and Scharnhorst and cruiser Prince Eugen. Two weeks later the Prince Eugen was torpedoed as she moved down the Norwegian coast.

A Beaufort bomber crew awaits its turn to take off as the R.A.F. launches a mass raid on the Ruhr at nightfall.

ts key points. A series of heavy raids continuing for days reduced Lubeck and Rostock to ashes; Lubeck was a major Baltic outlet for Nazi supplies going to Finland while Rostock was both a vital Baltic port and the site of the Nazi Heinkel aircraft plants. In April the R.A.F. began its now famous 1,000 plane raids on German industrial cities. Monster Wellington, Halifax, and Stirling bombers, taking off from airfields all over England, roared eastward to converge over one industrial center after another. Split-second timing was required to get the planes off, over the target, and home again without ramming one another. Thousands of incendiary bombs from the first planes lighted the target for the bombers with the heavy demolition bombs. The glare could be seen for 150 miles. They exceeded, both in planes and in the tons of bombs dropped, the worst raids on English towns the year before. The populace of the Ruhr Valley fled. Frantically the Nazis tried to move their remaining factories eastward out of the range of bombers.

ARING DAYLIGHT RAIDERS swoop down on Cologne's power ation in August, 1941. The R.A.F.'s great mass raids began by knock-g out Lubeck and Rostock, Nazi plane manufacturing centers, in April and May. On May 30, 1,250 planes dropped 6,000,000 pounds on Cologne in 90 minutes, completely demolishing city. Thousands of refugees streamed eastward to escape the new mass raids.

THE COAL-HANDLING PLANT of the Cologne power plant goes up in smoke. Though not as destructive as the mass night raids, the daring of the daylight raids did much to build up morale of the conquered peoples. The three-day continuous raiding of Rostock completely destroyed the Heinkel airplane factory there. Mannheim, Stuttgart, Copenhagen, Hamburg, Kiel, Trondheim, Pilsen, Essen were raided repeatedly, as was the entire coast of France and Paris. The picture below shows a daylight raid on a Poissy factory ten miles north of Paris. It had been producing 20 trucks a day for the Nazis. Note misses landing in the creek in the center foreground.

THESE PICTURES SHOW the Renault Works in Paris after they had been gutted by heavy R.A.F. raids in March. Pétain and Laval had turned French factories over to Nazi use, and the Renault plant was producing tanks for Hitler's spring offensive in Russia. The remarkable picture above shows some of the destruction. The circular object at the top of the photograph is a gas tank. By looking closely one can see some of the unfinished tanks in the extreme lower right corner. The picture below is a close-up of another section of the Renault plant. It shows the smoking ruins and the skeleton sheds that were left after the R.A.F. raid.

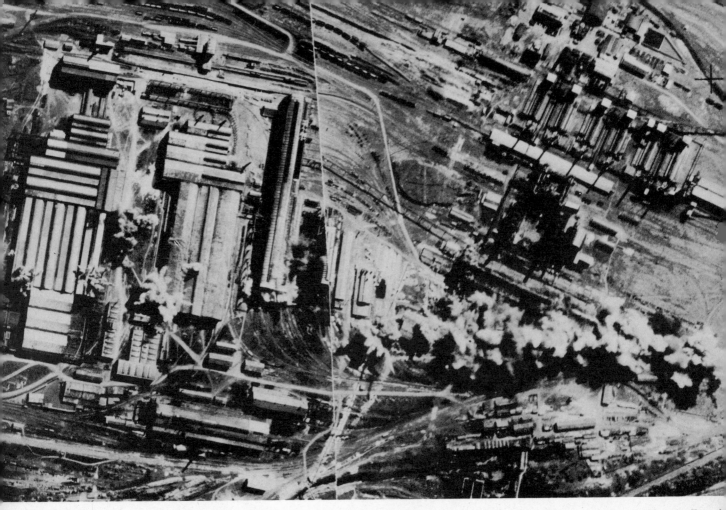

DIRECT HITS ARE SHOWN BEING MADE on a power station in northern France in the above picture. The power station is hidden by the smoke from the demolition bomb which hit it. An adjacent steel foundry was also attacked and hits may be seen exploding on its roofs. Crack running obliquely from top to bottom shows aerial photographer made two exposures, later pasted them together to make one photo-graph. The picture below shows British bombers attacking the French port of Le Havre. "A" shows a hit landing directly on the dock gates while "B" indicates hit landing among the barges tied up at the docks. Le Havre and all other ports along the invasion coast were bombed constantly. R.A.F. chiefs predicted three thousand-plane raids once U. S. air force joined them.

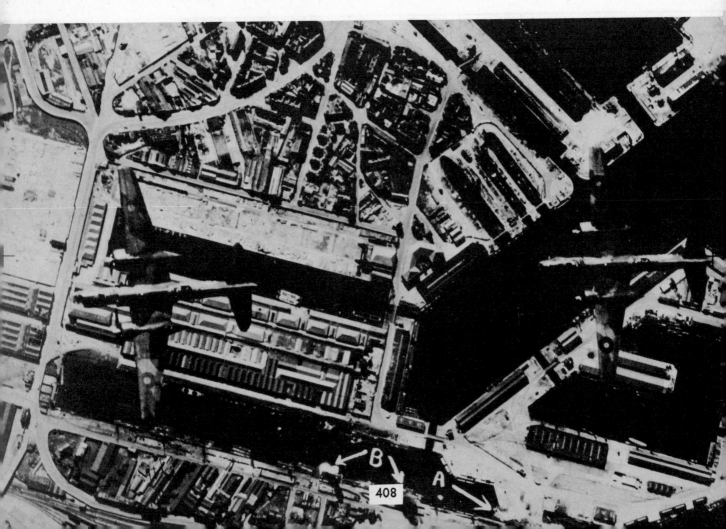

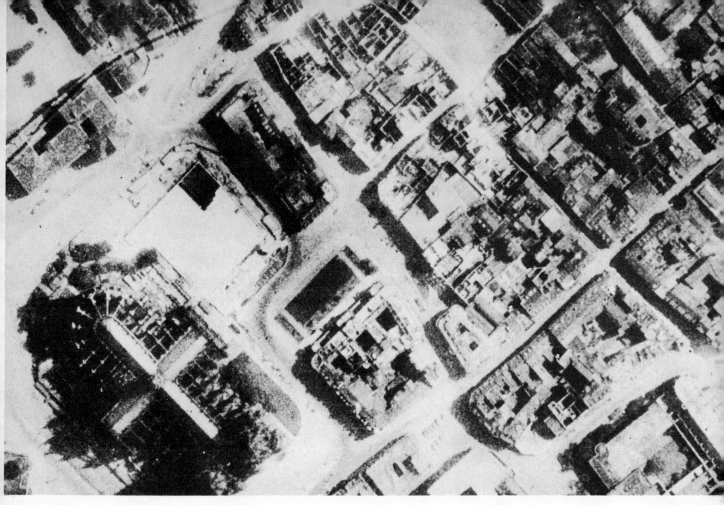

THIS R.A.F. PICTURE SHOWS THE DEVASTATION OF Cologne after it had been hit on consecutive nights by thousand-plane raids. The cross-shaped building in the left foreground is Cologne's famous Cathedral. After the smashing of Cologne the people of the Ruhr valley area began fleeing by the thousands eastward. In the picture below are some of the R.A.F. who participated in these raids. In some circles it was felt that these raids alone constituted a second front. However, while the raids did much damage, it was obvious that they in no way diminished the activity of the Nazi army and only after a long period of such raids would their effect begin to be felt by the Nazi war lords. But they were excellent preparation for the Allied invasion of the continent.

U. S. carrier planes hop off. They surprised part of Japanese fleet in Tulagi harbor in Coral Sea, sank or damaged 12 ships.

ON JAN. 31 U. S. NAVAL FORCES raided the Japanese supply bases on the Gilbert and Marshall islands and did much damage.

U. S. Fleet Wins
At Coral Sea and Midway

WHILE the Japanese moved swiftly southward into the Dutch East Indies, U.S. Pacific naval forces were reorganized under the command of Admiral Chester W. Nimitz, on whose shoulders fell the job of fitting a five-ocean strategy to a one-ocean navy. Early in March the Japanese began assembling in the New Guinea ports of Salamaua and Lae transports and warships for an assault on Port Moresby on the southern tip of New Guinea, a jumping-off point for an invasion of Australia. Japanese aircraft hammered Port Moresby, but the U.S. and Australian fliers based there hung on, struck back. On March 10 carrier planes from a task force commanded by Vice-Admiral Wilson Brown joined these shore-based planes in a ferocious attack on the assembling invasion fleet which ended with 20 Japanese ships sunk or badly damaged; delayed the Japanese for two months. Early in May the Japanese invasion fleet slipped into the Solomon Islands.

On May 7 U. S. planes hit main Japanese fleet, sank a cruiser, the carriers *Ryukaku* (above) and *Shokaku*. Note U. S. plane.

Admiral F. J. Fletcher

Admiral C. W. Nimitz

THE Japanese seized bases for land planes in the Solomon and Louisiade Island groups and making last-minute preparations for the assault on Port Moresby, began daily air reconnaissance over the Coral Sea. Yet their scouting force failed to discover the U.S. task force under Rear-Admiral Frank J. Fletcher operating near by. Fletcher's patrols, however, discovered part of the Japanese invasion fleet in the harbor of Tulagi on Florida Island. At dawn on May 4 squadrons of U.S. carrier planes, led by Lt. Commanders Joseph Taylor and William Burch, dropped out of the clouds over Tulagi. Called Taylor to Burch via his radiophone, "You hit 'em high and I'll git 'em low. From then on every man for himself." Yelling "Remember Pearl Harbor" to each other through their radiophones, the U.S. fliers dived on their unsuspecting prey. The attack caught the Japanese completely by surprise. Not until the attack was well under way did they get their anti-aircraft guns into operation. But it was too late. Every American flier had been assigned a specific ship as his target. Within a few minutes two Japanese heavy cruisers, three light cruisers, two destroyers, and two large transports had been sunk.

OTHERS were seriously damaged and had to be beached. The harbor was filled with smoking wreckage and sinking ships. U.S. losses: three planes. Meanwhile long-range, land-based U.S. bombers discovered the main Japanese fleet steaming southward through the Coral Sea, sank a heavy cruiser. On May 7 Admiral Fletcher's task force joined them off Misima and again the Navy dive bombers and torpedo planes led the attack. Within five minutes the new Japanese carrier *Ryukaku* had been sunk and a heavy cruiser set afire. American fliers shot down most of the Japanese planes. Meanwhile, scouting planes sighted two Japanese carriers 190 miles northward. Flights from the two U.S. carriers immediately took off, found the Japanese carrier *Zuikaku* in the midst of a rain squall, damaged it heavily, and left it burning. After some difficulty the American fliers found the other Japanese carrier known to be in the vicinity, the *Shokaku*. Coming in from all sides, the American fliers landed two 1,000-pound bombs on her as well as five torpedoes and left her sinking and burning. The Japanese, who had attacked Aleutians off Alaska to divert U.S. forces from Midway, were now forced to expand their Aleutian operations to save "face."

LEFT: A BADLY HIT JAPANESE BOMBER decides to "suicide" dive a U.S. carrier. Above, flight deck crew, salvaging plane hit by previous "suicider," tensely watches bomber come on.

WHILE THE U.S. PLANES were bombing the Japanese carriers, 108 Japanese planes from them attacked the U.S.S. *Lexington* and her sister carrier. Fifty-seven torpedo and dive bombers came at the *Lexington* simultaneously. Despite the work of defending fighters, two of 11 torpedoes and three bombs found their mark. The attack lasted only seven minutes, but the *Lexington*, most famous of U.S. carriers was afire in four places and listing. Meanwhile other Japanese planes had sunk the U.S. tanker *Neosho* and destroyer *Sims*. The *Lexington* crew put out the fires and landed their planes, just back from sinking the two Japanese carriers, as they headed back to port. Suddenly gasoline fumes, accumulating from leaking pipes below, exploded. New fires defied efforts of the crew to extinguish them. Destroyers

SSING THE CARRIER by a wide margin, the bomber drops ~~~ser and closer to the sea while the anti-aircraft units riddle its ~~elage. The plane is completely out of control.

BURNING FURIOUSLY, the bomber plunges into the sea. Japanese pilots frequently attempted "suicide" dives when their planes were disabled, but never succeeded in blowing up a ship.

~~me alongside, took off wounded men. Finally Admiral Fitch said to ~~r commander, Capt. F. C. Sherman, "I think we'd better get the ~~n off, Fred." The order to abandon ship was given. The picture ~~ove shows men sliding down ropes into the sea where they were ~~ked up. New explosions occurred as Captain Sherman, the last ~~n aboard slid down into the sea. The burning *Lexington* floated for several hours until a U.S. destroyer moved in and sank it with three torpedoes. Ninety-two per cent of the personnel escaped without injury. The battle had ended in an overwhelming victory for the United States, cost Japanese three of her newest, biggest carriers, four cruisers, two destroyers, and other craft. Yet neither the Japanese nor the U.S. ships fired a single shot from their big guns.

DESPITE their heavy losses in the Coral Sea the Japanese thought they had knocked out what remained of the U.S. Pacific Fleet after Pearl Harbor. The U.S. did not reveal the extent of its victory or its losses in an effort to lure the Japanese into a trap and deployed its forces from the Aleutian Islands off Alaska to the Panama Canal. The Japanese, rankling under their loss of "face" resulting from Gen. James Doolittle's daring raid on Tokyo, rose to the bait immediately. Two Japanese task forces, consisting of eighty ships, were sent out to capture Midway Island, north of Hawaii and an excellent base for operations against Hawaii. On the morning of June 3 a Navy PBY flying boat sighted one of the Japanese task forces 700 miles southwest of Midway. It consisted of destroyers, cruisers, and large troop transports carrying troops to occupy the island. A short time later the Japanese assault force, including the carriers *Kaga*, *Akagi*, *Soryu*, *Hiryu*, was found northwest of Midway. U.S. planes based on Midway immediately attacked, opening a battle which lasted for three days and three nights and ended in a disastrous rout of the Japanese. Army, Navy, and Marine forces participated in the battle, sinking the four Japanese carriers, two heavy cruisers, three destroyers, and damaging three battleships, one light and three heavy cruisers, and three destroyers. Several transports were also sunk and others were damaged. Over 4,800 Japanese were killed or drowned. U.S. losses amounted to only the sinking of the destroyer *Hammann*, heavy damage to the carrier *Yorktown*, and the loss of several scores of planes. Against the Jap losses, only 300 U.S. officers and enlisted men lost their lives. The smashing victory of the U.S. Fleet left the Japanese with little naval striking power, although their defensive power was admittedly still great. Marking a turning point in sea-power history, the battles of Midway and Coral Sea sealed the fate of the super-battleship;at Midway, as in the Coral Sea, no major ships had come within range of one another. The carrier had now become the backbone of the fleet. The Japanese losses put them in a desperate position, scarcely able to protect their long lines of communication southward to the China Sea. Meanwhile, to save "face" the Japanese expanded what had started to be a diversionist attack on Alaska when Midway was attacked into a full-scale invasion, seizing the distant islands Attu and Kiska. But the offensive had now passed into the hands of the U.S. Fleet and new blows would soon be forthcoming.

The Japanese heavy cruiser *Mogami* just before it sank.

A U.S. CARRIER, probably the *Yorktown*, stands off a torpedo plane, the long, flat object just above water near carrier. After this picture was taken the plane was downed.

AS SOON AS MIDWAY RECEIVED WORD of the Japanese approaching from the southwest, Army flying fortresses took off and bombed the oncoming ships, scoring hits on cruisers and transports. That night Navy patrol planes made a low-level torpedo attack in the moonlight, sinking one transport. At dawn, June 4, Army and Marine dive bombers and flying fortresses again attacked, concentrating